SAME-SEX MARRIAGE AND SOCIAL MEDIA

According to polls, from the early noughties to now, public support for same-sex marriage has increased dramatically. *Same-Sex Marriage and Social Media* asks how such a rate of attitude change came about and, more specifically, what role social media played.

Digital platforms like Facebook, Twitter, and YouTube have proved to be useful outlets for political expression, and Rhonda Gibson explores how this came to benefit the marriage equality movement. Drawing on a wealth of movement-related discourse, the book looks at:

- how marriage equality was framed by news companies online and in print;
- the digital strategies deployed by LGBT+ rights organizations and their opponents to gain support;
- the corporate response to the same-sex marriage debate;
- the effect of perceived public opinion and the concept of social identity on how the debate evolved online.

This book seeks to demonstrate how the unique ability of social networks to share personal stories on a mass scale, connect like-minded individuals regardless of geography, and leverage the bandwagon effect of viral content contributed to a seismic shift in visibility and public opinion around the issue of marriage equality. Students and researchers will find this a timely and accessible introduction to the impact of online networks on LGBTQ rights.

Rhonda Gibson is Associate Professor and Program Director of the Master of Arts in Technology and Communication in the School of Media and Journalism at the University of North Carolina at Chapel Hill, USA. Her research focuses on the media portrayal of sexual and gender minorities.

SAME-SEX MARRIAGE AND SOCIAL MEDIA

How Online Networks Accelerated the Marriage Equality Movement

Rhonda Gibson

Routledge
Taylor & Francis Group
LONDON AND NEW YORK

First published 2018
by Routledge
2 Park Square, Milton Park, Abingdon, Oxon OX14 4RN

and by Routledge
711 Third Avenue, New York, NY 10017

Routledge is an imprint of the Taylor & Francis Group, an informa business

British Library Cataloguing-in-Publication Data
A catalogue record for this book is available from the British Library

Library of Congress Cataloging-in-Publication Data
Names: Gibson, Rhonda, 1964- author.
Title: Same-sex marriage and social media : how online networks accelerated the marriage equality movement / Rhonda Gibson.
Description: Abingdon, Oxon ; New York, NY : Routledge, 2018. |
Includes index.
Identifiers: LCCN 2017037395 | ISBN 9781138894839 (hardback : alk. paper) |
ISBN 9781138894853 (pbk. : alk. paper) | ISBN 9781315179773 (ebook)
Subjects: LCSH: Same-sex marriage--United States. | Same-sex marriage--United States--Public opinion. | Social media--United States. | Mass media and public opinion--United States.
Classification: LCC HQ1034.U5 G53 2018 | DDC 306.84/80973--dc23
LC record available at https://lccn.loc.gov/2017037395

ISBN: 978-1-138-89483-9 (hbk)
ISBN: 978-1-138-89485-3 (pbk)
ISBN: 978-1-315-17977-3 (ebk)

Typeset in Bembo
by Taylor & Francis Books

CONTENTS

FIGURES

ACKNOWLEDGMENTS

So many smart and generous people contributed to this project. My colleagues at the University of North Carolina at Chapel Hill School of Media and Journalism have created an atmosphere that encourages both scholarship and friendship, and I consider it a privilege to work among them. Dean Susan King and Academic Dean Anne Johnston were unwavering in their support and provided me with the time needed to research and write. Professor Dan Riffe, who has given me invaluable advice for more than 25 years, assisted with the initial proposal for this book. When it comes to mentoring, Dan Riffe is truly the GOAT. My colleague Daniel Kreiss helped me understand that writing a book can be both gratifying and humbling, but that no matter what, it takes a lot of time.

Although I work with so many talented faculty and staff, it is actually my doctoral students who provide the most inspiration. Karen McIntyre and Joe Cabosky, both of whom are now talented scholars with their own academic careers, worked with me on LGBT-related projects that contributed to this book. Rachel Davis Mersey, Meredith Clark, and Scott Parrott turned the table on their former advisor and provided much-needed pep talks. Doctoral student Deborah Dwyer did some top-notch copy editing and managed to say "too many commas" in a nurturing way.

The media professionals, advocacy organization staffers, and academics I interviewed for this book were so very generous with their time and insights. I admire their passion for their work and the dignity they bring to public discourse about same-sex marriage. I also want to thank Leroy Aarons, who unfortunately isn't still around to thank in person. Mr. Aarons founded the National Lesbian and Gay Journalists Association, and his research is cited extensively in this book. I met him several years ago when he was working within the Association for Education in Journalism and Mass Communication to expand discussion of LGBT-related issues in journalism education. He encouraged my research in this area, and it made all the difference.

Alexandra McGregor and Kitty Imbert from Routledge were very helpful in pulling together all of the components of this book and keeping me on schedule. Their patience and support were much appreciated.

Lastly, I have two friends to thank. Olan Farnall has given me encouragement since we were in graduate school together, and he provided valuable input during the writing of this book. He also introduced me to my husband, Joe Bob Hester, 25 years ago. I'm not sure Joe Bob wants me to write another book anytime soon, but he certainly helped me write this one. He took care of our household and was a quietly supportive presence. I am glad to have finished this project before the start of college football season so that we can enjoy the games together.

ABBREVIATIONS

AE	Against Equality
FRC	Family Research Council
FOTF	Focus on the Family
FTM	Freedom to Marry
HRC	Human Rights Campaign
LGB	Lesbian, gay, and bisexual
LGBT+	Lesbian, gay, bisexual, transgender (plus other sexual and gender identities)
MADA	Marriage Anti-Defamation Alliance
NOM	National Organization for Marriage
RES	Red equal sign
SNS	Social networking site
SSM	Same-sex marriage
TDIP	Theory of dissonant identity priming

INTRODUCTION

The issue of same-sex marriage first surfaced in the U.S. news media – and thus public consciousness – in the early 1990s when the Hawaii state Supreme Court questioned the constitutionality of restricting marriage to heterosexual couples. In 1990 three same-sex couples had applied for marriage licenses in Hawaii and were turned down based on the state attorney general's opinion that marriage is between one man and one woman. The following year, the couples initiated *Baehr v. Lewin*, seeking to have the same-sex exclusion declared unconstitutional. The Lambda Legal Defense and Education fund, an LGBT+ civil rights organization, originally declined to take the case because of concern over the wisdom of publicly fighting for marriage equality. Eventually, Lambda Legal joined the case, and in 1993 the Hawaii Supreme Court ruled that limiting marriage to opposite-sex couples was presumed to be unconstitutional unless the state could present a compelling interest justifying the same-sex marriage (SSM) ban.

This ruling, which represented the first possibility of legalized SSM in the United States, pushed the topic onto the national stage. It also made the issue a high-priority concern for those who opposed LGBT+ civil rights. Although the Hawaii legal case was eventually rendered moot because voters approved a measure that restricted marriage to opposite-sex couples, the 1993 court ruling drew national attention to the fledgling SSM movement, particularly in state legislatures and the U.S. Congress. Concerned about the implications of a court decision opening the door to legal recognition of SSM, Congress passed the federal Defense of Marriage Act in May 1996. The legislation allowed states to refuse to recognize SSMs permitted by other states and prohibited same-sex married couples from receiving federal marriage benefits. With the passage of DOMA and national polls in 1996 showing a large majority of Americans in opposition to marriage equality, the SSM movement seemed dead. Yet just two decades later, DOMA is gone and SSM is legal in all 50 U.S. states.

A 2017 Gallup poll found public support for legal SSM at 64 percent, a record high and more than double the support (27 percent) recorded when the question was first asked in 1996. Famed statistician Nate Silver (2013) has analyzed the growth in public approval for SSM and found a steady increase from 2004 to 2013, with approval rates rising about 2 percentage points per year. Since then, however, growth has accelerated. For example, from March 2016 to June 2017, approval jumped 7 percentage points, from 55 percent to 62 percent (Pew Research Center, 2017). This rate of attitude change is astonishing when compared to public opinion about other social issues such as abortion or gun control (Baunach, 2011; Harrison & Michelson, 2017). Part of the dramatic about-face can be explained by older, more conservative generations dying off and being replaced by those who are younger and more progressive (Hart-Brinson, 2014). But some of the shift occurred because people from all age groups changed their attitudes (Baunach, 2011; Lewis & Gossett, 2008). In fact, a 2013 Pew report shows that 28 percent of individuals who indicated support for SSM also reported that they had shifted their opinion on the issue. *Same-Sex Marriage and Social Media* is concerned with how that shift came about. Specifically, this book will examine the role that persuasive messages about SSM – especially those disseminated through social media – played in the surprising turnaround in public opinion, ultimately creating a climate of support in 2015 that was conducive to a U.S. Supreme Court ruling in favor of marriage equality.

The marriage equality movement began years before popular social networking sites (SNSs) such as Facebook and Twitter emerged, and it's unreasonable to think that all the credit for the movement's success should be given to social media campaigns and other digital-based advocacy efforts. Early work by LGBT+ advocates and allies helped to reframe discussion of SSM in important ways, shifting the focus from traditional views about morality, sexuality, and deviance to a more contemporary consideration of civil rights, freedom, and equality. State-level campaigns helped national advocacy groups to form coalitions with progressive local organizations and officials, both gay and non-gay. These state-wide efforts to pass gay-friendly ballot initiatives were often unsuccessful, but they nonetheless helped educate the public about LGBT+ lives and relationships and the harm that same-sex couples and their families suffered because they were denied the legitimatization and rights of marriage. We should not overlook these early efforts because they were vital in growing public support for SSM from about a quarter of the population to about half, and they laid the groundwork for a final – and ultimately successful – push in the closing years of the movement. They allowed SSM advocates to focus their efforts on a particular segment of the population: those who were still undecided about marriage equality and who likely would be influenced by the opinions of members of their social networks. It was these citizens who were needed to push SSM approval to a more substantial majority and enhance its sense of inevitability. To reach these individuals, SSM advocates deployed a revamped digital media strategy that capitalized upon the ability of social networks to enhance users' sense of civic engagement, harness notions of shared identity, and leverage perceptions of public opinion. This book will take you through that process, showing how, as one marketing expert put it, the "inherent qualities of social media [made] the passage of same-sex marriage and equal rights for LGBT individuals and families inevitable" (Hoffman, 2012).

Social media use and civic engagement

Our understanding of the relationship between social media use and political engagement is expanding but by no means complete. Scholars seem to have transitioned from a vision of digital democracy as rational deliberation (Blumler & Gurevitch, 2001; Bucy & Gregson, 2001) to a focus on social networking practices that combine personal and social identity formation, status-seeking, entertainment, and political expression (Dahlgren, 2009; Donath & boyd, 2004; Loader & Mercea, 2011; Penney, 2015). Some are downright skeptical that online activities should even be considered political engagement. Futurist Malcolm Gladwell (2010), for example, has argued that the weak ties between individuals on social media are simply not sufficient to spur the level of activism needed to fuel actual political and social change. Similarly, social media campaigns that rely on symbolic action such as users changing their profile pictures have been derisively labeled as *slacktivism* or *clicktivism* (Babu, 2012; Karpf, 2010), suggesting that individuals who undertake such activities may feel good about themselves for their so-called civic engagement but will take no concrete steps to get involved. Others have been concerned about a substitution effect in which online activism takes the place of more traditional forms of political participation. These pessimistic hypotheses about the influence of digital political activities have been found generally lacking, with research suggesting that, if digital activism does have an effect on offline mobilization, it is most likely positive (Boulianne, 2015; Christensen, 2011).

One aspect of digital platforms that proved particularly beneficial for the SSM movement is that they allow ostensibly non-political users to casually come into contact with political ideas and discourse. This in turn allows individuals to decide for themselves whether to attend to and interact with political ideas and movements, and many are choosing to engage with political material online. Thus while social media platforms may have originally been associated with peer interaction and entertainment, they have also developed into a source of news and an outlet for political expression (Penney, 2015). We can see an illustration of how marriage equality benefitted from this dual nature of social networks by looking back at events that occurred in 2012. President Barack Obama, in a May 9 interview with ABC News, said publicly for the first time that he thought LGB couples should be able to get married. Obama, who had previously supported only civil unions for same-sex couples, said that his views had evolved and acknowledged that conversations with his two daughters about the issue had helped change his perspective. Not surprisingly, the president's statement received significant news media attention, but the conversation was even louder on social media. And although at the time the American public was evenly split over the issue of SSM, social media conversations leaned much more in favor of marriage equality (Hitlin & Tan, 2012).

The growing importance of social media to the marriage equality movement was also evident in spring 2013, when the U.S. Supreme Court was considering a pair of key cases regarding SSM rights. There were the usual legal arguments, friend-of-the-court briefs, and traditional communication efforts from advocacy groups, both supporting and opposing SSM. There was also the customary around-the-clock news media coverage of the landmark cases, as well as people taking to the streets to express their views. But supporters of SSM also took their voices online in an especially effective manner. A promotion started by the Human Rights Campaign, the nation's largest LGBT+ advocacy group, spread rapidly on Facebook and Twitter. Facebook users were encouraged to change their profile photos to a red square with a pink equal sign – a symbol of love and a variation of HRC's original blue and yellow logo – that was created specifically to call attention to and symbolize support for SSM in light of the upcoming Supreme Court hearings. Within hours of HRC's release of the new symbol on Facebook, it had been shared and "liked" hundreds of thousands of times (Bakshy, 2013). Proponents of marriage equality were also encouraged through social networks to wear red to show their support and to use specific Twitter hashtags such as #Equality and #LoveMustWin to increase visibility of the pro-marriage equality movement. The social media groundswell quickly caught the attention of traditional news media, as evidenced by a *Time* magazine story on March 26, 2013, that carried the headline "What is the red equal sign all over Facebook and Twitter?"

Political communication scholar Joel Penney (2015) used the RES campaign to examine the reasons social media users choose to participate in symbolic actions, specifically the posting of political-themed profile pictures. Penney conducted in-depth interviews with Facebook users who had adopted the RES image as their profile picture in 2013. Many interviewees said they hoped to persuade people who did not support marriage equality to reconsider their position, relying on the power of collective visibility to sway opinions. Still others described a strategic educational goal, hoping to draw people's attention to the issue of SSM without explicitly pushing a specific point of view. These attempts to leverage the power of public visibility and peer pressure are at the heart of a classic theory of public opinion influence – the spiral of silence – that helps to explain how social media campaigns such as the HRC's red equal sign were so influential in creating a positive climate for SSM.

The spiral of silence

The spiral of silence theory addresses the power of perceived public opinion on people's evaluation of and willingness to express their beliefs, especially with controversial issues such as SSM. Developed by German political scientist Elisabeth Noelle-Neumann (1974), SOS suggests that people are less willing to divulge their opinions in public when they believe those opinions are unpopular, primarily because people worry about negative social judgment and isolation. Even without access to polling data, individuals are able to develop a general sense of public sentiment about an issue, in large part nowadays through surveillance of social media. The more similar people think their own opinions are to the dominant opinion, the more willing they will be to share their views. Likewise, the farther from the majority opinion people perceive their own views, the less likely they will express them. SOS also suggests that people react to perceived *shifts* in majority opinions. If people perceive that public opinion has changed and their views are now similar to those held by the majority, they will likely speak out. However, if people find that their views are falling out of favor, they will likely stay silent. Because those who believe themselves to be in the majority usually express themselves often and with self-confidence while those in the perceived minority remain quiet, the former appear even stronger in public while the latter come across as weaker. This pattern – the spiral of silence – encourages others to either express themselves or not, depending on whether their views match up with the perceived majority or minority.

But how does SOS theory relate to the success of the SSM movement? Looking back to 2008 and the surprising outcome of California's Proposition 8, it's possible to identify key events that influenced both SSM proponents' and opponents' willingness to share their views on social media, creating a spiral effect in favor of pro-marriage-equality views. In 2008, conservatives shocked the country by securing enough votes to ban SSM in California, a victory that devastated marriage equality advocates but also got their attention. After the election, some gay activists used campaign finance disclosure laws to identify the names of people who had given money to defeat SSM and posted those individuals' names and personal details online, a controversial tactic known as doxing. Many anti-SSM donors were subsequently harassed online, and a few even faced protests at their homes and workplaces. The most famous of these protests forced Mozilla CEO Brendan Eich out of his position because of a boycott against his company. The result was a chilling effect for traditional marriage supporters, according to media accounts and an interview with Joe Grabowski, director of communication for the National Organization for Marriage (J. Grabowski, personal communication, June 19, 2017). Because of fears of online and offline intimidation, it was more difficult to get SSM opponents to participate in social media campaigns and publicly state their position. Meanwhile, marriage equality advocates were regrouping after Proposition 8, fine-tuning their message and putting substantially more resources into digital and social media. The result was a series of highly successful digital mini-campaigns focused on the personal stories of LGB couples and including simple yet meaningful visual images and hashtags that allowed SSM supporters to easily display and share their approval.

At the same time, SNSs were growing in popularity, especially among the pro-LGBT+ young demographic. The ability of gay advocacy organizations to secure the support of a few key celebrities and pubic officials with huge social media followings – Beyoncé, Barack Obama, and George Takei, for example – helped even further. Although public opinion polls at the time were barely showing half the country in favor of SSM, the message coming from social media – and news media reports of the activity on social media – was overwhelmingly pro-marriage equality. Taken together, these factors produced a classic SOS pattern: a point of view (in this case, SSM marriage opposition) that was held by almost half the country was unable to match its actual popularity with visibility online. The fear-based anti-SSM message, coupled with the intimidation likely felt by many traditional marriage supporters who dared share their views in SNSs, limited the anti-SSM movement's ability to get traction with digital campaigns. As marketing expert John Hoffman (2012) noted, stories of righteous indignation in defense of traditional marriage may invoke strong emotions, but they lack the emotional communion and social contagion provided by upbeat stories of same-sex couples who love each other and want to marry.

The power of identity

Numerous scholars have examined the ways that citizens use social media images such as profile pictures and avatars to illustrate and share their political identities through SNSs. This concept of identity is key to understanding how people make up their minds about controversial topics such as SSM, according to an interesting line of research by political science professors Brian Harrison and Melissa Michelson (2017). Central to their work is the notion of *social* identity, which suggests that an individual's sense of self is determined in large part by his or her real and perceived group memberships (Tajfel, 1982). Based on a series of experiments, Harrison and Michelson developed the *theory of dissonant identity priming* (TDIP), which predicts that messages that prime an individual's social identity can lead to attitude change. This suggests that people will be more supportive of SSM upon learning – in person or through mediated communication – that others within a shared-identity group are also supporters. Harrison and Michelson found, for example, that African Americans were more likely to support marriage equality after being told that then President Barack Obama was supportive. Messages that prime a shared in-group identity are effective because they reduce perceived social distance between the message's source and its receiver, increasing the likelihood that the receiver will pay attention to the message and be willing to accept its content (Harrison & Michelson, 2017). Interestingly, effects on attitude change are stronger when the delivered message is unexpected and yet plausibly held by other members of the primed in-group. This is because counter-stereotypical or dissonant messages, because of their surprising nature, are more likely to get the attention of their audiences and thus have a greater chance of persuasion.

The TDIP helps to explain why a series of targeted micro-campaigns developed by LGBT+ advocacy groups to increase support for same-sex marriage may have been especially effective in changing attitudes. As we'll discuss in Chapter 5, groups such as Freedom to Marry and the Human Rights Campaign produced videos featuring testimonials from same-sex couples and other marriage equality supporters from identity groups that weren't usually associated with LGBT+ rights. The campaigns targeted Southerners, members of the military, racial minorities, and political conservatives to persuade individuals in those communities to support SSM. The fact that these groups were sometimes considered hostile to SSM may have added an element of unexpectedness that caused people with shared identities to pay more attention to the videos and be more open to their calls for support for SSM.

Research into the power of shared identity can also help to explain why so many people otherwise unassociated with the LGBT+ rights movement were willing to change social media profile pictures and avatars or share memes supportive of marriage equality. Social psychology research shows that individuals choose to identify with or distance themselves from groups in an attempt to manage their social standing and self-esteem (Rubin & Hewstone, 1998). Likewise, people do not want to be viewed as being out-of-step with members of their in-groups, such as individuals in their social networks. Thus, when popular celebrities and political leaders – or even sought-after personal friends – changed their Facebook profile picture to a red-and-pink equal sign, individuals with shared identities were more likely to follow suit, even if they were undecided about SSM.

Hope and love win

As a movement, marriage equality was obviously able to harness the power of social networks through digital tools such as Facebook, Twitter, and YouTube, but it was by no means the only social movement to do so. Black Lives Matter and Occupy Wall Street were also very active on digital networks, as were international movements in countries such as Syria and Egypt. But there were aspects of marriage equality that differentiated it from other movements and afforded it greater visibility on social media and adoption by social networks. One key feature was the nature of the movement's primary message, that two people who love each other and want to share their lives together should be able to marry regardless of gender or sexual orientation. The message was simple and upbeat and lent itself nicely to visualization – and it aligned perfectly with two of social networks' primary functions: to tell and share stories.

Marketing expert John Hoffman (2012) analyzed this synergy in an essay he titled "Sharing our way toward equality: Social media and gay rights." Hoffman explained that opponents of marriage equality consistently argued that traditional marriage was under attack but found it difficult to produce emotion-inducing personal stories to illustrate their message. He suggested that stories and images of LGB couples – "beautiful brides and grooms and their families" – are more sharable than narratives featuring individuals who fear changes in the institution of marriage. Hoffman's professional experience-based assertion that "hope is viral" is supported by empirical research, which suggests that positive content, especially material that evokes high-arousal positive emotions such as awe, is more sharable than negative content (Berger & Milkman, 2012). Marriage equality advocates took full advantage of the opportunity to tell personal stories of LGB couples who wanted their love and commitment legally recognized by the state, sharing photos of smiling families, in additional to symbols such as the RES and rainbow-filtered profile pictures. Thus it was not surprising when, after the June 2015 U.S. Supreme Court ruling that SSM would be legal across the country, #LoveWins became the most viral hashtag related to the historic decision, garnering millions of tweets on the day of the ruling and eclipsing other less personal hashtags such as #MarriageEquality and #SupremeCourt.

Demographics also help to explain why marriage equality advocates were so successful with their digital education and persuasion campaigns. Online support for marriage equality should not come as a surprise given the younger demographics of those who populate social networking sites. In a Pew study of social media usage from 2005–2015, political scientist Andrew Perrin (2015) noted that young adults have always been the heaviest users of social media and by a considerable margin. Usage among those 65 and older is growing, but in 2015, the year of the landmark Supreme Court rulings on SSM, only about one-third of seniors reported using social media. According to the Pew Internet & American Life Project (Duggan, 2015), 60 percent of adults who use Twitter are 35 years old or younger. Other social media sites – Facebook, Instagram, and Tumblr – are also most popular for adults ages 18–29, and it's this age group that is driving support for marriage equality. A 2016 survey by the Pew Forum on Religion and Public Life showed that Millennials, people born in 1981 or later, are the generation most likely to support SSM, with 71 percent in favor. Support drops significantly among advancing age groups: 56 percent for Generation X (1965–1980), 46 percent for Baby Boomers (1946–1964), and just 38 percent for the Silent Generation (1928–1945). The generation gap in support for SSM persists even among conservatives. More than half of Republican Millennials favor allowing gays and lesbians to marry, compared to less than one-third of all Republicans (Pew Research Center, 2017).

So, in addition to the larger sociopolitical trend of digital civic engagement, there were unique aspects of the marriage equality movement's primary message and supporter demographics that allowed it to harness the power of social networks. But to what extent did the highly visible online support for SSM influence the movement's ability to achieve legal recognition? And what role did traditional communication patterns (those not deployed through social networks) by stakeholders such as the news media, advocacy organizations, opposition groups, and corporations play in the movement's success? A smattering of news articles and blog posts would suggest that social networks did it alone. For example, in 2012 *The Atlantic* featured a lengthy piece with the headline "The Social-Network Effect that is Helping Legalize Gay Marriage" (Scola, 2012) about how state-wide campaigns in Minnesota and Washington were using peer-to-peer networking tools such as Amicus to drum up support among friends, allies, and family for pro-marriage-equality initiatives.

But, of course, discourse about LGBT+ rights and marriage in particular was not limited to social media. Both proponents and opponents of SSM used other methods of communication to rally supporters and convince non-supporters to change their minds. In addition, the news media were a near constant source of information about the battle over marriage, especially in the last decade or so of the movement. And so, although a major focus of this book is the role of social media in advancing the marriage equality movement, that is not its only concern. In order to more fully understand how the movement was ultimately successful, *Same-Sex Marriage and Social Media* will take a broader look at movement-related discourse by examining messaging strategies – digital and otherwise – of multiple stakeholders, going back to the 1990s. Ultimately this book seeks to demonstrate how the unique abilities of social networks to share personal stories on a mass scale, connect like-minded individuals regardless of geography, and leverage the bandwagon effect of viral content contributed to a seismic shift in visibility and public opinion. Evidence will be drawn from (1) messages publicly disseminated by advocacy organizations, political and corporate entities, and the news media through social media and other digital platforms, in addition to traditional offline communication channels (2) scholarly and industry-based analyses of these activities, and (3) personal interviews with key players. Chapters will address communication strategies and output of advocates and opponents, political operatives, corporations, and the news media.

Overview of chapters

This book opens with an examination of social media platforms and networks, especially as they have been used by participants in the SSM movement. Chapter 1 traces the emergence of digital social media, explaining what they are, who uses them, and how they influence civic engagement. Chapter 2 provides a brief exploration of the cultural and legal history of marriage, with a focus on the factors that led a group of individuals to publicly suggest that same-sex couples should be allowed to join such a heterocentric institution.

The next two chapters deal with news coverage of SSM. Chapter 3 addresses the sociology of the newsroom, with a focus on the people who create news media messages to examine how individual attitudes and institutional practices have changed. It features material from surveys of LGBT+ journalists explaining how newsroom climate can influence the content produced, as well as material from blogs, columns, and social media posts that provide an insider's view of the decision-making processes regarding news coverage of SSM. Chapter 4 examines how traditional news media, as well as digital platforms such as blogs and Twitter, have framed marriage equality. It discusses scholarly research about the effects of news frames in general and specifically in terms of SSM, and traces shifts in framing of SSM-related news.

The next three chapters examine the rhetoric and communication strategies of organizations advocating for and against the right for LGB couples to marry. Chapter 5 focuses on the efforts of two national LGBT+ rights organizations most influential in the marriage equality movement: the Human Rights Campaign and Freedom to Marry. This chapter explores how organization leaders adjusted their messaging strategies to meet the needs of multiple stakeholders and to harness the power of social media. Chapter 6 introduces us to the organized opposition to LGBT+ civil rights and focuses on the communication strategies of conservative groups that have worked to defeat marriage equality initiatives. Chapter 7 examines the small but vocal minority of the LGBT+ civil rights movement that was not interested in fighting for marriage equality. This chapter will consider the historical foundations and communication strategies of the Against Equality movement, as well as media coverage of this aspect of the SSM issue.

Chapter 8 looks at corporate response to the SSM debate to review how companies have used social media platforms to either embrace or distance themselves from the issue, how they use their stand on the issue as part of the company brand, and how they manage controversy arising from executives who espouse public views about SSM. This chapter situates companies' activities within a larger critique of corporate appropriation of LGBT+ rights issues and markets and the resulting impact on queer identity and desire for radical social change.

The closing chapter is concerned with the final push in the SSM movement. It explores in detail how SSM supporters were able to adjust their messaging strategies to harness the power of social media and reach their ultimate goal. The chapter also applies two social psychology theories – spiral of silence and the theory of dissonant identity priming – to explain how perceived public opinion and the concept of social identity affect individuals' willingness to share their views and reconsider their positions based on exposure to social media content. The chapter ends with a look at the newest battle in the fight over marriage – the issue of religious freedom – and the conflict that arises when LGB couples' right to marry is weighed against individuals' faith-based opposition to participation in SSM-related activities.

References

Babu, C. (2012, April 8). Viral fever: Kony and slacktivism. *The Sunday Guardian*. Retrieved from http://www.sunday-guardian.com/artbeat/viral-fever-kony-a-slacktivism

Bakshy, E. (2013, March 29). Showing support for marriage equality on Facebook [Facebook note]. Retrieved April 4, 2017, from https://www.facebook.com/notes/facebook-data-science/showing-support-for-marriage-equality-on-facebook/10151430548593859

Baunach, D. M. (2011). Decomposing trends in attitudes toward gay marriage, 1988–2006. *Social Science Quarterly*, 92(2), 346–363. http://doi.org/10.1111/j.1540-6237.2011.00772.x

Berger, J., & Milkman, K. L. (2012). What makes online content viral? *Journal of Marketing Research*, 49(2), 192–205.

Blumler, J., & Gurevitch, M. (2001). The new media and our political communication discontents. *Information, Communication & Society*, 4(1), 1–13.

Boulianne, S. (2015). Social media use and participation: A meta-analysis of current research. Information, *Communication & Society*, 18(5), 524–538. http://dx.doi.org/10.1080/1369118X.2015.1008542

Bucy, E. P., & Gregson, K. S. (2001). Media participation: A legitimizing mechanism of mass democracy. *New Media & Society*, 3(3), 357–380. http://doi.org/10.1177/14614448010030030006

Christensen, H. (2011). Political activities on the Internet: Slactivism or political participation by other means? *First Monday*, 16(2). Retrieved from http://firstmonday.org/ojs/index.php/fm/article/view/3336/276

Dahlgren, P. (2009). *Media and political engagement*. Cambridge: Cambridge University Press.
Donath, J. & boyd, D. (2004). Public displays of connection. *BT Technology Journal*, 22, 71–82.
Duggan, M. (2015, August 19). Mobile messaging and social media 2015. Pew Research Center. Retrieved from http://www.pewinternet.org/2015/08/19/mobile-messaging-and-social-media-2015
Gallup. (2017, May 15). U.S. support for gay marriage edges to new high. Retrieved from http://www.gallup.com/poll/210566/support-gay-marriage-edges-new-high.aspx
Gladwell, M. (2010). Small change: Why the revolution will not be tweeted. *The New Yorker*. Retrieved from http://www.newyorker.com/magazine/2010/10/04/small-change-malcolm-gladwell
Harrison, B. F., & Michelson, M. R. (2017). *Listen, we need to talk: How to change attitudes about LGBT rights*. Oxford University Press. DOI: 10.1093/acprof:oso/9780190654740.001.0001
Hart-Brinson, P. (2014). Discourse of generations: The influence of cohort, period and ideology in Americans' talk about same-sex marriage. *American Journal of Cultural Sociology*, 2(2), 221–252. DOI: 10.1057/ajcs.2014.3.
Hitlin, P., & Tan, S. (2012, May 17). In social media, support for same-sex marriage. Pew Research Center. Retrieved from http://www.journalism.org/2012/05/17/social-media-support-samesex-marriage.
Hoffman, J. (2012, May 14). Sharing our way toward equality: Social media and gay rights. *Nonprofit Quarterly*. Retrieved from https://nonprofitquarterly.org/2012/05/14/sharing-our-way-toward-equality-social-media-and-gay-rights/
Karpf, D. (2010). Online political mobilization from the advocacy group's perspective: Looking beyond clicktivism, *Policy & Internet*, 2, 7–41.
Lewis, G. B., & Gossett, C. W. (2008). Changing public opinion on same-sex marriage: The case of California. *Politics & Policy*, 36, 4–30.
Loader, B. D., & Mercea, D. (2011). Networking democracy? Social media innovations and participatory politics. *Information, Communication, & Society* 14(6), 757–769.
Noelle-Neumann, E. (1974). The spiral of silence: A theory of public opinion. *Journal of Communication*, 24, 43–51. DOI: 10.1111/j.1460–2466.1974.tb00367.x.
Penney, J. (2015). Social media and symbolic action: Exploring participation in the Facebook Red Equal Sign profile picture campaign. *Journal of Computer Mediated Communication*, 20(1), 52–66. http://doi.org/10.1111/jcc4.12092
Perrin, A. (2015, October 8). Social media usage: 2005–2015. Pew Research Center. Retrieved from http://www.pewinternet.org/2015/10/08/social-networking-usage-2005-2015
Pew Research Center. (2013, March 20). Growing support for gay marriage: Changed minds and changing demographics. Retrieved from http://www.people-press.org/2013/03/20/growing-support-for-gay-marriage-changed-minds-and-changing-demographics
Pew Research Center. (2016, May 12). Changing attitudes on gay marriage. Retrieved from http://www.pewforum.org/2016/05/12/changing-attitudes-on-gay-marriage
Pew Research Center. (2017, June 26). Support for same-sex marriage grows, even among groups that had been skeptical. Retrieved from http://assets.pewresearch.org/wp-content/uploads/sites/5/2017/06/23153542/06-26-17-Same-sex-marriage-release.pdf
Rubin, M. & Hewstone, M. (1998). Social identity theory's self-esteem hypothesis: A review and some suggestions for clarification. *Personality and Social Psychology Review*, 2(1), 40–62.

Scola, N. (2012, November 30). The social-network effect that is helping legalize gay marriage. *The Atlantic*. Retrieved from https://www.theatlantic.com/politics/archive/2012/11/the-social-network-effect-that-is-helping-legalize-gay-marriage/265793

Silver, N. (2013, March 26). How opinion on same-sex marriage is changing, and what it means. FiveThirtyEight. Retrieved from https://fivethirtyeight.com/features/how-opinion-on-same-sex-marriage-is-changing-and-what-it-means

Tajfel, H. (1982). Social psychology of intergroup relations. *Annual Review of Psychology*, 33, 1–39.

1

SOCIAL MEDIA, SOCIAL NETWORKING, AND SOCIAL MOVEMENTS

It may seem that our personal and professional lives have always been filled with social media platforms such as Facebook, Twitter, LinkedIn, and YouTube, but networked sociality is, historically speaking, a relatively new phenomenon. Since the first commercially produced computers were made available to the public in the mid-twentieth century, users have sought ways to create computer networks that served professional – and eventually social – needs. However, it wasn't until the turn of the millennium with the development of Web 2.0 that networked communication evolved into what noted Dutch social media scholar Jose van Dijck (2013) refers to as "platformed sociality." Numerous social movements have taken advantage of these tools to promote ideas, mobilize participants, and influence public opinion and policy, with the U.S. same-sex marriage movement among the most successful. Before we examine the role of social media in the marriage equality movement specifically, this chapter will explore more broadly the evolution of social media and social networking sites (SNSs) and their place in social movements.

History of social media

Looking back, it is clear that computer networks were destined to become social networks. As early as 1978, public dial-up bulletin board systems allowed users to download files or games and post messages. Frequented by thousands of hobbyists and others looking for cyberfriends with similar interests, these online meeting places may seem primitive by today's standards, but they were revolutionary nonetheless, representing "the original home-brewed Internet" (Gilbertson, 2010). At about the same time, the United States' first major online service provider, CompuServe, gave subscribers the ability to send messages through electronic mail and participate in real-time virtual chats, and by the early 1980s, systems such as UseNet allowed individuals to interact through moderated computer news groups.

The 1990s saw the emergence of blogging sites such as Open Diary and LiveJournal, as well as the creation of more narrowly targeted affinity portals such as Gay.com, which served as both a community space for queer users as well as a ready-made online audience for advertisers (Campbell, 2007). SixDegrees.com, widely considered to be the first truly SNS (Kirkpatrick, 2010), premiered just before the new millennium. Unlike other social media sites that were oriented primarily toward special interest groups, SixDegrees focused on helping users identify and build *broader* social networks (Madej, 2016). Founded in 1997, it was named after the "six degrees of separation" concept that suggests all people in the world are six or fewer personal connections away from each other. SixDegrees allowed its members to upload a profile and list family, friends, and casual acquaintances on the site. Users could send messages and post bulletin board items to people in their closest "degrees" and see their connections to any other user on the site. SixDegrees folded in 2001, in part because of overly aggressive membership drives, but it was quickly followed by more commercially successful SNSs such as Friendster and Myspace.

Friendster was created in 2002 and capitalized upon the degree-of-separation concept popularized by SixDegrees in addition to technology that allowed users to see one another's profiles. The key selling point of Friendster, however, was its constantly updated and wide-ranging network: "Every time a homepage loaded, Friendster's servers calculated a single user's connection to other users within four degrees of separation, which could mean hundreds of thousands of individuals," giving users an immediate understanding of how they fit into their own social groups as well as into a larger community (Chafkin, 2007). Within a year of its launch, Friendster had more than three million registered members, but technology- and management-related troubles frustrated users, who eventually migrated to one of the many other SNSs that were popping up in the early 2000s (Madej, 2016). Myspace was one of those sites. Developed in 2003 by former Friendster employees and rooted in Southern California's music scene, Myspace was designed to be hipper than previous sites, allowing friends and music fans to connect with one another, as well as with their favorite artists (Cuthbertson et al., 2015). Myspace was immediately and immensely popular among the all-important young adult demographic, drawing user and media attention to the emerging social function of the Internet. It wasn't long until a *Fortune* magazine senior editor for technology noted the shift, suggesting "There may be a new kind of Internet emerging – one more about connecting people to people than people to websites" (Kirkpatrick, 2003).

From 2005 to 2009, Myspace was the king of social networking, even with the launch of Facebook in 2004 at Harvard University. Facebook remained campus-oriented for its first two years before opening to the public in 2006. With its insistence that users' profiles feature their real names and its increasingly business-friendly policies, Facebook soon became the darling of technology writers – as well as advertisers clamoring to gain access to its user base – and by April 2008, Facebook dethroned Myspace in the number of unique worldwide visitors and by May 2009 in the number of unique U.S. visitors. Quick to adapt to "fourth screen" mobile technology, Facebook made social media one of the most popular functions of the Internet and now stands as the undisputed global king of SNSs, available to users throughout the world (Cuthbertson et al., 2015). Joined in 2006 by microblogging site Twitter and later by niche SNSs such as Tumblr, Spotify, and Pinterest, Facebook has capitalized on the growing capabilities of smartphones. Other photo- and video-sharing applications such as the wildly popular Snapchat and Instagram exist almost entirely on mobile. The same is true for applications such as Foursquare, which allows users to check into various locations around the world through their smartphones, and the dozens of online matchmaking services.

Categories of social media

Given the vast number of online social platforms with a dizzying array of features, it is important to clarify some terminology and examine the difference between social media and social networking. Merriam-Webster's online dictionary, which says the term was first used in 2004, defines social media as "forms of electronic communication (such as websites for social networking and microblogging) through which users create online communities to share information, ideas, personal messages, and other content (such as videos)." Applying this definition, we can see that it is possible to use social media without actually networking – by simply posting messages, photos, or videos without overtly trying to make connections and interact with others. Social networking, a term that can be traced back to 1998, is defined by Merriam-Webster as "the creation and maintenance of personal and business relationships especially online." In their seminal article on the history of social networking, boyd and Ellison (2008) provide a more detailed definition of SNSs as "web-based services that allow individuals to (1) construct a public or semi-public profile within a bounded system, (2) articulate a list of other users with whom they share a connection, and (3) view and traverse their list of connections and those made by others within the system" (p. 211).

Social scientists Christakis and Fowler (2009), who have long studied humans' tendencies toward sociability, suggest that in the most basic sense, a social network consists of people and their connections. Some of these connections are formally organized, whereas others "evolve organically from the natural tendency of each person to seek out and make many or few friends, to have large or small families, to work in personable or anonymous workplaces" (p. 13). At their core, SNSs reflect offline interactions, allowing individuals to maintain contact with people they are otherwise tied to – some strongly and some weakly – but not organized around the introduction of strangers. Christakis and Fowler (2009) argue that people's inclinations to form social networks have ancient genetic roots: "The tendency to form social unions beyond reproductive ones is biologically encoded in humans; we seek out friends, not just mates" (p. 232). Their conclusion stems from research that analyzed the social networks of more than 1,000 twins drawn from a sample of 90,115 adolescents. They determined that genetic factors accounted for 46 percent of the variance in how popular – in terms of social connections – the children were.

Van Dijck (2013) has provided a useful typology for distinguishing among types of social media. In her book *The Culture of Connectivity* (2013), van Dijck puts SNSs such as Facebook, LinkedIn, and Twitter into their own category, suggesting that their primary purpose is to promote interpersonal, professional, and/or geographic connections – but relatively weak ties – between individuals or groups. She separates these from sites that feature user-generated content (UGC), arguing that the primary purposes of sites such as YouTube, Flickr, and Wikipedia are to support creativity, focus on cultural activity, and promote the exchange of content. A third category includes trading and marketing sites (TMSs) – think Amazon, Groupon, and eBay – that allow users to exchange products or sell them. Her final category consists of play and game sites (PGS), a genre with popular games such as Angry Birds and Candy Crush.

Regardless of which specific platforms are included in the discussion, it is clear that online SNSs have radically altered the ways that social networks form and interact. Christakis and Fowler (2009) have identified four major areas of influence: first is in their enormity, vastly increasing the size and scale of social networks; second is in communality, broadening the ability of members to share information and contribute to collective efforts; third is in their specificity, allowing users to be more particular in the connections they make; and lastly, in their virtuality, affording members the ability to assume virtual identities (p. 275). Of course, these influences of SNSs happen only for those individuals who venture online for networking purposes. It may seem as though everyone is on Facebook or Twitter, but that is not actually the case – not yet, at least.

Who uses social media?

The Pew Research Center's Internet & American Life Project has collected data about social media users for more than a decade. A 2016 Pew national survey of more than 1,500 adults showed that 86 percent of Americans reported using the Internet for some purpose (Greenwood et al., 2016). Online statistical portal Statista (2017) reports that in 2016, 78 percent of the U.S. population had some sort of social media profile, a figure that has continued to climb every year since it began collecting data in 2008. The Pew survey identified Facebook as by far the most popular SNS in the U.S.: Nearly four-fifths of Americans who use the Internet are on Facebook (79 percent), which is more than double the number who use Twitter (24 percent), Pinterest (31 percent), Instagram (32 percent), or LinkedIn (29 percent) (Greenwood et al., 2016). Facebook use continues to increase, with 2016 figures showing a seven-percentage-point jump over the previous year. As of mid-2017, Facebook had 2 billion active users worldwide.

While young adults continue to be the heaviest users of Facebook, older adults are increasingly attracted to the site (Greenwood et al., 2016). In 2016, 88 percent of online adults age 18–29 were Facebook adopters, whereas 62 percent of Internet users age 65 and up reported being on Facebook, a whopping 14-point jump in one year. Women use Facebook at higher rates than men: 83 percent of female

Internet users and 75 percent of male Internet users are on Facebook. Facebook remains the most popular social media platform, with its users visiting the site more regularly than users of other social media sites. Roughly three-quarters (76 percent) of Facebook users report that they visit the site daily – with a whopping 55 percent of those visiting several times a day.

Only about one-fourth of online adults (24 percent) use Twitter, statistically unchanged from a survey conducted in 2015 (23 percent) (Greenwood et al., 2016). Younger Americans are more likely than older ones to be on Twitter; 36 percent of online adults ages 18–29 are on the microblogging site, compared to 10 percent of online adults age 65 and older who are Twitter users. Twitter is also more popular with those who have higher levels of education. About 30 percent of Internet users with college degrees use Twitter, compared with 20 percent of those with a high school degree or less. According to Pew, Twitter is joined by mobile photo-sharing platform Instagram in the "middle tier" of social media sites in terms of the share of users who log in daily. Roughly half (51 percent) of Instagram users access it on a daily basis, with 35 percent saying they do so several times a day, whereas 42 percent of Twitter users indicate that they are daily visitors, with 23 percent saying they visit more than once a day.

Sexual minorities and social media

Gays and lesbians have been heavier-than-normal social media users from the very beginning; in fact media and sexuality scholar Larry Gross suggests that "queers were among the first to realize the potential" of the Internet and social media (2007, p. ix). From the early days of chat rooms, news groups, and affinity portals such as Gay.com, sexual minorities have connected with like-minded individuals online and used social media platforms to develop communities and participate in civic engagement activities (Campbell, 2007; Wakeford, 2002). The urban queer community was among the original groups that populated Friendster and helped to define that site's culture (boyd, 2008). Gay men commonly perceived Friendster as a queer dating site and invited other gay men to join. Likewise, queer youth who may not have access to a supportive geographically local community have found that social media allow them to develop a sense of community with people they have met online (Wakeford, 2002). LGBT+ individuals who participated in the early online groups related to sexual identity felt less socially isolated and more accepted (McKenna & Bargh, 1998). Similarly, the Internet has been attractive to sexuality and gender nonconformists as a medium "where sex and gender can lose their meaning" and not be limited to a male/female dichotomy (Laukkanen, 2007, p. 81).

Although Pew's annual surveys of Internet and social media usage do not segment LGBT+ users, there is survey evidence to suggest that sexual minorities are among the heaviest users. A 2010 Harris Interactive national online survey of 2,412 U.S. adults – 271 of whom self-identified as gay or lesbian – found that LGBT+ adults choose to connect online through SNSs more often than their heterosexual counterparts. According to the survey (Harris Interactive, 2010), 73 percent of

LGBT+ adults reported using Facebook, compared to 65 percent of heterosexual adults. When it comes to the business-oriented SNS LinkedIn, 22 percent of LGBT+ respondents reported being members, while 16 percent of heterosexual adults were. Almost twice the number of gay male and lesbian respondents (29 percent) than heterosexual respondents (15 percent) used Twitter. In addition, 55 percent of gay men and lesbians said they visit SNSs at least once a day, compared to only 41 percent of heterosexual adults. As Bob Witeck, CEO of a communications company that aided Harris Interactive in conducting the study, noted: "Over this past decade, through many comparative measures – we see first-hand that online media consumption for gays and lesbians is strong and growing stronger" (Harris Interactive, 2010). Witeck referred to blogging and SNSs as "the virtual, new gay community centers and marketplace," a claim that is supported by survey data showing that more than half of U.S. gay, lesbian, and bisexual Internet users have "liked" a business page on Facebook, and four in five have clicked on a Facebook ad (Bennett, 2014).

Facebook appears to be the platform of choice for sexual minorities in the United States. A June 2014 poll by Community Marketing Inc. (Bennett, 2014) found that 88 percent of lesbian and bisexual female Internet users and 79 percent of gay and bisexual males used Facebook. These groups were far more likely to have interacted with business pages on Facebook than on Twitter, with 55 percent of lesbian/bisexual females and 51 percent of gay/bisexual men having "liked" a brand's Facebook Page, which finished first of all the digital interactions in the poll. Clicking on a Facebook ad finished second, cited by 36 percent of lesbian/bisexual females and 45 percent of gay/bisexual men. Conversely, only one in 10 respondents to the survey had tweeted during a TV show or tuned into a TV show after seeing related tweets. Although LGBT+ use of Facebook is high, some queer users may feel constrained by the limited anonymity afforded by the SNS. Specifically, those users who are not fully out about their sexual orientation with members of their networks do not feel comfortable posting information about their identity or support for LGBT+ issues on Facebook (Fox & Warber, 2015).

Social networking sites, civic engagement, and social movements

Since the notion of a virtual public sphere emerged in the late twentieth century (Hague & Loader, 1999), scholars have debated the role of digital media in civic engagement and social movements. Early models included Blumler and Gurevitch's cautiously optimistic vision of the "vulnerable potential" of digital media to enhance public discourse and democracy (2001, p. 2) and Bucy and Gregson's (2001) suggestion that the symbolic civic participation afforded by social media allows citizens to cultivate a sense of civic identity that leads to more traditional participation in public affairs. Even before the development of Facebook, Twitter, and YouTube, Bucy and Gregson predicted that the "open-mike access to a wide audience" (p. 375) afforded by digital media would allow users some degree of persuasive influence over their peers – an observation that is especially relevant to the same-sex marriage movement. Castells' model (2007) was even bolder in its optimism, arguing that the development of interactive horizontal networks of communication through SNSs has produced a new form of communication – "mass self-communication" (p. 238) that can serve as a potent political weapon, allowing social movements to distribute alternative messages counter to those from more powerful sources and thus enhancing emerging social movements' influence over public discourse. Drawing on empirical evidence from a series of studies of young social media users, Mascheroni (2013) notes that for some people, the sense of community created by the actions of like-minded individuals on Facebook can be an important first step toward more concrete political activism.

Of course, not all visions of Internet influence on political participation are so optimistic. In a widely read piece in *The New Yorker*, futurist Malcolm Gladwell (2010) scoffed at the notion that social media activists represent hope for the future. Gladwell suggests that the "weak ties" between individuals on social media (who may have thousands of digital friends but very few in real life) simply do not translate into the "high-risk activism" needed to fuel actual political and social change. Similarly, social media–related campaigns that focus on symbolic action such as users changing their profile pictures or sharing a video clip have been criticized for promoting what some have labeled *slacktivism* (Babu, 2012; Christensen, 2011), where the main effect of online activities is self-satisfying individual expression that allows participants to feel good about themselves for so-called civic engagement but that results in little actual political impact and occurs at the expense of organized action. In an effort to determine whether the slacktivism accusation is warranted, Christensen (2011) examined the empirical literature regarding the effectiveness of social media campaigns in affecting real-life political decisions, in addition to the "substitution effect" – whether Internet activism takes the place of more traditional forms of political participation. He found no evidence of the substitution effect, concluding that, if there is an effect of the Internet on offline mobilization, it is actually a positive one. On the other hand, Fenton and Barassi (2011), in their study of the role of social media among British trade union activists, found some evidence of a substitution effect. They suggest that leaders of the activist groups believed that participating in political-related action on SNSs "distorted people's understanding of collective action by reinforcing the idea that simply joining a Facebook group was enough" (pp. 186–187).

In spite of the possibility that online activism may, for some SNS users, substitute for offline engagement, there is substantial evidence to support the more optimistic models of Internet influence on civic engagement. For example, results from a massive Facebook experiment indicate that persuasive messaging on SNSs can influence voting behavior and information sharing (Bond et al., 2012). The study involved more than 60 million Facebook users who accessed the site on Election Day in November 2010. Individuals who logged into Facebook that day were randomly assigned to a "social message" group, an "informational message" group, or a control group. Those in the social message group saw a statement at the top of their news feed that encouraged the user to vote, provided a link to identify polling sites, included a clickable button saying "I Voted," displayed a counter showing how many other Facebook users had reported voting, and showed up to six randomly selected profile pictures of the user's Facebook friends who had already clicked the "I Voted" button (Bond et al., 2012). Individuals in the informational message group saw the message, poll information, counter, and "I Voted" button but did not see any faces of friends. Those in the control group didn't see any message atop their news feed. Results of the study indicate that the presence of a Facebook social message increased voting behavior directly by about 60,000 voters and indirectly through social contagion by another 280,000 voters (Bond et al., 2012). Messages involving images of close friends were found to be even more influential, dramatically increasing the effectiveness of the mobilization message.

Likewise, in a study about what encourages people to express themselves politically and the influence of such expression on political participation, SNS use among American adolescents was found to be strongly predictive of engagement with traditional political participation in the 2008 U.S. presidential election cycle (Bode et al., 2014). From this study, the authors developed the concept of "political SNS use," which they define as "using a social networking site for explicitly political purposes, like displaying a political preference on one's profile page or becoming a 'fan' of a politician" (p. 415). The authors consider political SNS use to represent a new form of online political expression that focuses more on the public element of expression rather than the interpersonal discussion often emphasized by previous measures of online expression. As such, they conclude that "political SNS use is unique to SNSs, and meaningfully different from generic online political participation, in that it captures the ability of individuals to not only exchange information about politics but also to publicly affiliate themselves with a group" (p. 415). The authors note that SNSs influence political behaviors in multiple ways, among the most important being identity formation and expression and the creation of social capital. They suggest that for the youth of America, SNS use – for multiple purposes, including political expression – is part of their everyday activities: "This ease of use, paired with the extreme connectedness facilitated by SNSs, represents an important new space in which politics may occur – somewhere between communication and participation – while incorporating both" (Bode et al., 2014, p. 424).

This process of civic identity formation lies at the center of newer culturally oriented models of Internet influence on civic engagement and social movements. These models focus on individuals' use of SNS to participate in lifestyle and identity politics (Dahlgren, 2009; Loader & Mercea, 2011), which can eventually lead to more formal participation in political processes. Joel Penney (2015), who has studied digital civic participation in the same-sex marriage movement, notes that recent scholarship has focused on social networking platforms' ability to "integrate politically themed expression and discussion into a broader sphere of sociocultural interaction" (p. 53) that also includes entertainment and socializing activities. Embedded in this approach is Dahlgren's (2009) assertion that SNSs allow for the development of a shared sense of civic identity that can lead to what Bakardjieva (2009) has conceptualized as "subactivism," a pro-social process in which everyday online activities related to personal and political identity formation create a sense of civic initiative in users.

In his examination of Facebook's red equal sign profile picture campaign in 2013 (which will be discussed in greater detail in Chapters 5 and 9), Penney helps us trace marriage equality proponents' paths from casual online interaction to a stronger sense of community to civic engagement and eventually, for some, to more organized activism and fuller political participation. Of course, the same-sex marriage movement has not been the only one to harness the power of SNSs to spread messages and drum up support. Other scholars have documented the efforts of Occupy Wall Street, the Arab Spring, Black Lives Matter, and the Kony 2012 campaigns to disseminate their messages through social media in an attempt to rally supporters, draw newcomers to the cause, attract media attention, and eventually influence policy (Bennett & Segerberg, 2012; Fominaya, 2014; Theocharis et al., 2014). The Kony campaign was especially effective at getting supporters to share a video promoting the fight against Joseph Kony, a brutal Ugandan warlord. The Kony video became the most rapidly disseminated human rights video ever, was one of the most popular topics on Twitter and Facebook, and received substantial news media attention, although it did not necessarily lead to much actual political action on the part of U.S. residents (Gregory, 2012; Penney, 2015). Based on this research, Penney (2015) suggests that, instead of viewing social media as a one-way platform for message distribution, movement leaders are increasingly devising ways to use their supporters as "nodal distribution agents" to further spread the movement's message widely across multiple social networks (p. 55). As we'll see throughout this book, the same-sex marriage movement's ability to consistently create highly sharable content and motivate supporters to serve as distribution agents was vital to its success.

Also important is the concept of social capital, which is key to understanding the role of SNSs in furthering social movements. In its simplest form, social capital is "investment in social relations with expected returns in the marketplace" (Lin, 2001, p. 19). In the context of SNSs, social capital can be thought of as resources embedded within a person's social networks that can be accessed or mobilized though other ties in the network. Based on a survey of undergraduate students, Ellison, Steinfield, and Lampe (2011) have expanded the notion of social capital to include "the benefits individuals receive from their social relationships and interactions: resources such as emotional support, exposure to diverse ideas, and access to non-redundant information" (p. 873). Ellison et al. (2011) also emphasize the relational aspect of social capital and consider it to include interpersonal trust, norms, and social relations. Donath and boyd (2004) suggest that SNS use can serve the important function of enhancing an individual's *bridging* social capital, allowing users to maintain and increase more diverse social networks. Importantly, this social capital can be harnessed by individuals involved with social movements to share information and attract recruits. Indeed, research indicates that use of SNSs can bridge social ties

(Boase & Kobayashi, 2008), mobilize people to attend protests (Tufekci & Wilson, 2012), and change political attitudes and behaviors (Vitak et al., 2011). For example, Becker and Copeland (2016) found that LGBT+ individuals who use social media for connective activities such as meeting new friends or to discuss LGBT+ issues are more likely to engage in boycotts or buycotts to promote gay rights.

As we'll see going forward, the same-sex marriage movement was uniquely able to take advantage of its emotional and upbeat message (love wins), harness supporters to share the personal stories and compelling images created by advocacy organizations involved with the movement, and ultimately shift public opinion in a way that presented legislative and judicial officials with a new lens through which to consider the issue of same-sex marriage. The following chapters will examine this process, looking at how specific groups related to same-sex marriage – stakeholders, as well as institutions such as the news media – harnessed social media and SNSs for their particular purposes, whether it be to support or oppose marriage equality or to inform the public about the debate. First, however, we take a detour to visit the history of marriage.

References

Babu, C. (2012, April 8). Viral fever: Kony and slacktivism. *The Sunday Guardian*. Retrieved from http://www.sunday-guardian.com/artbeat/viral-fever-kony-a-slacktivism

Bakardjieva, M. (2009). Subactivism: Lifeworld and politics in the age of the internet. *e Information Society* 25, 91–104.

Becker, A. B., & Copeland, L. (2016). Networked publics: How connective social media use facilitates political consumerism among LGBT Americans. *Journal of Information Technology & Politics*, 13(1), 22–36. http://dx.doi.org/10.1080/19331681.2015.1131655

Bennett, S. (2014, September 23). Want to reach lesbian, gay and bisexual Internet users? Use Facebook (not Twitter). *ADWEEK*. Retrieved from http://www.adweek.com/digital/lgbt-social-media-study

Bennett, W. L., & Segerberg, A. (2012). The logic of connective action. *Information, Communication, & Society*, 15(5), 739–768.

Blumler,J., & Gurevitch, M. (2001). The new media and our political communication discontents. *Information, Communication & Society*, 4(1), 1–13.

Boase, J., & Kobayashi, T. (2008). Kei-Tying teens: Using mobile phone e-mail to bond, bridge, and break with social ties – a study of Japanese adolescents. *International Journal of Human-Computer Studies*, 66, 930–943.

Bode, L., Vraga, E. K., Borah, P., & Shah, D. V. (2014). A new space for political behavior: Political social networking and its democratic consequences. *Journal of Computer-Mediated Communication*, 19, 414–429. DOI:10.1111/jcd4.12048

Bond, R. M., Fariss, C. J., Jones, J. J., Kramer, A. D. I., Marlow, C., Settle, J. E., & Fowler, J. H. (2012). A 61-million-person experiment in social influence and political mobilization. *Nature*, 489, 295–298. DOI:10.1038/nature11421

boyd, d. m. (2008). Why youth (heart) social network sites: The role of networked publics in teenage social life. In D. Buckingham (Ed.), *Youth, identity, and digital media* (pp. 119–142). http://doi.org/10.1162/dmal.9780262524834.119

boyd, d. m., & Ellison, N. B. (2008). Social network sites: Definition, history, and scholarship. *Journal of Computer-Mediated Communication*, 13, 210–230.

Bucy, E. P., & Gregson, K. S. (2001). Media participation: A legitimizing mechanism of mass democracy. *New Media & Society*, 3(3), 357–380. http://doi.org/10.1177/14614448010030030 06

Campbell, J. (2007). Virtual citizens or dream consumers: Looking for civic community on Gay.com. In K. O'Riordan & D. Phillips (Eds.), *Queer online: Media, technology, & sexuality* (pp. 177–196). New York: Peter Lang.

Castells, M. (2007). Communication, power, and counter-power in the network society. *International Journal of Communication*, 1, 238–266.

Chafkin, M. (2007, June.) How to kill a great idea! *Inc. Magazine*. Retrieved from https://www.inc.com/magazine/20070601/features-how-to-kill-a-great-idea.html

Christakis, N. A., & Fowler, J. H. (2009). *Connected: The surprising power of our social networks and how they shape our lives*. New York, NY: Little, Brown, & Co.

Christensen, H. (2011). Political activities on the Internet: Slactivism or political participation by other means? *First Monday*, 16(2). Retrieved from http://firstmonday.org/ojs/index.php/fm/article/view/3336/276

Cuthbertson, R., Furseth, P.I., & Ezell, S.J. (2015). *Innovating in a service-driven economy*. London: Palgrave Macmillan UK.

Dahlgren, P. (2009). *Media and political engagement*. Cambridge: Cambridge University Press.

Donath, J. & boyd, D. (2004). Public displays of connection. *BT Technology Journal*, 22, 71–82.

Ellison, N.B., Steinfield, C., & Lampe, C. (2011). Connection strategies: Social capital implications of Facebook-enabled communication practices. *New Media & Society*, 13(6), 873–892. DOI: 10.1177/1461444810385389

Fenton, N., & Barassi, V. (2011). Alternative media and social networking sites: The politics of individuation and political participation. *The Communication Review*, 14(3), 197–196. http://dx.doi.org/10.1080/10714421.2011.597245

Fominaya, C. F. (2014). *Social movements & globalization: How protests, occupations and uprisings are changing the world*. New York, NY: Palgrave Macmillan.

Fox, J., & Warber, K. M. (2015). Queer identity management and political self-expression on social networking sites: A co-cultural approach to the spiral of silence. *Journal of Communication*, 65, 79–100. DOI:10.1111/jcom.12137

Gilbertson, S. (2010, February 16). February 16: 1978: Bulletin Board goes electronic. *Wired*. Retrieved from https://www.wired.com/2010/02/0216cbbs-first-bbs-bulletin-board

Gladwell, M. (2010). Small change: Why the revolution will not be tweeted. *The New Yorker*. Retrieved from http://www.newyorker.com/magazine/2010/10/04/small-change-malcolm-gladwell

Greenwood, S., Perrin, A., & Duggan, M. (2016, November 11). Facebook usage and engagement is on the rise, while adoption of other platforms holds steady. Pew Research Center. Retrieved from http://www.pewinternet.org/2016/11/11/social-media-update-2016

Gregory, S. (2012). Kony 2012 through a prism of video advocacy practices and trends. *Journal of Human Rights Practice*, 4(3), 463–468. DOI:10.1093/jhuman/hus024

Gross, L. (2007). Foreword. In K. O'Riordan & D. J. Phillips (Eds.), *Queer online: Media technology & sexuality* (pp. vii–x). New York: Peter Lang.

Hague, B.N., & Loader, B. (1999). *Digital democracy: Discourse and decision making in the information age*. New York: Routledge.

Harris Interactive. (2010, July 13). Gay and lesbian adults are more likely and more frequent blog readers: Social networks, blog popularity remain high for gay Americans over past three years. *PR Newswire*. Retrieved from http://www.prnewswire.com/news-releases/gay-and-lesbian-adults-are-more-likely-and-more-frequent-blog-readers-98317299.html

Kirkpatrick, D. (2003, October 13). I get by with a little help from my friends of friends of friends. *Fortune Magazine*. Retrieved from http://archive.fortune.com/magazines/fortune/fortune_archive/2003/10/13/350905/index.htm

Kirkpatrick, D. (2010). *The Facebook Effect: The inside story of the company that is connecting the world*. New York: Simon & Schuster.

Laukkanen, M. (2007). Young queers online: The limits and possibilities of non- hetero-sexual self-representation in online conversations. In K. O'Riordan & D. J. Phillips (Eds.), *Queer online: Media, technology & sexuality* (pp. 81–100). New York, NY: Peter Lang.

Lin, N. (2001). *Social capital: A theory of social structure and action*. London: Cambridge University Press.

Loader, B. D., & Mercea, D. (2011). Networking democracy? Social media innovations and participatory politics. *Information, Communication, & Society* 14(6), 757–769.

Madej, K. (2016). *Interactivity, collaboration, and authoring in social media*. New York, NY: Springer International.

Mascheroni, G. (2013). Performing citizenship online: Identity, subactivism and participation. *Observatorio*, 7(3), 93–119.

McKenna, K. Y. A., & Bargh, J. A. (1998). Coming out in the age of the Internet: Identity "demarginalization" through virtual group participation. *Journal of Personality and Social Psychology*, 75(3), 681–694. http://dx.doi.org/10.1037/0022-3514.75.3.681

Penney, J. (2015). Social media and symbolic action: Exploring participation in the Facebook Red Equal Sign profile picture campaign. *Journal of Computer Mediated Communication*, 20(1), 52–66. http://doi.org/10.1111/jcc4.12092

Statista. (2017). Social media: Statistics & facts. Retrieved February 12, 2017, from https://www.statista.com/topics/1164/social-networks

Theocharis, Y., Lowe, W., van Deth, J. W., & Garcia-Albacete, G. (2014). Using Twitter to mobilize protest action: Online mobilization patterns and action repertoires in the Occupy Wall Street, Indignados, and Aganaktismenoi movements. *Information, Communication & Society*, 18(2), 202–220.

Tufekci, Z., & Wilson, C. (2012). Social media and the decision to participate in political protest: Observations from Tahrir Square. *Journal of Communication*, 62(2), 363–379. DOI: 10.1111/j.1460–2466.2012.01629.x

Van Dijck, J. (2013). *The culture of connectivity. A critical history of social media*. New York: Oxford University Press.

Vitak, J., Zube, P., Smock, A., Carr, C. T., Ellison, N., & Lampe, C. (2011). It's complicated: Facebook users' political participation in the 2008 election. *Cyberpsychology, Behavior, and Social Networking*, 14(3), 107–114. https://doi.org/10.1089/cyber.2009.0226

Wakeford, N. (2002). New technologies and "cyber-queer" research. In D. Richardson & S. Seidman (Eds.), *Handbook of lesbian & gay studies* (pp. 115–144). Thousand Oaks, CA: Sage.

2

THE HISTORY OF MARRIAGE IN THE UNITED STATES

The legal history of same-sex marriage in the United States is a relatively modern one, dating back to the early 1970s when the first lawsuits were filed challenging the notion that marriage rights should be limited to heterosexual couples. But we must travel further back in time to fully understand the broader historical context of marriage and its economic, political, religious, and cultural implications. According to historian and marriage expert Stephanie Coontz (2005), marriage has for centuries served as a stabilizing force for society, but it has also in various ways excluded and/or discriminated against women and racial and sexual minorities. For much of Western history, marriage served as a mechanism for securing power through wealth, family alignments, and property rights. Historically, marriages were arranged through a system in which women were viewed as property and "purchased" through dowries based on the best interests of the families involved (Coontz, 1999, 2005). Within this context, marriage provided a structure for organizing a society's economy and for asserting control over sexuality, race, and gender (Graff, 1999).

Of course, marriage has not historically been available to everyone. For example, slaves in the United States were never allowed to legally marry, and slave families were routinely separated. In the 1600s, the colonies of Maryland and Virginia passed legislation prohibiting interracial marriage, a practice that was adopted by the other colonies, and eventually all states, within a few decades. With the abolition of slavery in the mid-1800s, freed slaves were granted marriage rights, but only with other members of minority groups – they were still prohibited from marrying Whites (Coontz, 2005). In 1883, in *Pace v. Alabama*, the U.S. Supreme Court gave its stamp of approval to these laws, unanimously ruling that state-level bans on interracial marriage did not violate the Equal Protection and Due Process clauses of the U.S. Constitution's Fourteenth Amendment. It was not until 1967 that the U.S. Supreme Court unanimously overturned *Pace*, ruling in *Loving v. Virginia* that state bans on interracial marriage were indeed in violation of the Fourteenth Amendment. Interestingly, the Supreme Court's decision in *Loving* was made despite prevailing public opinion (73 percent) that overwhelmingly opposed such marriages, a judicial/ public opinion split that has also emerged in the battle for marriage equality.

Attitudes about the *purpose* of marriage have also shifted over time, and the idea of marrying for love is a relatively recent concept (Coontz, 2005). It was not until the 1800s that couples began to value marriage for its ability to provide companionship and intimacy, although still within a framework of rigid gender roles and with some degree of parental control. Psychologist and sexual prejudice expert Gregory Herek points to this shift, which accompanied a transition from an agrarian society to an industrialized one, as evidence that marriage is an adaptable institution: "As cultural definitions of marriage have evolved in the United States and other Western countries, relationship quality and its constituent components have become increasingly central to the meaning of that institution" (Herek, 2006, p. 609). Under this new conceptualization, marriage was valued not only for the reproduction of children, but also for personal fulfillment and accompanying privileges. Other well-documented marriage trends include delayed age of marriage, increased cohabitation, a growing single population, and more childbearing outside of marriage (Cherlin, 2004), additional evidence that marriage in the United States is not a static institution. Adaption has not always been swift, but marriage customs and laws are constantly in flux, in spite of some claims (Sprigg, 2004) that marriage has remained unchanged for centuries.

Early evidence of same-sex unions

Same-sex marriage may not have received nationwide legal approval in the United States until 2015, but there is evidence of publicly recognized – although usually not state-sanctioned – queer unions dating back to antiquity. In ancient Rome, for example, there are numerous examples of men taking other men as a spouse, sometimes celebrating their unions with elaborate wedding ceremonies. The Roman emperor, Nero, who lived from 37–68 AD, famously married at least one man and likely more (Kiefer, 2012). Historians have also identified documents that demonstrate the existence of institutionalized same-sex unions in ancient Greece, early modern Japan, dynastic China, some American Indian nations, twentieth-century African groups, and many other regions of the world (Boswell, 1994).

However, by the time Europeans founded the "new world" in North America, such same-sex unions were no longer accepted, and colonists were shocked to learn that versions of them existed among Native American populations (Abbott, 2011). Multiple indigenous tribes historically have recognized a third gender in the *berdache*, individuals considered to be of "two spirits," possessed of both femaleness and maleness and sometimes permitted to marry partners of the same sex (Jacobs et al., 1997). But the Founding Fathers rejected this practice, instead creating a framework grounded in the Anglo-American ideal of heterosexual Christian monogamy, which they considered to be morally superior. Although it may seem surprising now, for many years same-sex marriage was not explicitly prohibited by U.S. law – it simply would not have occurred to most people that such a thing would be considered (D'Emilio & Freedman, 1988). At that time, the concept of same-sex physical attraction was taboo; in fact, the term "homosexuality" was not coined until the mid-nineteenth century (Mondimore, 1996). French philosopher and historian Michel Foucault (1978) likewise has suggested that homosexuality as a form of personal or group identification did not develop until the 1800s. Indeed, early U.S. statutes did not address gay or lesbian individuals but instead focused on behavior, specifically "sodomy," which usually included all forms of nonreproductive sexual activity.

In spite of this lack of public awareness of homosexuality, same-sex couples were known to live together in romantic relationships. Among upper-class women in the northeast United States, monogamous, marriage-like relationships were common enough to be known as "Boston marriages" (Faderman, 1981). Whether most such relationships included sexual intimacy is unknown, although surviving letters and diaries often suggest some degree of romantic physicality (D'Emilio & Freedman, 1988). Also in the 1800s, some women and even a few men adopted the characteristics and social role of the other sex, "passing" so effectively that some of them were able to secure legal licenses and marry their romantic partners (D'Emilio & Freedman, 1988).

The modern same-sex marriage movement

It was not until the second half of the twentieth century that the notion of marriage rights for same-sex couples entered the public consciousness in the United States. Numerous scholars (Bronski, 2011; D'Emilio, 1983; Fejes, 2008; Gross, 2001) have positioned the Stonewall riots of June 28, 1969, as the symbolic beginning of the U.S. gay rights movement, coming after years of social and political marginalization and following the many successes of the women's and Black civil rights movements (van Eeden-Moorefield & Alvarez, 2015). After years of raids and harassment by police, a group of queer patrons at New York City's Stonewall Inn fought back against authorities, leading to subsequent demonstrations, marches, and calls for basic civil liberties – and eventually attracting nationwide press attention. This set the scene for the 1970s, the decade in which the organized marriage equality movement was born. From the beginning, the country was polarized regarding the notion of rights for sexual minorities, with some celebrating the emergence of organizations such as Lambda Legal Defense and Education Fund and the National Gay Task Force and a much-publicized decision by the American Psychiatric Association to declassify homosexuality as a disorder (Bronski, 2011). But others cheered the Save Our Children campaign started by entertainer Anita Bryant in 1977, the first widely known organized opposition to LGBT+ rights (Fejes, 2008). In 1977, Gallup first measured public opinion about relations between gays and lesbians – ambiguous wording that did not specifically address the issue of marriage – and found that only 43 percent of the public believed such relations should be legal (Saad, 2012).

As LGBT+ individuals in the 1970s started forming more visible communities and working to end discrimination based on sexuality (Herek, 2006), some of those who were in committed relationships began to question their inability to access the recognition and benefits afforded to married couples (Nardi, 1997). Two such young men likely unknowingly launched the modern same-sex marriage movement. On May 18, 1970, University of Minnesota students Jack Baker and Mike McConnell applied to the Hennepin County District Court clerk for a marriage license, but the application was denied because both applicants were male. Baker and McConnell sued, claiming that Minnesota marriage law made no mention of gender. The trial court ruled in favor of the county, as did the Minnesota Supreme Court, which ruled that a state law limiting marriage to persons of the opposite sex did not violate the U.S. Constitution. The case was appealed to the U.S. Supreme Court, which dismissed it on October 10, 1972, "for want of a substantial federal question," making it the first major case ruling on same-sex marriage and establishing it as precedent for subsequent rulings (van Eeden-Moorefield & Alvarez, 2015). The following year, in 1973, Maryland made history by becoming the first state to pass a state-wide law explicitly banning marriage between same-sex couples. More bad news for the fledgling marriage equality movement followed with a 1974 ruling by the Washington State Court of Appeals that same-sex marriage was not allowed under their state law and a 1976 U.S. Supreme Court ruling that upheld the validity of Virginia's sodomy laws. As a whole, the 1970s represent a dubious beginning for the same-sex marriage movement with all of the legislative setbacks. History shows, however, that these events began to draw important public attention to the secondary status of LGBT+ individuals, laying the groundwork for later challenges to marriage restrictions – in addition to public opinion.

The emergence of the AIDS epidemic in the 1980s pulled the spotlight away from other LGBT+-related issues, including the right to marry (Bronski, 2011). Responding to the framing of AIDS as a "gay disease" by the news media (Alwood, 1996) and many elected officials, public support for the legality of relations between gays and lesbians dropped from 44 percent in the early 1980s to just 33 percent later in the decade (Saad, 2012). However, the AIDS epidemic and resulting anti-gay backlash did serve to galvanize the queer community, leading to the formation of two additional LGBT+ advocacy organizations, the Human Rights Campaign and ACT UP. There was also some good news for gay rights activists on the political front: On August, 11, 1980, the Democrats became the first major U.S. political party to endorse the rights of gays and lesbians in its platform, and not long after, in 1982, Wisconsin made history by becoming the first state to ban discrimination based on sexual orientation in employment, housing, and public accommodations (Umhoefer, 2014). There was little activity explicitly connected to marriage rights during the 1980s, although one very public event on October 10, 1987 – a mass wedding of approximately 2,000 same-sex couples as part of the March on Washington for Gay and Lesbian Rights – served as a symbolic celebration and a direct political challenge to opponents of marriage equality (Dunak, 2013).

The 1990s may be fondly remembered as the "gay '90s" (Bronski, 2011) because of increased queer visibility in the media, but it was a mixed bag for marriage activists. Both California and Hawaii began to offer domestic partnership benefits to same-sex couples, but the vast majority of federal, state, and municipal legislation was designed to deny marriage rights to sexual minorities. Defense of Marriage statutes emerged as a strategic maneuver for states to protect against other states that might expand marriage rights. In March 1995, Utah became the first state to adopt such a law, stipulating that it did not have to recognize out-of-state marriages. The following year, then President Bill Clinton signed the Defense of Marriage Act, which defined marriage for federal purposes as the union of one man and one woman and permitted all states to refuse to recognize same-sex marriages issued by other states. In addition, two states (Arkansas, 1997; Hawaii, 1998) passed constitutional amendments banning same-sex marriage.

Interestingly, we begin to see a pattern in the 1990s that van Eeden-Moorefield and Alvarez (2015) suggest is unique among Western countries that have legalized same-sex marriage: divergent pathways in legislative and judicial activity. Whereas most political or legislative activity in the 1990s rejected the right of same-sex couples to marry, court decisions began to question the constitutionality of excluding specific classes of people from marriage rights. One major court ruling, *Baehr v. Lewin* (1993), stemmed from a case in Hawaii in 1990 when three same-sex couples applied for marriage licenses and were turned away based on the state attorney general's opinion that marriage was limited to one man and one woman. The couples sued, seeking to have the same-sex exclusion declared unconstitutional. As noted in the introduction to this book, the Lambda Legal Defense and Education Fund originally declined to accept the case because its leaders thought marriage rights an unattainable goal. Nonetheless, Lambda Legal eventually joined the case, and in 1993 the Hawaii Supreme Court ruled that the statute limiting marriage to opposite-sex couples was presumed to be unconstitutional unless the state could present a compelling interest justifying the same-sex marriage ban. In another ruling that had implications for the marriage equality movement, the U.S. Supreme Court in 1996 struck down Colorado's Amendment 2, which had been approved by voters in 1992 and prohibited local entities from passing measures that protected lesbian, gay, or bisexual individuals from discrimination. In 1996, in *Romer v. Evans*, the U.S. Supreme Court ruled that Amendment 2 did not satisfy the Equal Protection Clause of the Fourteenth Amendment to the U.S. Constitution, signaling official questioning of legislative discrimination against lesbians and gay men (van Eeden-Moorefield & Alvarez, 2015). Finally, as the decade was coming to a close, the Vermont Supreme Court ruled in December 1999 that the state was constitutionally required to extend to same-sex couples the same benefits afforded heterosexual couples. The ruling included a requirement that the state legislature take action, which resulted in Vermont passing the country's first civil unions law the following year, granting the full benefits of marriage (but not the same legal status) to same-sex couples.

For those interested in the nuances of public opinion polling, the 1990s also provided a historic event: In 1996 Gallup for the first time began polling the public specifically on their beliefs about same-sex marriage (as opposed to the more ambiguous "gay and lesbian relations"), asking "Do you think marriages between same-sex couples should or should not be recognized by the law as valid, with the same rights as traditional marriages?" Just over a quarter of survey respondents (27 percent) said they should be valid in 1996, a figure that rose to 35 percent by 1999 (Saad, 2012).

Marriage equality moves into the twenty-first century

The dawn of the twenty-first century saw a flurry of activity regarding marriage rights, creating highs and lows for those involved in the debate and leading to a continuing state of ambiguity as to the changing status of same-sex couples (van Eeden-Moorefield & Alvarez, 2015). Some states – often under judicial pressure – were moving forward with expanded marriage rights, whereas many others were amending state constitutions to limit marriage to one man and one woman. Internationally, marriage rights were advancing, with the Netherlands becoming the first country to legalize same-sex marriage in 2001 and Belgium following suit in 2003. In the United States, Vermont established civil unions for same-sex couples in 2000, the same year that Nebraska approved a constitutional ban on same-sex marriage. Nevada followed with its own constitutional ban in 2002.

Marriage equality proponents cheered a major court victory the following year on November 8, 2003, when the Supreme Judicial Court of Massachusetts ruled four–three in *Goodridge v. Department of Public Health* that under the state constitution's guarantee of equal protection, marriage rights could not be limited to heterosexual couples. With its ruling, the court issued a 180-day stay that expired May 17, 2004, at which point the first legal same-sex marriages in the United States took place. Within a week, about 2,500 LGB couples had applied for licenses in the state (MacDonald & Dedman, 2004). In response to efforts in Massachusetts and other states to expand marriage rights, then President George W. Bush announced in October 2003 that he supported limiting marriage to one man and one woman, and within a few months he publicly supported an amendment to the U.S. Constitution. The president insisted that the American public did not want same-sex marriage, and indeed, polls conducted that fall showed that a majority of adults in the United States opposed expansion of marriage rights to include same-sex couples – 59 percent against, according to the Pew Research Center (2016), and 61 percent against, according to Gallup (Kiefer, 2003).

Although it did not explicitly address marriage rights, another U.S. Supreme Court ruling in 2003 was of vital importance to the marriage equality movement. In June 2003, the Supreme Court in *Lawrence v. Texas* struck down a Texas law that criminalized homosexual sodomy, which the court considered an infringement on the exercise of liberty under the Due Process Clause of the U.S. Constitution (*Lawrence v. Texas*, 2003). Same-sex marriage proponents quickly saw this as paving the way for nationwide marriage equality with the assumption that "In time, one would assume, state and federal courts will apply the same rationale exhibited in

Lawrence in recognition of enduring personal bonds between same-sex couples" (van Eeden-Moorefield & Alvarez, 2015, p. 69). But even with the two key favorable court rulings in 2003, the marriage equality movement still faced well-organized opposition, much of it from state-wide ballot initiatives. In 2004, constitutional amendments denying same-sex marriage were passed in 13 states, with seven more following in 2006. Yet courts in some parts of the country were starting to rule in favor of challenges to such measures. We need only look to California to see the conflict between forces for and against marriage equality and to see how legislative and judicial reasoning was often at odds. California had established domestic partnership rights in 1999, but the following year voters passed Proposition 22, which legally defined marriage as only between one man and one woman. Then in September 2005, both houses of the California State Legislature approved a bill legalizing same-sex marriage, making California's legislature the first in the nation to approve a same-sex marriage bill without judicial pressure. However, Governor Arnold Schwarzenegger vetoed the measure, a pattern that was repeated again in 2007. Meanwhile, in February 2004, San Francisco Mayor Gavin Newsom had drawn national attention when he announced the city would issue marriage licenses to same-sex couples and allow them to be married at City Hall. Approximately 4,000 same-sex marriages were performed before the California Supreme Court on August 12, 2004 voided those marriages, ruling that Newsom had overstepped his authority. Marriage licenses were again issued and many same-sex couples married in 2008 after the California Supreme Court ruled that limiting marriage to opposite-sex couples was unconstitutional, but the process was halted when a November 2008 voter referendum in California passed Proposition 8 to again ban same-sex marriage. Proposition 8 was ruled unconstitutional by a federal judge in August 2010, an opinion that was eventually upheld by the U.S. Supreme Court in 2013. California's example was extreme, but it was not the only state where both proponents and opponents of same-sex marriage may have felt as though they spent the first decade of the new century on one long rollercoaster ride.

One of the most widely publicized milestones of the marriage equality movement didn't actually have anything to do with a court case or state-wide ballot initiative. In a May 9, 2012, interview with ABC News reporter Robin Roberts, Barack Obama became the first sitting U.S. president to publicly support the right for LGB couples to marry. Obama, who was running for re-election, established his position at odds with Republican presidential nominee Mitt Romney, who had already made it clear that he opposed same-sex marriage (Gast, 2012). The president had previously himself declined to publicly support same-sex marriage, although as an Illinois State Senate candidate from Chicago, Obama apparently had signed a questionnaire in 1996 saying that he supported marriage for LGB couples – a fact that was known to his advisers but not the general public (Becker, 2014). In 2012, he acknowledged that his (public) views had changed, and it became a continuing campaign issue. At the time of Obama's announcement, half of the country agreed with him: A Gallup Poll indicated that 50 percent of Americans thought same-sex marriages should be recognized by law as valid, with 48 percent saying such marriages should not be legal (Gast, 2012).

Legislative and judicial marriage-related activities continued at a frenetic pace through 2013, with many occurring in relation to each other – state laws proposed in reaction to a court decision expanding marriage rights, and court decisions based on challenges to the constitutionality of state laws. Possibly the most important judicial event of 2013 was *United States v. Windsor* (2013), which addressed a direct challenge to the federal Defense of Marriage Act signed in 1996. The five–four *Windsor* ruling on June 26, 2013 declared a major component of DOMA to be unconstitutional and a deprivation of the liberty protected by the Fifth Amendment (Socarides, 2013). Also on June 26, 2013, the U.S. Supreme Court issued the final ruling in *Hollingsworth v. Perry* (2013), a series of court cases that concerned Proposition 8 and the issue of same-sex marriage in California. This decision dismissed an earlier challenge to the Proposition 8 ruling, thus making same-sex marriage legal once again in California. Perhaps as a sign of things to come, for the first time in Pew Research Center polling history, a May 2013 survey showed that just over half (51 percent) of Americans favored same-sex marriage. Possibly more importantly, nearly three-quarters of the survey's respondents – 72 percent – said that legal recognition of same-sex marriage is "inevitable," a group that included 85 percent of marriage equality supporters, as well as 59 percent of its opponents (Pew Research Center, 2013).

The biggest court decision of all occurred exactly two years to the day after the *US v. Windsor* and *Hollingsworth v. Perry* rulings. On June 26, 2015, the U.S. Supreme Court issued its ruling in *Obergefell v. Hodges*, a group of six consolidated cases challenging same-sex marriage bans in Ohio, Michigan, Tennessee, and Kentucky. The historic decision, by a five–four vote, declared simply that the U.S. Constitution guarantees a right to same-sex marriage. Writing for the majority, Justice Anthony M. Kennedy stated, "No longer may this liberty be denied. No union is more profound than marriage, for it embodies the highest ideals of love, fidelity, devotion, sacrifice, and family. In forming a marital union, two people become something greater than once they were" (*Obergefell v. Hodges*, 2013). The ruling was cheered internationally by LGBT+ rights advocates, and the Obama administration showed its support by illuminating the White House in rainbow colors. Opponents were stunned, and news coverage focused as well on the opinions of dissenting justices, featuring some of the more pointed comments from Chief Justice John Roberts, as quoted by *The New York Times*: "If you are among the many Americans – of whatever sexual orientation – who favor expanding same-sex marriage, by all means celebrate today's decision. Celebrate the achievement of a desired goal. Celebrate the opportunity for a new expression of commitment to a partner. Celebrate the availability of new benefits. But do not celebrate the Constitution. It had nothing to do with it" (Liptak, 2015).

By the time of the historic June 26, 2015 U.S. Supreme Court ruling, 37 states had legalized same-sex marriage. Three had done so through popular vote, eight by votes of the state legislature, and 26 by court decision. The other 13 states had same-sex marriage bans, either by state law and constitutional amendment or constitutional amendment only. *Obergefell* brought a halt to the constantly changing legal landscape by setting the same standard for all 50 states and U.S. territories. At the time of the ruling, Gallup polls showed that about 60 percent of adults in the United States indicated support for same-sex marriage (McCarthy, 2016).

Response from the opposition

Soon after the Supreme Court decision, lead plaintiff Jim Obergefell predicted that those opposed to same-sex marriage would continue their fight, and he was certainly correct (Wolf, 2016). The primary strategy thus far has been a push for religious exemptions to a wide range of LGBT+ rights laws, not just those related to marriage. In a July 2015 column for *U.S. News & World Report* (Roff, 2015), a senior fellow at the conservative Frontiers of Freedom think tank made it clear that opponents would work tirelessly to seek relief through legislation based on religious freedom. Peter Roff (2015) argued that "The founders believed that no one group of people should be allowed to bully everyone else into conformity and that the rights of those who did not agree must not be infringed upon."

Since long before same-sex marriage became legal, Americans have disagreed over how governments should guarantee religious liberty. The federal Religious Freedom Restoration Act passed by Congress in 1993 prohibited governments at any level from placing substantial burden on a person's exercise of religion, stating that rights of individuals can only be limited by the least restrictive means of advancing a compelling government interest (Nussbaum, 2008). A few years later, the U.S. Supreme Court in *City of Bourne v. Flores* (1997) ruled that the Religious Freedom Restoration Act applied only to the federal government, not to states and municipalities within them. As a result, 21 states have passed their own RFRAs (NCSL, 2016), and other states have such legislation in the works. Although they may vary in scope, usually at a minimum these measures prevent religious officials from having to officiate a marriage that is counter to their religious beliefs (NCSL, 2016). Many such measures are in flux because of legal challenges to their scope. The Family Research Council, which lobbied heavily for years against legalized same-sex marriage, sponsors a Center for Religious Liberty that provides a comprehensive run-down on its website of the state and federal protections for those who oppose same-sex marriage on religious grounds.

In writing the majority opinion for the *Obergefell* ruling, Justice Anthony Kennedy had acknowledged there would likely be pushback from those with religious objections to same-sex marriage. In actuality, this opposition was in place years before the *Obergefell* decision – efforts to establish legal avenues for religious objections began not long after Massachusetts in 2004 became the first state to marry same-sex couples. More recently, there is a push to extend religious liberty measures beyond protection of government officials to include private citizens and businesses. An article in *The Atlantic* (Green, 2016) noted that legislators in 20+ states have considered some sort of new religious-freedom-protection bill in the two years since the *Obergefell* ruling. Many of these bills seek to expand protections to businesses, so that owners can choose not to provide goods and services "in a manner inconsistent with adherence to that person's sincerely held religious belief" (Green, 2016). A Pew Research Center survey from 2016 found Americans to be closely divided about whether businesses that provide wedding services should be required to provide those services for same-sex couples (49 percent) or whether they should be allowed to refuse service based on religious objections to homosexuality (48 percent). The U.S. Supreme Court has indicated its willingness to weigh in on the matter, announcing in June 2017 that it would hear a case involving a baker in Colorado who refused to create a wedding cake for a gay male couple.

References

Abbott, E. (2011). *A history of marriage*. New York, NY: Seven Stories Press.

Alwood, E. (1996). *Straight news: Gays, lesbians, and the news media*. New York, NY: Columbia University Press.

Baehr v. Lewin, 74 Haw. 530, 852 P.2d 44(1993)

Becker, J. (2014, April 16). How the President got to 'I Do' on same-sex marriage. *New York Times Magazine*. Retrieved from https://www.nytimes.com/2014/04/20/magazine/how-the-president-got-to-i-do-on-same-sex-marriage.html

Boswell, J. (1994). *Same-sex unions in premodern Europe*. New York, NY: Vintage Books.

Bronski, M. (2011). *A queer history of the United States*. Boston, MA: Beacon Press.

Cherlin, A. J. (2004). The deinstitutionalization of American marriage. *Journal of Marriage and Family*, 66(4), 848–861. http://doi.org/10.1111/j.0022-2445.2004.00058.x

Coontz, S. (1999). (Ed.) *American families; A multicultural reader*. London: Routledge.

Coontz, S. (2005). *Marriage, a history: From obedience to intimacy, or how love conquered marriage*. New York, NY: Viking.

D'Emilio, J. (1983). *Sexual politics, sexual communities: The making of a homosexual minority in the United States, 1940–1970*. Chicago, IL: University of Chicago Press.

D'Emilio, J., & Freedman, E.B. (1988). *A history of sexuality in America*. Chicago, IL: University of Chicago Press.

Dunak, K. M. (2013, September, 8). The secret history of gay marriage: Same-sex weddings were happening in this country for decades before the Supreme Court permitted it. *Salon*. Retrieved from http://www.salon.com/2013/09/08/the_secret_history_of_gay_marriage

Faderman, L. (1981). *Surpassing the love of men: Romantic friendship and love between women from the Renaissance to the present*. New York, NY: William Morrow.

Fejes, F. (2008). *Gay rights and moral panic: The origins of America's debate on homosexuality*. http://dx.doi.org/10.1057/9780230614680

Foucault, M. (1978). *The history of sexuality*. New York, NY: Pantheon Books.

Gast, P. (2012, May 9). Obama announces he supports same-sex marriage. CNN. Retrieved from http://www.cnn.com/2012/05/09/politics/obama-same-sex-marriage

Graff, E. J. (1999). *What is marriage for?* Boston, Mass: Beacon Press.

Green, E. (2016, January 6). Can states protect LGBT rights without compromising religious freedom? *The Atlantic*. Retrieved from https://www.theatlantic.com/politics/archive/2016/01/lgbt-discrimination-protection-states-religion/422730

Gross, L. (2001). *Up from invisibility: Lesbians, gay men, and the media in America*. New York, NY: Columbia University Press.

Herek, G. M. (2006). Legal recognition of same-sex relationships in the United States: A social science perspective. *American Psychologist,* 61(6), 607–621. http://doi.org10.1037/0003-066X.61.6.607

Hollingsworth v. Perry, 507 U.S. __ (2013).

Jacobs, S. E., Thomas, W., & Lang, S. (Eds.). (1997). *Two-spirit people: Native American gender identity, sexuality, and spirituality.* Urbana, IL: University of Illinois Press.

Kiefer, H. M. (2003, November 11). How would same-sex marriages affect society? Gallup. Retrieved from http://www.gallup.com/poll/9670/how-would-samesex-marriages-affect-society.aspx

Kiefer, O. (2012, November 12). *Sexual life in ancient Rome.* London, England: Routledge.

Lawrence v. Texas, 539 U.S. 558 (2003).

Liptak, A. (2015, June 26). Supreme Court ruling makes same-sex marriage a right nationwide. *The New York Times.* Retrieved from https://www.nytimes.com/2015/06/27/us/supreme-court-same-sex-marriage.html?_r=0

MacDonald, C., & Dedman, B. (2004, June 17). About 2,500 gay couples sought licenses in 1st week. *Boston Globe.* Retrieved from http://archive.boston.com/news/local/massachusetts/articles/2004/06/17/about_2500_gay_couples_sought_licenses_in_1st_week?pg=full

McCarthy, J. (2016, May 19). Americans' support for gay marriage remains high, at 61%. Gallup. Retrieved from http://www.gallup.com/poll/191645/americans-support-gay-marriage-remains-high.aspx

Mondimore, F. M. (1996). *A natural history of homosexuality.* Baltimore, MD: Johns Hopkins University Press.

Nardi, P. M. (1997). Friends, lovers, and families: The impact of AIDS on gay and lesbian relationships. In M. P. Levine, P. M. Nardi, & J. H. Gagan (Eds.), *In changing times: Gay men and lesbians encounter HIV/AIDS* (pp. 55–82). Chicago, IL: University of Chicago Press.

National Conference of State Legislatures (2016). 2016 state Religious Freedom Restoration Act legislation. Retrieved from http://www.ncsl.org/research/civil-and-criminal-justice/2016-state-religious-freedom-restoration-act-legislation.aspx

Nussbaum, M. (2008). *Liberty of conscience: In defense of America's tradition of religious equality.* New York, NY: Basic Books.

Obergefell v. Hodges, 135 S. Ct. 2584 (2015).

Pew Research Center. (2013). In gay marriage debate, both supporters and opponents see legal recognition as "inevitable." Retrieved from http://www.people-press.org/2013/06/06/in-gay-marriage-debate-both-supporters-and-opponents-see-legal-recognition-as-inevitable

Pew Research Center. (2016, September 28). Where the public stands on religious liberty vs. non-discrimination. Retrieved from http://assets.pewresearch.org/wp-content/uploads/sites/11/2016/09/Religious-Liberty-full-for-web.pdf

Roff, P. (2015, July 31). Defend religious freedom: Congress must act to ensure that the Supreme Court's gay marriage decision isn't wielded as a cudgel. *U.S. News & World Report.* Retrieved from https://www.usnews.com/opinion/blogs/peter-roff/2015/07/31/congress-must-defend-religious-freedom-after-gay-marriage-decision?int=opinion-rec

Saad, L. (2012, May 14). U.S. acceptance of gay/lesbian relations is the new normal. Gallup. Retrieved from http://www.gallup.com/poll/154634/acceptance-gay-lesbian-relations-new-normal.aspx

Socarides, R. (2013, June 26). How the court ruled on DOMA and Prop. 8. *The New Yorker.* Retrieved from http://www.newyorker.com/news/news-desk/how-the-court-ruled-on-doma-and-prop-8

Sprigg, P. (2004). *Outrage.* Washington, DC: Regnery Publishing.

Umhoefer, D. (2014, June 22). Mark Pocan says Wisconsin was the first state to ban employment discrimination against all gay and lesbian people. *PolitiFact Wisconsin*. Retrieved from http://www.politifact.com/wisconsin/statements/2014/jun/22/mark-pocan/mark-pocan-says-wisconsin-was-first-state-ban-empl

U.S. v. Windsor, 699 F. 3d 169 (2013).

van Eeden-Moorefield, B. V., & Alvarez, A. (2015). The social, political, and judicial contexts of queer marriage in the United States. *Journal of GLBT Family Studies*, 11(1), 57–81. http://doi.org/10.1080/1550428X.2014.883560

Wolf, R. (2016, May 29). Gay marriage victory at Supreme Court triggering backlash. *USA Today*. Retrieved from https://www.usatoday.com/story/news/politics/2016/05/29/gay-lesbian-transgender-religious-exemption-supreme-court-north-carolina/84908172

3

INSIDE THE NEWSROOM: SHIFTING ATTITUDES ABOUT HOW TO COVER SAME-SEX MARRIAGE

Of all the stories, graphics, and photos included in *USA Today*'s extensive coverage of the two landmark U.S. Supreme Court rulings in favor of same-sex marriage rights in June 2013, one picture in particular drew the most attention. The front-page Associated Press photograph of two men kissing in front of the Supreme Court building, accompanied by the banner headline "Rainbow rulings," drew hundreds of responses – both pro and con – from media critics, activists, politicians, and readers. Executive Editor David Colton, in a post to the newspaper's "Inside *USA Today*" blog, defended the photo, arguing that it adequately captured the jubilation that same-sex couples felt after learning of the rulings. But Colton acknowledged that just a few years before, when a lower-court ruling was issued in favor of same-sex marriage, he had decided against using a similar photo because it might upset readers. Colton said that staffers predicted the 2013 kissing photo would draw strong responses from readers, and so for balance, they included another smaller photo of a preacher praying in opposition to the ruling. But, as Colton recalls, that didn't stop the complaints. Nonetheless, Colton believes that his staff made the right decision: "In the end, we think the kissing photo captured not only the historic nature of the decision but also the very human impact of the day" (Colton, 2013).

USA Today's situation illustrates the difficulty that newsrooms face when dealing with contentious issues, a situation that can be complicated by shifting social norms and public opinion. It's certainly not a new dilemma. Back in 1993, *Hartford Courant* ombudsman Henry McNulty wrote about facing angry subscribers after his newspaper published a profile of an openly gay state legislator in the paper's Sunday magazine. Readers were especially offended by the magazine's cover, which featured a full-page photograph of the legislator kissing a former lover on the mouth. As McNulty (1993) acknowledged, reporters and editors in his newsroom were not in agreement over how to handle gay-themed content, simultaneously facing pressure from LGBT rights groups to increase coverage and from some subscribers to eliminate it altogether. Fast forward 20 years, and the staff at *USA Today* were still asking some of the same questions, although in a very different political climate.

This chapter will examine the decisions that news organizations and personnel made regarding coverage of the same-sex marriage movement and the outside pressures that may have affected their decision-making processes, using the hierarchy of influences model (Shoemaker & Reese, 2014) as a theoretical framework. This model was developed in the early 1990s to allow for systematic evaluation of multiple levels of influence on media content, from the individual to social system level. Reese and Shoemaker (2016) have updated their model to address ways that technology-enabled social networks have disrupted the traditional levels of influence, an adjustment that is particularly valuable when considering the manner in which news personnel and organizations handled coverage of the same-sex marriage movement. This chapter will focus primarily on three of the five levels of influence: the individual, routines/practices, and media organizational levels. We'll also take a brief look at how changing public opinion and U.S. Supreme Court rulings regarding same-sex marriage – components of the social-systems level of the hierarchy of influences model – have affected news practices. Evidence suggests that news coverage of the movement has been influenced by shifting societal-level ideologies regarding sexuality, gender, and the institution of marriage; shrinking resources available to journalists; changing newsroom routines and demographics; and increasing support of LGBT issues by individual producers of content.

Individual level of influence: the journalists themselves

Characteristics of the individual media practitioner comprise the most micro level of influence on media content contained in the original hierarchy of influences model. Although an updated version (Shoemaker & Reese, 2014) discourages positioning individual news workers as lone decision-makers, it nonetheless continues to acknowledge the influence of communicators' personal and professional characteristics on the content they produce. Characteristics such as gender, sexual orientation, and race – as well as religious, education, and political backgrounds – can indirectly influence media content by contributing to personal attitudes and values that in turn influence professional roles and behavior.

It is well documented that heterosexual journalists have not always joyfully welcomed their queer colleagues into the newsroom (Aarons, 1990; Aarons & Murphy, 2000; Camblos, 2006). In 1989, the American Society of Newspaper Editors sponsored a first-of-its-kind survey of LGBT journalists in the workplace, discovering that anti-gay discrimination was widespread. The survey itself was controversial, with many editors "vociferously" opposed, according to project director Leroy Aarons (1990, p. 7). Numerous LGB reporters declined to participate, and of the 205 who did, only 59 percent reported being out to their colleagues at work (ASNE, 1990). Aarons explained that although a majority of respondents described their newsrooms as largely hospitable to LGB journalists, "they also harbor a palpable undercurrent of bias" stemming from attitudes of some anti-gay news colleagues and supervisors (1990, p. 9). Likewise, most of the survey respondents rated their news outlet's coverage of LGBT issues and individuals as mediocre to poor (ASNE, 1990), results that should not have been terribly surprising given the media focus in the 1980s on the emerging AIDS epidemic at the expense of other important LGBT concerns (Alwood, 1996; Camblos, 2006; Gross, 2001). A survey of 227 senior newspaper editors two years later (Bernt & Greenwald, 1992) suggested a gap between queer journalists' assessments of LGBT-related coverage and the assessments of their bosses, who were less critical of coverage in every area except AIDS. When asked to evaluate their newspapers' overall coverage of issues of concern to lesbians and gays, 40 percent of senior editors rated it excellent or good, compared to 29 percent of LGBT journalists.

So, what kind of people work in newsrooms, and which of their attributes are likely to influence news coverage of same-sex marriage? Little research has explicitly addressed the attitudes of news personnel related to sexual orientation, but data from the Pew Research Center does provide some illumination. Results from a 1995 survey of journalists – which are presented along with survey data from subsequent years in a 2004 report titled "Values and the Press" – identified notable differences between journalists and the general public when it came to attitudes toward morality and homosexuality (Pew Research Center, 2004). In 1995, 75 percent of local journalists and 83 percent of national journalists answered "yes" to a question asking whether homosexuality is a way of life that should be accepted by society. By contrast, a 1996 national Gallup poll showed that 50 percent of respondents indicated that they did *not* feel that homosexuality should be considered an acceptable alternative lifestyle (Yang, 1999). By 2004, the "homosexuality way of life" approval figures for local and national journalists were 74 and 88 percent, respectively, compared to just over half (51 percent) of the general public (Pew Research Center, 2004).

Pew data also show differences in religious views. A 2002 survey (Pew Research Center, 2004) showed that about three-fifths of Americans (58 percent) believe that it is necessary to believe in God to be a moral person. However, regardless of whether they work at a national or local news organization, journalists' views differ. About 91 percent of those who work at national news organizations say it is not necessary to believe in God to be moral, with 78 percent of local journalists sharing that view (Pew Research Center, 2004). Survey data released in May 2004 by the Pew Research Center also identified key differences between journalists and the general public in regards to political ideology. Although most local and national news reporters and editors, as well as 41 percent of the general population, describe themselves as political moderates, journalists (especially those who work for national news organizations) are more liberal and less conservative than the general public (Pew Research Center, 2004). Specifically, just over one-third of national journalists (34 percent) and just under one-fourth of local journalists (23 percent) describe themselves as liberals, compared to 19 percent of the general public (Pew

Research Center, 2004). Just 7 percent of national news personnel and 12 percent of local ones label themselves as conservatives, compared to one-third of the American public. Politically, Internet journalists were found to be similar to local print journalists: 57 percent describe themselves as moderates, whereas 27 percent say they are liberals and 13 percent conservatives (Pew Research Center, 2004). Pew data showed that local television and radio news personnel included the lowest percentage of liberals of any of the journalist groups surveyed (15 percent). However, even among local TV and radio journalists, just 13 percent labeled themselves as conservatives.

Reporters who are socially and politically liberal might be expected to produce more favorable content regarding LGBT issues. But data from David Weaver and his colleagues' extensive surveys of journalists (Weaver et al., 2007) indicate that even though news personnel are still more often politically liberal than conservative, surprisingly the percentage of journalists who identified as Democrats was the lowest in 2002 than it had been since 1971. Likewise, more reporters identified as Republicans than before (Weaver et al., 2007). Journalists were not asked explicitly about same-sex marriage in Weaver et al.'s surveys, but they were queried about other social issues. Regarding the legality of abortion, journalists tended to hold more liberal views, but their opinions were closer to the opinions of the public at large in 2002 than a decade earlier. In addition, 2002 survey data showed that journalists have become less religious (Weaver et al., 2007), which may be expected to affect coverage of same-sex marriage, given that it has often been framed as a religious issue (Weaver et al, 2007; Woodford et al., 2012).

The media routines and practices level

The second level of influence in Shoemaker and Reese's (2014) hierarchy of influences model concerns journalistic routines and practices, including unstated but understood rules that can wield considerable influence. Journalists' routines influence the ways that issues and events are covered, affecting the focus and sourcing of the stories that journalists tell. As with other professions, journalism routines have developed over time in response to day-to-day challenges of newsgathering to help journalists do their jobs effectively, efficiently, and ethically (Lecheler & Kruikemeier, 2015; Reese & Shoemaker, 2016). These routines are important to all of us because they affect the social reality portrayed by the media (Shoemaker & Reese, 1996). For this level, we will take a look inside the newsrooms themselves, examining how both official policies and unofficial practices developed and evolved to address shifting attitudes and legalities related to sexual orientation and marriage. As Reese and Shoemaker (2016) note, news routines serve the needs of journalists and their employers, but they also take into consideration audience needs and interests – therefore this section will also examine how news personnel have adjusted content production to address audience demands and reactions.

The news media have long struggled with how to cover topics related to sexuality, balancing traditional notions of newsworthiness with changing public norms and, of course, a desire to attract readers and viewers. Early news coverage of homosexuality tended toward the sensational, focusing on criminality and deviance in line with legal and medical classifications of the times (Alwood, 1996). When same-sex marriage emerged as an issue in the 1970s, public attitudes toward gays and lesbians were in flux, but there was still significant stigma against LGBT individuals and laws preventing them from holding certain jobs. Newsrooms were not immune to these stigmatizing attitudes, a point made clear by results of the initial American Society of Newspaper Editors survey of LGBT news personnel conducted in 1989 (ASNE, 1990). The ASNE president who commissioned the study, Loren Ghiglione (1990), was disturbed by survey findings that showed LGB employees routinely endured wisecracks and sometimes even severe reprisals related to their sexual orientation. Respondents said they knew of instances – although rare – when journalists were demoted or even fired for being lesbian or gay. About four-fifths said they had heard general derogatory LGBT-related remarks, and nearly half had heard such remarks directed specifically at LGB employees (Aarons, 1990). Writing about the historic ASNE survey in his book *Straight News*, former broadcast journalist Edward Alwood said many of the LGB journalists working across the country at that time were concerned about filling out the survey because they "feared they might lose their jobs if their names fell into the wrong hands" (Alwood, 1996, p. 288). Although some survey respondents were willing to be quoted by name, 87 percent were not. In addition, these individuals were dissatisfied with the quality of news coverage about LGBT issues, disappointed by a lack of thoughtful and nuanced coverage (ASNE, 1990). Alwood (1996) explained that "journalists felt that the homophobia they observed in the newsrooms was reflected in the pages of the newspapers at which they worked" (p. 288).

As noted earlier, the ASNE survey was directed by Leroy Aarons, who was then executive editor of *The Oakland* (Calif.) *Tribune* and a (somewhat) closeted gay man himself. During his presentation of the study's results at the 1990 ASNE convention, Aarons came out to his nationwide peers as gay and soon after founded the National Lesbian and Gay Journalists Association. Ten years later, he directed another survey, this one involving 363 print and broadcast journalists who were recruited from the NLGJA, ASNE, and the Radio and Television News Directors Association. In the second survey, most of the respondents (92 percent) reported being open about their sexuality in the newsroom, feeling that workplace climates had improved (Aarons & Murphy, 2000). As then NLGJA president Robert Dodge noted, "never before have LGB journalists felt so comfortable being out in the workplace" (Aarons & Murphy, 2000). Survey results also showed that nearly half of respondents were afforded domestic partner benefits, and 89 percent said they would feel comfortable bringing a same-gender date to company events. Survey coordinators concluded that results provided evidence of two major trends from the 1990s: an "onrush" of journalists who risked going public about their sexuality and a growing commitment within the news industry to equal treatment (Aarons & Murphy, 2000, p. 10).

The initial ASNE study received coverage in several major news outlets, as did the formation and activities of the NLGJA. An *Editor & Publisher* article (Case, 1993) about the NLGJA's second annual convention marveled at the large number of working journalists present (about 600) and the attendance of high-profile newspaper executives and politicians. The story cautioned that newfound acceptance in newsrooms did not mean that anti-gay biases had disappeared but acknowledged that increased numbers of LGBT journalists "have helped improve coverage of gay issues" (Case, 1993, p. 10). The report noted, however, that such coverage wasn't universally appreciated, providing an anecdote from Geneva Overholser, at the time editor of the *Des Moines Register*, who had dozens of readers cancel their subscriptions after the paper prominently ran a photograph of a lesbian couple. Likewise, in her historical analysis of newsroom diversity efforts, Gwyneth Mellinger (2013) suggested that the rapid growth of NLGJA showed that "clearly, gay and lesbian journalists had developed the organizational infrastructure to advocate for their inclusion" (p. 156), but she also pointed out that sexual minorities were left out of a major initiative by ASNE to achieve racial parity by the year 2000 or sooner. This left LGBT journalists "on the margins of the newsroom diversity movement" (Mellinger, 2013, p. 156).

One newsroom that attracted widespread attention – much of it unfavorable – for its early coverage of LGBT topics was that of *The New York Times*. Although more recently it has been identified as producing a higher volume of LGBT-related content than other national news outlets such as *USA Today* and *The Wall Street Journal* (Capuzza, 2016; Gibson & Etheridge, 2017), it received harsh criticism for its paucity of coverage in the 1980s during the emergence of the AIDS epidemic in New York City. Much of the newspaper's early reluctance to write about AIDS and other LGBT topics has been attributed to the influence of Abe Rosenthal, who was *The New York Times* executive editor from 1977 to 1986 (Alwood, 1996; Gross, 2006; Signorile, 2012). An expert in media portrayals of LGBT topics, Larry Gross wrote an obituary of sorts not long after Rosenthal's death in 2006. Gross (2006) acknowledged Rosenthal's contribution as one of the dominant figures in journalism in the late twentieth century, but noted that Rosenthal also had a homophobic side that significantly influenced his newspaper's output by creating an atmosphere of paranoia and fear for queer employees. Gross explained how Rosenthal was often hostile to staff members who dared produce LGBT-related stories and that it was a well-known but unwritten policy in Rosenthal's newsroom that homosexuality was best left in the closet: "The most important rules are those learned by editors and reporters by observing what happens when someone breaks one. Such critical incidents provide everyone in a news organization with dramatic evidence that an unwritten rule exists and must be observed, and it was in this way that editors and reporters at *The New York Times* learned that the topic of homosexuality was not popular with the higher-ups" (Gross, 2006). After Rosenthal, who for years insisted that the word "gay" not be used in the paper to describe gay men and lesbians (Alwood, 1996; Gross, 2001), reached the mandatory retirement age of 65, he was replaced as executive editor by Max Frankel. According to Gross

(2006), Frankel quickly let the newsroom know that policies would change regarding attitudes toward LGBT individuals and the stories that affected them, a change that was soon apparent in the paper's increased coverage of AIDS. Gross (2006) recalls that within a few months of Frankel's ascension, *The New York Times* published a four-part series of articles about the effect of AIDS on New York City. Within a year, *The New York Times*' AIDS coverage was considered among the best (Gross, 2006).

Author and talk-show host Michael Signorile (2102) also attributes changes at the *Times* to the presence of gay staffer Jeff Schmalz. In a piece titled "Out at *The New York Times*: Gays, lesbians, AIDS, and homophobia" written for *The Advocate* in 1992 and republished on *The Huffington Post* 20 years later, Signorile interviewed Schmalz, a well-respected *NYT* reporter and editor who for many years kept his homosexuality a secret. In 1990 Schmalz suffered a seizure in the newsroom, an event that led doctors to an AIDS diagnosis. After telling his editors about both his medical condition and sexual orientation, Schmalz returned to work and started to cover the AIDS epidemic. Signorile (2012) suggests that Schmalz's revelation changed the course of LGBT issues reporting at *The New York Times*. As other media covered Schmalz's situation at the *NYT*, reporters and editors there began to expand AIDS coverage, in addition to covering other aspects of the LGBT movement. Schmalz's revelation, Signorile suggests, seemed to open the door for others to come out in the newsroom.

Since the early 1980s, LGBT advocates have attempted to work with media organizations to improve their coverage of issues and events related to their community. American University historian Rodger Streitmatter (1990) has written specifically about efforts to increase coverage in *The Washington Post*, noting that leaders of the LGBT+ community in the nation's capital who met with newsroom executives compared the *Post* to a huge ocean liner: "They don't like the Post's coverage, but they know a newspaper, like an ocean liner, can't turn around instantly" (p. 29). Similar efforts were taking place in other cities, and one of today's best-known LGBT advocacy organizations, the Gay and Lesbian Alliance Against Defamation (now just known as GLAAD), was formed in 1985 in New York City specifically to pressure media organizations to stop what was viewed as sensational and defamatory AIDS-related coverage. Since then, other organizations have also begun advising media outlets about reporting best practices, and two groups, GLAAD and NLGJA, even provide style guides for reporters to use when covering LGBT-related issues.

As the same-sex marriage movement gained momentum in the 1990s, LGBT advocacy organizations began to issue advisories on topics such as marriage-related terminology, the handling of same-sex wedding announcements, and even whether LGBT reporters should be allowed to cover a story so relevant to their personal lives. Now that LGB couples have the constitutional right to marry in all U.S. states and territories, both GLAAD's and NLGJA's websites recommend that reporters not modify the term "marriage" – such as in "same-sex marriage" or "gay marriage" – because that implies marriage for same-sex couples is somehow different from marriage for opposite-sex couples. Instead they recommend "marriage equality" and "marriage for same-sex couples." The NLGJA website (Association for LGBT Journalists, n.d.) notes that when there is a need for shorthand language, "same-sex marriage" is preferred because it is considered more inclusive than "gay marriage," which may be seen to refer only to gay men. In 1991, the American Psychological Association, yet another professional organization that recommends style guidelines for language usage, recommended using the term "gay" only when referring to gay men (American Psychological Association, 1991). The term has evolved to include both sexes, but research has shown that even when people know it refers to both men and women, it's likely to evoke images of gay men only (Herek et al., 1991).

An informal survey of staffers from eight LGBT publications conducted in 2012 by *Press Pass Q*, a trade publication for LGBT media professionals, showed that "same-sex marriage" was the preferred and most commonly used term in news reports (Colbert, 2012). *The New York Times Manual of Style and Usage* (Siegal & Connolly, 2015) has also begun to recommend "same-sex marriage" instead of "gay marriage," a shift from earlier policies, and an analysis of *New York Times* content shows the newer policy is indeed being followed. Hackl et al. (2013) examined sexual orientation labels that modified the words "marriage," "couples," and "individuals" in the context of same-sex marriage in *The New York Times*, comparing usage in 2004 and 2012. In 2004, reporters used "gay" as a modifier in the majority of same-sex marriage references (52 percent gay compared to 47 percent same-sex). In 2012, the pattern was substantially reversed, with reporters overwhelmingly using the term "same-sex" to modify marriage references (82 percent same-sex compared to 18 percent gay). The *Times*' shift may well affect how reporters at smaller news outlets refer to marriage for same-sex couples, given the fact that U.S. journalists are more likely to read *The New York Times* than any other news outlet (Weaver et al., 2007).

The *Associated Press Stylebook*, widely used by newspapers in the United States, has provided relatively little guidance related to same-sex marriage, but an internal AP memo about marriage terminology drew a lot of criticism in early 2013. One sentence in the memo, which was leaked to influential journalism blogger Jim Romenesko, referred to use of the terms "husband" and "wife," stating that "*Generally AP uses couples or partners to describe people in civil unions or same-sex marriages*" (Romenesko, 2013). There was swift pushback from other news outlets, marriage equality advocates, and even some AP staffers. Associated Press reporter David Crary, who covers LGBT issues for the wire service, insisted he would not abide by his own company's guidelines, explaining, "I will continue to depict them on equal terms, linguistically and otherwise, with heterosexual married couples, with no hesitation about using husband and wife in the cases where that's the appropriate term" (Aravosis, 2013, February 13). Jen Christensen, then president of the Association for LGBTQ Journalists (the new name for NLGJA), wrote an open letter to the AP criticizing the differential treatment for same-sex couples and asking for a revision in the style advisory. Referring specifically to AP's recommendation that the terms "couples" or "partners" be used for legally married same-sex couples, Christensen argued that, "Such guidance may be appropriate for referring to people in civil unions, for which there are no established terms and the language is still evolving, but it suggests a double standard for same-sex individuals in legally recognized marriages" (Christensen, 2013). Eventually, the AP capitulated, revising its guidelines to allow the use of "husband" or "wife" in all references to individuals in a legally recognized marriage regardless of sexual orientation (Vanasco, 2013). Research has shown that language use regarding the same-sex marriage movement is important because it can affect how people think about the issue. In a 2011 poll of New Jersey residents conducted by the Eagleton Institute of Politics and Rutgers University, 51 percent of respondents said "gay marriage" should be legal. When pollsters changed the wording to "marriage equality," however, 61 percent of respondents expressed support (Colbert, 2012).

Terminology use is not the only issue that newsrooms have dealt with in their coverage of the marriage equality movement. Since civil unions were instituted in Vermont in 2000 and same-sex marriage was legalized in Massachusetts four years later, editors have wrestled with policies regarding marriage announcements from same-sex couples. One historically conservative newspaper in New Hampshire, *The Manchester Union Leader*, made headlines for its refusal to print such announcements, even though same-sex marriage was legal in the state. A CNN story (Phillips, 2010) invited readers to respond to Publisher Joe McQuaid's explanation of the newspaper's decision: "This newspaper has never published wedding or engagement announcements from homosexual couples. It would be hypocritical of us to do so, given our belief that marriage is and needs to remain a social and civil structure between men and women and our opposition to the recent state law legalizing gay marriage." Reader comments about the story were mostly critical of McQuaid's position.

Another issue that newsrooms have grappled with is whether LGBT journalists who cover news related to marriage equality represent a conflict of interest, either real or perceived. Editors at *The San Francisco Chronicle* in 2004 drew both criticism and support (Halloran, 2004) for a decision they made to not allow two female journalists who had recently married each other to participate in the newspaper's coverage of the marriage beat. In a memo to *Chronicle* staffers about the situation (Bronstein, 2004), editors were upfront about what they described as a difficult and painful decision-making process, concluding that "The majority of editors involved in the story, and in the discussions, were in agreement on one aspect: that *Chronicle* journalists directly and personally involved in a major news story – one in whose outcome they also have a personal stake – should not also cover that story." Not everyone agreed; in fact, a number of San Francisco city officials and LGBT community leaders advocated for keeping the two women on the same-sex marriage beat, arguing that being married should not keep a reporter from covering any topic (Halloran, 2004). NLGJA did not take a position, calling it a teaching moment and stating, "Overall, there is an increasing need for transparency in newsrooms and the acknowledgement that every person who comes into the newsroom has biases" (Halloran, 2004).

After the key U.S. Supreme Court decisions in favor of marriage equality in the summers of 2013 and 2015, news personnel also had to consider whether they should personally or professionally show support for the rulings through social media. One specific debate concerned the use of Twitter hashtags such as #LoveWins or #LoveisLove to label content. Writing for *Poynter*, AJ+ Deputy Producer Shadi Rahimi (2015) acknowledged that her news outlet, which is an online news and current events channel run by the Al Jazeera Media Network, has cut back on hashtag use. She explained that at first, hashtags were incorporated into copy to save space and streamline content, but over time, journalists began to wonder if they were editorializing by using certain hashtags. *Poynter* columnist and former news director Al Thompkins (2015) has cautioned journalists about using trending hashtags that carry an editorial message, suggesting that it may undercut their intentions to appear to be fair, accurate, and open to multiple sides of the story. After the *Obergefell* decision in 2015, Thompkins was concerned about reporters using #LoveWins and media outlets changing their social media avatars to include visible elements of support (usually the rainbow flag) for the court's decision. Thompkins suggested, "A good measure for how to handle this would be whether you would use a hashtag or change your logo if the Court had decided differently. Would you use #HateWins or #LoveLoses? Would you have used the rainbow flag colors no matter what the decision?"

A reporter or news outlet's decision to change a social media avatar in relation to a specific issue can have repercussions beyond the issue of objectivity; it can also antagonize audiences or future news sources who interact with the journalist on Facebook or Twitter. Back in 2013 in advance of the two key pro-marriage equality U.S. Supreme Court rulings, *Poynter* columnist Nisha Chittal asked journalists about their views and the possible repercussions of switching avatars to show support for an issue. Sara Morrison, then an assistant editor at *Columbia Journalism Review* who changed her Facebook profile photo to the Human Rights Campaign logo, said it's unrealistic to think journalists are objective to begin with: "I don't think changing my avatar compromises my objectivity since it wasn't there to begin with. I have opinions about things. We all do" (Chittal, 2013). Morrison said she is able to report a story fairly regardless of her personal views. "Both my readers and my sources trust me to do this, and I take that trust very seriously. If a few potential sources feel antagonized by my avatar, well, of course that's not good. But I feel strongly enough about this – and know and love too many people affected by this – that it really would've been dishonest for me not to do it" (Chittal, 2013). After a series of interviews, Chittal (2013) concluded that journalists who changed their profile pictures were more likely to work for entrepreneurial and digital media outlets, whereas journalists from legacy news outlets such as NPR, *The New York Times*, and Associated Press tend not to do so. Chittal noted that in many cases, traditional media organizations have developed social media ethics codes or policies that discourage news personnel from sharing their personal opinions through social media. She also learned that journalists who did not specifically cover the same-sex marriage beat were more likely to publicly show their support for marriage equality. Interestingly, many of those who did change their avatars were bloggers and opinion writers, pundits "whose credibility is enhanced rather than undermined by taking a stance on a contentious political issue" (Chittal, 2013). Sarah Blazucki, former editor of the *Philadelphia Gay News* and current NLGJA vice president for print and online, suggests that reporters who work for newer digital news outlets often develop their "brands" through social media and are not as likely to face backlash for posting avatars or other images showing support for SSM (S. Blazucki, personal communication, July 17, 2017). But she considers it more acceptable for journalists to use images such as the rainbow flag, which signifies support for LGBT+ rights in general, as opposed to a red equal sign or some other logo that is related to a specific organization. "Reporters might be covering that organization, so it's probably best to avoid their specific logos," Blazucki said.

The Poynter column that called attention to journalists' use of pro-gay avatars was written two years before the landmark June 2015 U.S. Supreme Court ruling in favor of same-sex marriage, but the avatar issue was still a concern in 2015. For example, *Politico* writer Dylan Byers questioned the decision by *Buzzfeed, Huffington Post*, and *Mashable* to change their Twitter avatars to feature the rainbow flag. Byers (2015) suggested it signaled an endorsement of the rulings, showing "how comfortable some news outlets have become with backing certain political causes." He argued that although columnists and contributors from news organizations may write opinions on the matter, the generally accepted view – at least with legacy news organizations – is that news divisions should report on, but not advocate for, political causes. Byers specifically called out *BuzzFeed* editor-in-chief Ben Smith, who had defended the decision to feature the rainbow flag and had been criticized (Hemingway, 2015) for his explanation that, "We firmly believe that for a number of issues, including civil rights, women's rights, anti-racism, and LGBT equality, there are not two sides" (Byers, 2015). Byers pointed out that *BuzzFeed*'s professional standards guide encouraged journalists to remain neutral, and he suggested the standards guide was not being followed.

For his part, *BuzzFeed*'s Ben Smith did not back down, pushing forward with his belief that there aren't two reasonable arguments to the debate over same-sex marriage. In a podcast interview (Hewitt, 2015), he argued that for people who work at *BuzzFeed*, "the marriage issue is really singular," and they want to be honest with readers about that. He said other news outlets, including traditional ones such as *The Washington Post* and *The New York Times*, have implicit values such as opposing racism and favoring free speech that are "baked into" their coverage (Hewitt, 2015). Smith made it clear that, for *BuzzFeed*, supporting same-sex marriage rights was a core value, although he stressed that he didn't want to silence other points of view. Smith's belief that his company could both cover same-sex marriage as a news issue and publicly support it as a matter of principle may have sounded familiar to readers of *The Huffington Post.* Two years before, in March 2013, *Huffington Post* executives had publicly announced the company's support for marriage equality. Noah Michelson, editor of *HuffPo*'s microsite Gay Voices, assured readers in an interview with Politico (Weinger, 2013) that the site's news coverage would not change. As part of its announcement, *HuffPo* changed its avatars on Facebook and Twitter to a rainbow "H" as a symbol of solidarity.

The question of whether journalists have a responsibility to cover "all sides" of an issue certainly did not originate with the same-sex marriage debate. A Nieman Reports article published just as same-sex marriage was heating up as a political issue examined journalistic notions of objectivity and balance in relation to socially divisive issues (McNulty, 1993). It suggested that journalists traditionally follow one of two models when framing social issues in terms of morals and values. The first is the "two-reasonable-arguments" model in which journalists make an effort to uphold professional norms such as objectivity and fairness by dedicating relatively equal time and space to both sides of a moral issue. This model has been used for subjects such as immigration, abortion or gun control, which are topics the public is divided about. Alternatively, journalists may use the "one-reasonable-argument" model when they cover an issue for which the dominant view is that only one position is morally tenable, such as with reporting on civil rights or human trafficking. As an example, McNulty (1993) points out that a reporter who interviewed a member of the NAACP would not also interview a member of the Ku Klux Klan because the dominant view in the U.S. is that racial discrimination is morally wrong. McNulty suggested that in 1993, when he wrote about these models, the media had not decided which one was appropriate for LGBT+ stories.

Sociologist Gaye Tuchman (1972) has written on the ways journalists have incorporated strategies aimed at achieving objectivity into journalism routines. These strategies include the practice of selecting sources to provide a sense of balance. Thus, if one source makes a truth-claim, a reporter should take measures to include an opposing source's truth-claim as well, which allows for claims of objectivity because neither side has been favored in writing the story (Tuchman, 1972, p. 665). However, Tuchman has pointed out that this strategy may not lead to actual objectivity because the reporter, if unable to verify the accuracy of either source, has merely presented the reader with two unverifiable opposing statements. Johnson-Cartee (2004) has also suggested that attempts to balance sources can limit journalists' perceptions of issues to include two sides only, even when many issues contain multiple nuanced points of view.

A series of in-depth interviews in 2005 with reporters at two metropolitan daily newspapers in North Carolina (Camblos, 2006) showed that, as individual states started to legalize civil unions and marriage for same-sex couples, reporters were hyper aware of journalistic norms of fairness and balance, a focus that routinely led them to consider the "two sides" of the issue. This "two-reasonable-arguments" approach produced reporting practices that routinely pitted LGBT+ activists against conservative (and often anti-gay) sources, resulting in news stories that were often focused on opponents' rhetoric and conflict, rather than exploring issues important to both groups. This approach also left some reporters reluctant to identify neutral sources to provide analysis for news articles (Camblos, 2006).

BuzzFeed's approach to covering same-sex marriage suggests that more recently, at least some media outlets have adopted the one-reasonable-argument model, working under an assumption that the dominant public view favors marriage equality for same-sex couples. Indeed, public opinion polls have shown that a majority of U.S. residents support same-sex marriage rights (Pew Research Center, 2016), although in 2016, more than one-third of survey respondents were opposed. The U.S. Supreme Court, in multiple rulings, has affirmed the right of gays and lesbians to marry as a fundamental civil right, and as we will see in Chapter 4, a significant amount of media coverage of same-sex marriage has framed it as a civil rights issue (Hitlin et al., 2013; Moscowitz, 2013). Likewise, reaction to the infamous 2013 Associated Press memo – which limited use of "husband" or "wife" to descriptions of heterosexual couples – was derided by some for its double standard, described by a *Gawker* writer who compared it to racial segregation as a "jarring 'separate but equal' standard for married couples" that is inherently unequal (Kessler, 2013). Gay activist and radio show host Michael Signorile (2015) has called upon LGBT+ rights supporters to pressure media outlets "to stop legitimizing defamation as rational debate" (p. 137). Signorile specifically condemns news outlets that showcase the views of anti-gay organizations such as the Family Research Council, which has been included among a list of extremist groups by the Southern Poverty Law Center.

But not everyone agrees that the one-reasonable-argument model is appropriate for media coverage of the marriage debate. Conservative columnist Cal Thomas, in a Fox News Watch discussion in 2013, accused the news media of being cheerleaders for the same-sex marriage movement and ignoring the millions of Americans who, for religious or other reasons, do not believe marriage rights should have been extended to same-sex couples (Scott, 2013). He specifically criticized journalists Savannah Guthrie and Natalie Morales for participating in events sponsored by the Association for LGBTQ Journalists, suggesting that it compromises their credibility in covering news related to LGBT+ issues.

Results from a Pew Research Center analysis of media coverage of same-sex marriage (Hitlin et al., 2013) provide evidence that journalists have most often deployed a two-reasonable-arguments model in their news reports, although they may favor one of those arguments over another. The Pew study found almost equal numbers of stories providing either affirming or neutral coverage of same-sex marriage, but a smaller amount of coverage sympathetic to the arguments of those opposed to it. Results showed that 44 percent of stories were relatively neutral, but in stories that largely reflected one side or the other, statements supportive of marriage equality dominated those opposing it by a 5-to-1 margin. NPR's Folkenflik (2013) has surmised that journalists covering same-sex marriage are wrestling with objectivity, reflecting shifts in public opinion, and, in many cases, addressing their own beliefs that same-sex marriage is a civil right similar to interracial marriage in earlier decades. He suggests that much of the resulting news coverage seems to embody a sense that opponents to gay marriage are on the wrong side of history. Even *The New York Times*, once vilified for its insufficient coverage of AIDS in the

1980s, has been accused of favoring pro-marriage equality arguments in its coverage. In his farewell column as the *Times*' public editor, Arthur Brisbane (2012) implied that the newspaper's coverage of the marriage equality movement may have been too progressive, a product of like-minded staffers who treated topics such as the same-sex marriage and Occupy movements "more like causes than news subjects."

Newsrooms must also consider how they will address the aftermath of *Obergefell v. Hodges*, which legalized same-sex marriage in all U.S. states. Writing a few days after the 2015 historic ruling, Poynter's Al Thompkins (2015) chastised journalists who had publicly celebrated the Court's decision. Thompkins, who has co-authored a series of ethics guides for journalists, cautioned journalists not to assume the *Obergefell* decision signaled a conclusion to the marriage debate, warning that a complicated and contentious future lie ahead. He predicted – correctly, as it turns out – that the next battles would be related to churches and religion, a complex arena in which effects of the U.S. Supreme Court decision may not be entirely clear. Suggesting that the decision would "no doubt, ignite great debates inside churches about how to comply with the law while adhering to the canons of their faith" (Thompkins, 2015), he encouraged reporters to cover the situation with an understanding that it will be different from covering the political and social issues around same-sex marriage, specifically because of constitutional limits on government intervention in church activities. Thompkins admonished journalists that whether they agree with the many religious institutions that oppose same-sex marriage or "believe those beliefs are outdated or nonsensical should not shape your reporting when it comes to covering matters of faith" (Thompkins, 2015). He advised reporters to avoid labeling those who oppose marriage equality as nuts or zealots just as they would avoid stereotyping gays and lesbians in their reporting, suggesting that "the job of the journalist is to help your audience have an informed conversation with itself" (Thompkins, 2015).

The media organizations level

This level of Shoemaker and Reese's (2014) hierarchy of influences model focuses on media company structure, the resources they provide to employees, and how they respond to customer demand. Camblos' 2006 study of the decision-making practices at newspapers in North Carolina may have found that news routines led reporters to produce conflict-driven stories that often pitted opposing viewpoints against each other, but it concluded that organizational-level factors such as newspaper resources and location were more influential on news output (Camblos, 2006). The two newspapers studied had very different levels of resources, with *The* (Raleigh) *News & Observer* featuring a larger staff and bigger budget than *The* (Durham) *Herald-Sun*. Because they often had the luxury of more time to write articles about same-sex marriage, *News & Observer* reporters were more likely to write issue stories, whereas reporters from the smaller paper, the *Herald-Sun*, focused more on events. Likewise, executives of the *News & Observer*, which had a circulation that reached beyond the metropolitan market of Raleigh–Durham to include more rural and conservatives areas of the state, were more concerned about perceptions of bias in favor of LGBT+-related issues than were executives from the Durham paper, whose subscribers lived primarily in metropolitan areas (Camblos, 2006). As a result, stories in the Durham paper were less likely to include sources that opposed marriage equality.

Organizational-level influences can also be seen in approaches to coverage of same-sex marriage taken by digital native media outlets such as *The Huffington Post* and *BuzzFeed*. Both organizations have younger and more technologically savvy audiences, and both have publicly stated their support for same-sex marriage. In a 2013 study of media coverage in the months before the landmark June 26 U.S. Supreme Court rulings in support of same-sex marriage (Hitlin et al., 2013), the Pew Research Center analyzed coverage of national media outlets, LGBT+ outlets, Twitter, and *The Huffington Post*. (Pew explained that *HuffPo* was analyzed separately simply because of the high volume of stories it produced.) It should not come as a surprise that LGBT+-focused media outlets' coverage of the same-sex marriage movement was found to be overwhelmingly favorable (Hitlin et al., 2013), with 64 percent of stories including twice as many supportive statements as opposing ones, compared to only 4 percent of stories that had opposition statements outnumbering supporting statements by at least 2:1. Likewise, LGBT+-focused media were more likely to include LGBT+-identified sources than were national media. Content from *The Huffington Post*, which has a microsite dedicated to "Gay Voices," was very similar in tone to that of LGBT+ outlets, with 62 percent of *HuffPo* stories including twice as many supportive stories as opposing ones, compared to only 47 percent of national media stories with that pattern. These findings suggest that LGBT+ media outlets, as well as companies such as *The Huffington Post* and *BuzzFeed* that reach younger and likely more politically liberal audiences (Quantcast, n.d.), have organizational-level policies that push content toward support for marriage equality.

It is important to recognize that the influences discussed in this chapter are not independent of each other, but instead overlap. Journalist demographics and beliefs, newsroom practices and routines, and media organizational policies are in constant play when it comes to news coverage of issues such as same-sex marriage. Societal-level concerns such as shifting public opinion and political and judicial ideologies also influence journalistic output. The next chapter will examine news media coverage of same-sex marriage, tracing patterns over the past 40 years and synthesizing research findings about the effects of such coverage on public opinion and policy.

References

Aarons, L. (1990). Survey brings a minority into focus for first time. In American Society of Newspaper Editors (Ed.), *Alternatives: Gays & lesbians in the newsroom* (pp. 7–19). Washington, DC: American Society of Newspaper Editors.

Aarons, L., & Murphy, S. (Eds.). (2000). *Lesbians and gays in the newsroom, 10 years later.* Los Angeles: Annenberg School for Communications, University of Southern California.

Alwood, E. (1996). *Straight news: Gays, lesbians, and the news media.* New York, NY: Columbia University Press.

American Psychological Association Committee on Lesbian and Gay Concerns. (1991). Avoiding heterosexual bias in language. *American Psychologist*, 46(9), 973–974. http://doi.org/10.1037/0003-066X.46.9.973

American Society of Newspaper Editors. (1990). *Alternatives: Gays & lesbians in the newsroom: American Society of Newspaper Editors Human Resources Committee report.* Washington, DC: American Society of Newspaper Editors.

Aravosis, J. (2013, February 13). AP reporter: I won't follow new anti-gay rule banning terms "husband" "wife." [Blog post]. Retrieved from http://americablog.com/2013/02/dissension-at-ap-over-ban-on-using-husband-wife-for- legally-wed-gays.html

Association for LGBT Journalists (n.d.). *Stylebook.* Retrieved from http://www.nlgja.org/stylebook/marriage

Bernt, J. P., & Greenwald, M. S. (1992). Differing views of senior editors and gay/lesbian journalists regarding newspaper coverage of the gay and lesbian community. *Newspaper Research Journal*, 13(4), 99–110.

Brisbane, A. S. (2012, August 25). Success and risk as *The Times* transforms. Retrieved from http://www.nytimes.com/2012/08/26/opinion/sunday/success-and-risk-as-the-times-transforms.html

Bronstein, P. (2004, March 12). Memo to staff. Grade the News. Retrieved from http://www.gradethenews.org/pages2/marriage.htm

Byers, D. (2015, June 26). Should news outlets declare allegiances? [Blog post]. Retrieved from http://www.politico.com/blogs/media/2015/06/should-news-outlets-declare-allegiances-209576

Camblos, G. Z. (2006). Getting the story straight: Newspaper reporters' decision-making process in coverage of same-sex marriage at The (Durham) Herald-Sun and The (Raleigh) News & Observer (Master's thesis). Retrieved from Carolina Digital Repository Theses and Dissertations database. (UUID: 0ad0958a-614f-4a48–8133-ffe3306ef1da.)

Capuzza, J. (2016). Improvements still needed for transgender coverage. *Newspaper Research Journal*, 37(1), 82–94.

Case, T. (1993). Gay journalists ponder obstacles: Newfound acceptance in newsrooms does not mean biases are gone. *Editor & Publisher*, 126(40), 10–12.

Chittal, N. (2013, March 27). Journalists share arguments for, against using same-sex marriage symbols on social media profiles. *Poynter.* Retrieved from https://www.poynter.org/2013/journalists-share-arguments-for-against-using-same-sex-marriage-symbols-on-their-social-media-profiles/208523

Christensen, J. (2013). Open letter to AP Stylebook Editor. Retrieved from http://www.nlgja.org/blog/2013/02/open-letter-to-ap-stylebook-editor

Colbert, C. (2012, January). "Gay marriage" or "marriage equality"?: New polling shows semantics make a difference, but LGBT media not in agreement over best phrase. *Press Pass Q*, 13(10). Retrieved from http://www.presspassq.com/detail.cfm?id=124

Colton, D. (2013, June 30). INSIDE USA TODAY: All about that front page photo … *USA Today.* Retrieved from http://www.usatoday.com/story/opinion/2013/06/30/gay-marriage-usa-today-front-page-kissing-photo-colton/2476953

Folkenflik, D. (2013, June 27). Is there bias in media's coverage of gay marriage fight? NPR. Retrieved from http://www.npr.org/templates/story/story.php?storyId=196338157

Ghiglione, L. (1990). Why ASNE surveyed gay and lesbian journalists. In American Society of Newspaper Editors (Ed.), *Alternatives: Gays & lesbians in the newsroom* (pp. 5–6). Washington, DC: American Society of Newspaper Editors.

Gibson, R. & Etheridge, C. (2017). Identity negotiation within the family: How transgender television characters challenge gendered family roles, by. Paper presented to the LGBTQ Studies Interest Group of the International Communication Association, May 2017.

Gross, L. (2001). *Up from invisibility: Lesbians, gay men, and the media in America.* New York, NY: Columbia University Press.

Gross, L. (2006, May 16). Larry Gross: Abe Rosenthal's reign of homophobia at The New York Times. *Truthdig.* Retrieved from http://www.truthdig.com/report/item/20060516_larry_gross_abe_rosenthal_homophobia

Hackl, A. M., Boyer, C. R., & Galupo, M. P. (2013). From "gay marriage controversy" (2004) to "endorsement of same-sex marriage" (2012): Framing bisexuality in the marriage equality discourse. *Sexuality & Culture,* 17(3), 512–524. http://doi.org/10.1007/s12119-012-9159-9

Halloran, L. (March 24, 2004). News ethics in flux: Who should cover same-sex issue? *The Hartford Courant.* Retrieved from http://articles.courant.com/2004-03-24/features/0403240205_1_same-sex-marriage-marriage-issue-cover-same-sex-issue

Hemingway, M. (2015, June 30). BuzzFeed's journalistic struggles on same-sex marriage, in GIFs. *The Federalist.* Retrieved from http://thefederalist.com/2015/06/30/buzzfeeds-journalistic-struggles-on-same-sex-marriage-in-gifs/

Herek, G. M., Kimmel, D. C., Amaro, H., & Melton, G. B. (1991). Avoiding heterosexist bias in psychological research. *American Psychologist,* 46(9), 957–963. http://doi.org/10.1037/0003-066X.46.9.957

Hewitt, H. (Interviewer). (2015, June 29). Interview with Ben Smith [Audio podcast]. Retrieved from http://www.hughhewitt.com/wp-content/uploads/06-29hhs-smith.mp3

Hitlin, P., Jurkowitz, M., & Mitchell, A. (2013, June 17). News coverage strong momentum for same-sex marriage. *Pew Research Center.* Retrieved from http://www.journalism.org/2013/06/17/news-coverage-conveys-strong-momentum/

Johnson-Cartee, K. S. (2004). *News narratives and news framing.* Lanham, MD: Rowman & Littlefield.

Kessler, R. (2013, February 12). Associated Press: "Husband" and "wife" are for heterosexual couples only. *Gawker.* Retrieved from http://gawker.com/5983747/associated-press-husband-and-wife-are-for-heterosexual-couples-only

Lecheler, S., & Kruikemeier, S. (2015). Re-evaluating journalistic routines in a digital age: A review of research on the use of online sources. *New Media & Society,* 18(1), 156–171. http://doi.org/10.1177/1461444815600412

McNulty, H. (1993). Are there two reasonable views or is there just one? *Nieman Reports,* 47(3), 80–81.

Mellinger, G. (2013). *Chasing newsroom diversity: From Jim Crow to affirmative action.* http://dx.doi.org/10.5406/illinois/9780252037382.001.0001

Moscowitz, L. M. (2013). *The battle over marriage: Gay rights activism through the media.* http://dx.doi.org/10.5406/illinois/9780252038129.001.0001

Pew Research Center. (2004, May 23). Bottom-line pressures now hurting coverage, say journalists: IV. Values and the press. Retrieved from http://www.people-press.org/2004/05/2/iv-values-and-the-press

Pew Research Center. (2016, May 12). Changing attitudes on gay marriage. Retrieved from http://www.pewforum.org/2016/05/12/changing-attitudes-on-gay-marriage

Phillips, K. (2010, October 25). Blocked gay marriage announcement. CNN. Retrieved from http://newsroom.blogs.cnn.com/2010/10/25/blocked-gay-marriage-announcement

Quantcast. (n.d.). Buzzfeed.com demographics. Retrieved February 1, 2017, from https://www.quantcast.com/buzzfeed.com#trafficCard

Rahimi, S. (2015, June 10). We're using hashtags less than ever. Here's why. *Poynter*. Retrieved from http://www.poynter.org/2015/were-using-hashtags-less-than-ever-heres-why/350121

Reese, S. D., & Shoemaker, P. J. (2016). A media sociology for the networked public sphere: The hierarchy of influences model. *Mass Communication and Society*, 19(4), 389–410. http://doi.org/10.1080/15205436.2016.1174268

Romenesko, J. (2013, February 12.) What the AP does when a man refers to his "husband" or a woman mentions her "wife." [Blog post.] Retrieved from http://jimromenesko.com/2013/02/12/what-the-ap-does-when-a-man-refers-to-his-husband/

Shoemaker, P. J., & Reese, S. D. (1996). *Mediating the message: Theories of influences on mass media content* (2nd ed.). White Plains, NY: Longman.

Shoemaker, P. J., & Reese, S. D. (2014). *Mediating the message in the 21st century: A media sociology perspective*. New York, NY: Routledge.

Scott, J. (2013, March 30). Same-sex marriage coverage leans left. Fox News. Retrieved from http://www.foxnews.com/on-air/fox-news-watch/2013/04/01/same-sex-marriage-coverage-leans-left

Siegal, A. M., & Connolly, W. (2015). *The New York Times Manual of Style and Usage* (5th ed.) New York, NY: Three Rivers Press.

Signorile, M. (2012, November 28). Out at The New York Times: Gays, lesbians, AIDS and homophobia inside America's paper of record. *The Huffington Post*. Retrieved from http://www.huffingtonpost.com/2012/11/28/new-york-times-gays-lesbians-aids-homophobia_n_2200684.html

Signorile, M. (2015). *It's not over: Getting beyond tolerance, defeating homophobia, and winning true equality*. Boston, MA: Houghton Mifflin Harcourt.

Streitmatter, R. (1990). Washington gay leaders seek changes at the Post. In American Society of Newspaper Editors (Ed.), *Alternatives: Gays & lesbians in the newsroom* (pp. 29–32). Washington, DC: American Society of Newspaper Editors.

Thompkins, A. (2015, June 29). Same-sex marriage: Covering the battles ahead. *Poynter*. Retrieved from http://www.poynter.org/2015/same-sex-marriage-covering-the-battles-ahead/353883

Tuchman, G. (1972). Objectivity as strategic ritual: An examination of newsmen's notions of objectivity. *American Journal of Sociology*, 77(4), 660–679.

Vanasco, J. (2013, February 22). Behind AP's new "husband and wife" guideline. *Columbia Journalism Review*. Retrieved from http://archives.cjr.org/minority_reports/when_the_ap_appeared_to_be_lim.php

Weaver, D. H., Beam, R. A., Brownlee, B. J., Voakes, P. S., & Wilhoit, G. C. (2007). *The American journalist in the 21st century: U.S. news people at the dawn of a new millennium*. Mahwah, NJ: Erlbaum.

Weinger, M. (2013, March 26). HuffPo officially comes out in support of gay marriage. *Politico*. Retrieved from http://www.politico.com/blogs/media/2013/03/huffpo-officially-comes-out-in-support-of-gay-marriage-160264

Woodford, M. R., Walls, N. E., & Levy, D. L. (2012). Religion and endorsement of same-sex marriage: The role of syncretism between denominational teachings about homosexuality and personal religious beliefs. *Interdisciplinary Journal of Research on Religion*, 8, 1–29.

Yang, A. S. (1999). From wrongs to rights: Public opinion on gay and lesbian Americans moves toward equality. *National Gay and Lesbian Task Force*. Retrieved from http://www.thetaskforce.org/static_html/downloads/reports/reports/1999FromWrongsToRights.pdf

4

MEDIA FRAMING OF THE MARRIAGE DEBATE

It's a good bet that few people saw the first U.S. magazine cover devoted to the topic of SSM. It was published in August 1953 at a time when homosexuality was a crime and gays and lesbians were considered a danger to children and a threat to national security. The unassuming cover of *ONE* magazine featured no photographs, just a simple two-word question: "Homosexual Marriage?" *ONE* had been founded earlier that year by members of the secretive Mattachine Society, a group of gay men in Los Angeles who, as part of the emerging homophile movement, wanted to increase both the visibility and rights of gays and lesbians. The monthly magazine was sold openly in Los Angeles and quickly attracted the attention of local officials who were determined to shut it down. The U.S. Post Office in short time banned the publication as obscene, with the marriage-themed issue making history as the first one censored by the postal service (Savage, 2015). A decade later, *ONE* once again put marriage on its cover, this time with a more optimistic cover story headlined "Let's Push Homophile Marriage" (Stewart-Winter, 2006). Author Randy Lloyd (1963, p. 6) advocated for recognition of existing relationships among what he referred to as "the homophile married set." There was less pushback from officials this time, as homosexuality was being discussed more openly in newspapers and on television. But still, the topic of SSM wasn't taken seriously.

As we know now, it took years before an organized SSM movement developed in the United States and even longer before the mainstream press paid any attention to it. Since the mid-1990s, however, media attention has steadily increased, with some larger newspapers having beats dedicated to the subject. This chapter will examine that media coverage, which has for the most part relied on two key frames when addressing SSM: morality and civil rights. This chapter will also build upon the previous one's discussion of the "two reasonable arguments" model, in which news reporters are careful to provide equal coverage of sources on both sides of a debate. We'll see if there is evidence that SSM coverage has shifted in favor of the "one reasonable argument" model where only one side of an argument is presented as acceptable because the other side is deemed by many to be morally distasteful. But first, it's important to situate this discussion within the theoretical tradition of media framing, a social constructivist approach that acknowledges the fact that journalists do more than simply recount the details of events. Rather, they *frame* social phenomena in ways designed to help audiences make sense of them, emphasizing some points over others and in the process, shaping public understanding of the issues involved. This process is especially important when news stories focus on social movements, where research has shown that media accounts can influence public opinion by casting one side or another as more legitimate (Bronstein, 2005).

Media framing, public opinion, and social movements

Our contemporary understanding of the news media's ability to influence public discourse through the construction of frames can be traced back to 1922's *Public Opinion*, a book by the influential journalist and public intellectual Walter Lippmann. His now-famous premise is that people form opinions about social phenomena based upon the "pictures in their heads," which arise from the media's interpretative frames of those events and issues. In this context, news frames help people organize their knowledge, opinions, and impressions about topics in the news, be they a controversial event, legal case, or social issue. These mental images help audiences to simplify real-world complexities, but individuals typically lose sight of the fact that the images are just interpretations and not a window into reality. Indeed, Lippmann insisted that a news story not be considered a first-hand report of reality; instead he referred to it as "a report of that material after it has been stylized" (1922, p. 219). This concept of stylization is what we now refer to as framing, a theoretical approach to the study of media influence that is popular across disciplines. The term "frame" came from sociologist Erving Goffman, who used the simple yet elegant analogy of a picture frame that serves as a structure to hold together individuals' "pictures" of life experiences, helping them to "locate, perceive, identify, and label" those experiences (1974, p. 21). Research in this tradition has examined ways that journalists create frames in their news reports, as well as how audiences interpret those frames and use them to form opinions about topics in the news (Entman, 1993; Scheufele, 1999). Within this constructionist approach, media audiences are considered to be active in their discussions and interpretations of public events, yet also reliant on the news media to produce understandable frames of reference for important issues (Price et al., 2005).

As a theory, framing has its detractors and has been described as lacking a disciplined approach to the conceptualization and operationalization of variables (Scheufele, 1999). Media scholar Robert Entman's now classic critique of framing as a "fractured paradigm" notes that despite its popularity in multiple fields, there is "no one statement of framing theory that shows exactly how frames become embedded within and make themselves manifest in a text, or how framing influences thinking" (1993, p. 51). Nonetheless, Entman acknowledges the value of examining both frame production and interpretation processes because of their ability to help us understand the ways that media texts influence people's reasoning and opinion formation. Likewise, numerous researchers have provided evidence that media frames can exert substantial influence over the public's understanding of social issues (Brewer, 2002; Bronstein, 2005; Entman, 1993; Iyengar, 1991), especially under circumstances where that understanding is shifting (Warren & Bloch, 2014; Nelson et al., 1997), as has been the case with issues related to sexual and gender identities. As such, it is important to examine the ways in which journalists have framed the decades-old debate over SSM.

Media framing of homosexuality and SSM

As noted in Chapter 1, the media paid scant attention to LGBT+-related topics until after the 1969 Stonewall riots in New York City and the subsequent emergence of a more organized and visible gay rights movement. Political scientist John Zaller, whose research has sought to explain how people acquire and are influenced by political information from the media and other sources, analyzed early news media coverage of LGBT+ issues. Zaller's analysis (1992) revealed that news reports in the 1970s generally characterized homosexuality in one of two ways: (1) as a psychological disorder to be treated with therapy or (2) as a civil rights issue similar to those faced by racial minorities and thus subject to government efforts to promote equality. However, analysis of news coverage of California's Proposition 6, a 1978 measure that sought (unsuccessfully) to prevent LGBT+ individuals from working in the state's public school system, identified a more uniformly defamatory framing pattern. The qualitative study (Adams, 2013) compared *Los Angeles Times*' coverage of Prop 6 with its coverage 30 years later of Proposition 8, the now infamous measure that voters passed to outlaw SSM in California. Adams discovered several frames, in addition to terminology use, prevalent in the 1978 coverage that media professionals would now likely find problematic: the use of sexual "preference" instead of "orientation" to describe homosexuality, the implication that homosexuals prey on children, the belief that homosexuality can be taught, an absence of support for homosexuality, and a fear of publicly opposing Proposition 6. By the time Prop 8 made headlines years later, Adams found that the phrase "sexual preference" had disappeared from the *L.A. Times*.

Moving into the 1980s and 1990s, frames equating gay rights to civil rights became more common in news coverage, a trend Haider-Markel and Joslyn (2013) attribute to the emergence of deeply partisan politics surrounding the question of sexual orientation during that time period. Democrats, a party that historically had responded (mostly) positively to civil rights–based social movements, began to increase the number of LGBT+ delegates at the state and national levels, and by the early 1990s, sexual minorities were considered an important component of the Democratic political coalition (Haider-Markel, 2001). It makes sense, then, that

Democrats pushed for media and public consideration of LGBT+ issues from a civil rights perspective, relying on a genetics-based explanation for homosexuality to support their assertions that individuals should not be denied rights based on an innate characteristic such as sexual orientation. Republicans, on the other hand, rejected the comparison of homosexuality to racial or gender identity, arguing that being gay is a choice and thus not deserving of civil rights protections. They also characterized anti-LGBT+-discrimination legislation proposed in some cities across the country as "special rights" (not civil rights), thus differentiating LGBT+ individuals from heterosexuals (Haider-Markel, 2001). As you can see, even with such divergent positions staked out by the two political parties, regardless of which side of the debate journalists drew sources from, their resulting news reports would likely feature some version of a civil rights frame, albeit with different conclusions. This phenomenon can be seen in even the earliest mainstream media coverage of marriage-related court rulings. A *Washington Post* story about the Hawaii Supreme Court's 1993 ruling that states may not be able to prohibit same-sex couples from marrying included as a source an ACLU official who was clearly positioning the issue as a civil rights–based one: "When a man is allowed to marry a woman, but a woman is not allowed to marry a woman, that is a form of discrimination" (Biskupic, 1993, p. A10). A *New York Times* article from the same day (May 7, 1993) provided the counter argument that restricting marriage to heterosexual couples wasn't discrimination but an acknowledgment of the biological ability of a union between a man and woman to produce children. The story quoted from the Hawaii court ruling's dissent by Justice Walter Heen, who insisted that the intent of laws restricting marriage did not represent bias, "but a recognition that heterosexual couples further the propagation of the species" (Schmalz, 1993, p. A14).

As medical and psychiatric professionals in the 1970s began to distance themselves from earlier classifications of homosexuality as a mental disorder, so too did news frames. By the time media reports about SSM emerged in the 1990s, the psychological disorder frame had largely disappeared, with opponents of SSM instead positioning their arguments within the realm of morality, arguing that homosexuality as a lifestyle violates natural law and religious teachings. This morality frame appeared regularly in news reports, joining the civil rights frame as the most common ones employed by journalists, according to numerous analyses of news coverage of SSM (e.g., Brewer, 2002, 2003; Gordon et al., 2007; Liebler et al., 2009; Moscowitz, 2010; 2013; Pan et al., 2010; Rimmerman et al., 2000).

The result was a barrage of news content focused on opposing values-based frames. We can look to news stories following the *Lawrence v. Texas* ruling in 2003 to see great examples of how these frames played out. As you'll recall, one of the most newsworthy aspects of that ruling was the implications it had for the future of SSM. This served to galvanize both proponents and opponents of marriage equality and attracted a lot of news attention. A typical example of a morality-framed news story appeared in *The New York Times* on July 31, 2003, featuring this lead: "Worried about the spread of laws that recognize same-sex couples, the Vatican today urged Roman Catholic lawmakers and others to fight back, calling support for such legislation 'gravely immoral'" (Semple, 2003). The story quoted at length from the Vatican dictate: "There are absolutely no grounds for considering homosexual unions to be in any way similar or even remotely analogous to God's plan for marriage and family… Marriage is holy, while homosexual acts go against the natural moral law" (Semple, 2003). Equally strong values-based language was used in stories featuring an equality/civil rights frame, as we can see in yet another *NYT* article from 2003, this one quoting Evan Wolfson from the advocacy group Freedom to Marry about the implications of the *Lawrence v. Texas* ruling for marriage equality: "The Supreme Court has said in the strongest possible terms that love and intimacy and family have deep constitutional protection for all Americans and that gay people have an equal right to participate. This gives us a tremendous tool for moving forward to end discrimination" (Kershaw, 2003).

There have been so many scholarly analyses of media coverage of SSM that it's impossible to review them all. A select few will be reviewed here to show how coverage changed over time and varied depending upon the medium and news outlet under consideration. A study of SSM news coverage from 2002–2004 (Pan et al., 2010) suggests that the type of value frame (equality vs. morality) applied to the marriage debate depended upon the news company being studied. This project analyzed framing patterns in *The New York Times* and *Chicago Tribune* in the months just before and after Massachusetts legalized SSM in 2004. The newspapers were chosen because of their differing ideological reputations to determine if framing, topic, and sourcing patterns would be dissimilar. Results indicated that *The New York Times*, which has the more liberal reputation, more often emphasized an equality/civil rights frame, especially after SSM began in Massachusetts, at which point the authors describe *NYT* personnel as becoming "activists" for marriage equality (Pan et al., 2010, p. 630). A March 2004 *NYT* editorial provides an example of its supportive language: "This debate follows the same narrative arc as women's liberation, racial integration, disability rights, and every other march of marginalized Americans into the mainstream" (New York Times, 2004, p. 82). The editorial suggested that SSM had gone from being considered outlandish to being branded offensive, but that the final destination would be eventual acceptance. Alternatively, the *Chicago Tribune* was more likely to employ a morality frame suggesting that legalization of SSM would be detrimental to American traditions, families, and religious teachings.

Analysis of media coverage of key court rulings and political events from 2002–2003 (Gordon et al., 2007) also indicated that news coverage of SSM relied heavily on two key frames, equality and traditional moral values. However, there were some unusual patterns in the findings. Results showed that traditional values frames were slightly more prevalent than equality frames, with a combination of the two frames within one story representing the most common story format. The researchers suggest that the prevalence of this combination pattern was likely due to reporters' attempts to handle story assignments in an objective or balanced manner. Interestingly, in spite of the fact that traditional frames were more prevalent than equality frames, sourcing patterns were more pro-SSM: In the study sample, 35 pro-SSM and 26 anti-SSM interest groups were quoted or referenced at least once. A later study of sourcing patterns in marriage coverage in U.S. newspapers (Li & Liu, 2010) examined content from five large metropolitan daily newspapers in 2004. The researchers focused on the issue of balance, suggesting that it is something reporters can control to help reduce the anxiety of producing stories about such a controversial issue. This study defined "balance" simply as including sources both for and against SSM, and results showed it to be quite common. Of the 209 news stories analyzed, 87 percent contained sources from both sides (pro or con), 8 percent involved only pro-SSM sources, and 3 percent involved only anti-SSM sources.

A few years later, news coverage of the battle over California's Proposition 8 in 2008 (Warren & Bloch, 2014) was found to rely heavily on equality framing. Proposition 8, a voter initiative limiting marriage to heterosexual couples, was among the most expensive ballot measures ever. Warren and Bloch compared content frames from three newspapers, the *San Francisco Chronicle, New York Times,* and *Washington Post* from May 2008 to August 2010, a time period extending from a few months prior to the Prop 8 vote through two court challenges. The researchers examined more than 500 news articles, editorials, and letters to the editor, and discovered that the civil rights/equality frame appeared most often, occurring – somewhat surprisingly – regardless of an article's position (pro or con) on the issue. In much of the coverage, same-sex couples were portrayed as targets of unequal treatment, and their opponents were portrayed as discriminatory. A January 6, 2009, news story quoting then California Attorney General Jerry Brown included typical language illustrating this civil rights frame: "Because the court's May ruling equated a person's right to marry with the rights to liberty and privacy, it should be recognized as an inalienable right that voters can't generally overturn" (Wildermuth, 2009, p. A1). Warren and Bloch's study also found that overall, pro-SSM frames were represented more prominently than those in opposition, noting that the majority of documents were either balanced in coverage or skewed in support of SSM. Articles focused on opposition to SSM were most often framed within a context of protecting heterosexual marriage and respecting the vote of the people in California regarding the definition of marriage.

Leigh Moscowitz, whose 2013 book *The Battle Over Marriage* provides a critical look at media coverage of the marriage movement, has closely examined the visual and spoken content that has accompanied news reports of SSM. Looking specifically at television news coverage from 2003–2004, Moscowitz's (2010) analysis of sourcing patterns and sound-bite length shows coverage was dominated by conventionally "straight" perspectives. Although LGB couples were visually prevalent in news stories from the national network news broadcasts, they were largely "seen and not heard" (p. 24). Moscowitz concludes that LGB couples who appeared in the news were essentially used just for visual ornamentation. Moscowitz (2013) has also examined visual narratives in print news, noting that a large majority of news reports included some type of visual representation of gays and lesbians. However, she suggests that many of the early news stories about marriage equality featured non-threatening images that helped to mainstream SSM and that did not challenge traditional notions of masculinity and femininity. As an example, Moscowitz discusses a split-run cover featured by *Newsweek* in July 2003 after the *Lawrence v. Texas* ruling. The cover featured either an attractive lesbian or gay male couple in an embrace and looking directly at the camera. The cover story – headlined "Is Gay Marriage Next?" – addressed the implications of *Lawrence v. Texas*, which many predicted would pave the way for marriage rights for same-sex couples. Both cover photos exemplified a pattern in mainstream media depiction: a focus on white middle- to upper-class couples, nonthreatening in appearance and usually in a long-term relationship.

In a similar critical approach to examining media framing practices, Liebler, Schwartz, and Harper (2009) analyzed 572 news articles focused on SSM from 2004–2005. The researchers were interested in whether the press, in reporting on state ballot initiatives banning SSM, had reinforced the traditional moral and legal structure of marriage by privileging standards of heteronormativity, or whether coverage had challenged traditional boundaries of marriage and family. They also wanted to examine the power relations at work in newspaper coverage of SSM through analysis of sourcing patterns and topic frames. Their project involved content and frame analyses of stories from daily papers and wire services, in addition to a deeper textual analysis of a portion of that content. Based on their findings, the researchers suggest that news coverage did little to challenge heteronormative definitions of marriage, and that although SSM-friendly frames were more common than traditional-marriage frames, the latter actually wielded more power over the structure of the marriage debate. Liebler et al. (2009) concluded that media typically craft frames that privilege heterosexuality without challenging traditional gender and sexuality norms within the institution of marriage. Results showed that this was accomplished through source selection that relied on viewpoints considered "comfortable" for heterosexual audiences and avoided those with more controversial perspectives (p. 656).

One analysis of news coverage of the state-level marriage amendments took a somewhat different approach to evaluating framing patterns. Sociologist Katherine McFarland (2011) suggested that researchers had been too quick to position the marriage debate between two opposite-minded sides – conservatives who resist change versus liberals who embrace diversity and change. McFarland examined the use of themes in news articles and editorials written by journalists and prominent contributors to the news, as compared to letters to the editor written by non-elite members of the public. She pulled content from print newspapers in the seven states that voted on marriage-related state ballot initiatives banning gay marriage in November 2006. Results revealed a variety of frames, 17 in total. Seven were supportive of the amendments, nine opposed, and one neutral. Although the study found that a version of the traditional morality frame was most prevalent among those in support of the amendments and an equality/rights frame was most prevalent among those in opposition to the amendments, many of the remaining frames went beyond arguments of equality vs. morality. For example, to explain their support of the amendments, letter writers argued that heterosexuality has always been a component of the definition of marriage, that religious teachings are important to follow, and that it is beneficial to provide children with a mother and father. Frames also revolved around the appropriate role of government in the extension of civil rights. Likewise, those who opposed the amendments did so by calling for increased tolerance for diversity, expressing concern for the legal ramifications for existing same-sex couples and their children. McFarland characterized her findings as contradicting previous research that has focused on polarization of values. Instead, a more nuanced examination shows that debates also invoke broader themes including support of children, competing claims of harm, and separation of government powers.

Although a substantial amount of traditional university-based research has analyzed framing patterns in media coverage of SSM, perhaps the broadest examination was conducted in 2013 by the nonpartisan Pew Research Center. Their project included analysis of non-traditional media and social media, and thus it's worth a detailed discussion. Involving multiple staffers, the study involved examination of content from March 18 to May 12, 2013, when the U.S. Supreme Court was considering two key cases (*U.S. v. Windsor* and *Hollingsworth v. Perry*) regarding marriage rights. The subsequent report (Hitlin et al., 2013) was titled "News coverage conveys strong momentum for SSM" and received substantial media attention, with opponents of marriage equality interpreting it as confirmation of media bias against supporters of traditional marriage. So, how did Pew come to the conclusion that media coverage had conveyed such a "strong momentum" for SSM? To measure content tone and framing patterns, staffers analyzed a wide variety of sources: 11 newspapers (including national papers such as *USA Today* and *The New York Times* and regional ones such as *The Houston Chronicle* and the *Traverse City Record-Eagle*); morning and evening news programs from the three main network news outlets (ABC, CBS, and NBC) and PBS; a mix of programs from three cable TV channels (CNN, Fox News, and MSNBC), talk radio, NPR, and six websites (such as *Politico, BuzzFeed*, and *The Daily Caller*). The study also separately analyzed content from *The Huffington Post*, a mix of 11 LGBT+ news outlets, and Twitter.

As noted in Chapter 3, the key takeaway highlighted in Pew's report – and the focus of much media attention – was that stories with more statements supporting SSM outweighed those with more statements opposing it by a five-to-one margin. Of the 488 items that were coded by researchers, almost half of them (47 percent) primarily focused on support for marriage equality, with 9 percent largely focused on opposition, and 44 percent mixed/neutral.[1] The focus on support appeared in both news articles and opinion pieces and across almost all of the media outlets examined, including Fox News. The only exceptions were two conservative talk radio programs included in the sample, those of Sean Hannity and Rush Limbaugh. Not surprisingly, the largest percentage of stories supporting SSM appeared in the LGBT+ media outlets (64 percent), with *The Huffington Post* not far behind (62 percent). Only 4 percent of LGBT+ news outlet stories contained more statements opposing SSM than supporting it, a figure that was 7 percent for *The Huffington Post*. Interestingly, Twitter showed the most balanced sentiment in terms of support for or opposition to SSM, with 31 percent of assertions on Twitter labeled as supporting, 28 percent as opposing, and 42 percent as mixed/neutral. Pew's report noted that content on Twitter aligned more closely with public opinion than with the news media in terms of support/opposition percentages. At the time, public opinion polls put public support for SSM at 51 percent, with 42 percent opposed.

The Huffington Post was found to contain far more same-sex-marriage-related content than any other media outlet studied. On one day alone – March 27, the second day of the U.S. Supreme Court hearings – *HuffPo* produced 77 separate items on the subject. Most of this content appeared on *HuffPo*'s microsite Gay Voices, which was launched in 2011. *Huffington Post* content also more often included LGBT+-identified individuals as sources than did other media outlets. Coincidentally, during the timeframe of the Pew study, *The Huffington Post* officially announced its public support for marriage equality, with Gay Voices editor Noah Michelson stating in an interview with *Politico* that it would not affect the site's reporting. Michelson explained his position: "I think that we can have accurate, smart and also neutral reporting on the issues and also say that we think that LGBT+ rights are not only the right thing to do, but the future of this country" (Weinger, 2013).

Pew's study also focused on the arguments for and against SSM included in media coverage. It found that the central argument among supporters was that it was a civil rights issue (mirroring much of the academic research we've discussed thus far), whereas opponents focused on the idea that SSM would be detrimental to society and the institution of traditional marriage (Hitlin et al., 2013). Those arguing for SSM had a more consistent message, with half of the stories in the news media content studied focused on the argument that LGB couples should be allowed to marry because of ideals of equality, an argument that was also the most common in LGBT+ media and *The Huffington Post*. This strategy emphasized the importance of marriage in legitimizing relationships and argued that denying these rights to gays and lesbians relegates them to a second-class status. It also tended to compare the movement for marriage equality to previous equality movements, such as the one for race-based civil rights. Other arguments supporting marriage equality included a focus on shifting public opinion (22 percent of stories), the assumption that it would benefit families (12 percent), and that government (in the form of ballot initiatives or state legislation) should not determine marriage restrictions (10 percent). Marriage equality opponents provided a wider variety of arguments, with the most common argument being that it would harm society and traditional marriage, a focus of about one-fifth of news items studies. Other anti-same-sex-marriage arguments featured the view that homosexuality is immoral based on religious teachings and natural law, and that the government should not force on people a new definition of marriage that deviates from the traditional notion of one woman and one man.

In addition to the primary arguments for and against expansion of marriage rights for lesbian and gay couples, 17 percent of stories included the view that the U.S. Supreme Court should not have taken on the issue of SSM and that it should be left up to individual states to determine marriage status. This was usually put forth by legal scholars/sources and occasionally by opponents. LGBT+ news outlets tended to focus on local and state laws more than other media outlets, which were more focused on national issues. Many of the news stories that were coded as supportive of marriage equality included evidence that it was gaining approval from the general public as well as public figures such as President Barack Obama. On the other hand, stories that were coded as opposing marriage rights for same-sex couples were more likely to include profiles of individuals or organizations working to maintain the marriage status quo.

Given this book's emphasis on the role of social media messaging in the success of the SSM movement, it's important to delve more deeply into Pew's findings in relation to Twitter. Pew began monitoring social media trends in 2009, and its data indicate that the marriage battle has regularly been a "hot-button cultural topic," sparking large amounts of conversation on blogs and Twitter (Hitlin & Tan, 2012). The online debate has generally been fueled by an event or court ruling, and for the most part supporters of SSM have outnumbered foes. In the 2013 study (Hitlin et al., 2013), Twitter posts related to SSM encompassed political and religious opinions, as well as more personal material. The big-picture results from analysis of more than 2.4 million public Twitter posts showed balance overall, with 31 percent of the content supportive of SSM, 28 percent opposed, and 42 percent mixed or neutral. During the eight weeks involved in the analysis timeframe, there were surprisingly large swings in sentiment. The week of the actual U.S. Supreme Court hearings (March 25–29) featured the most content, with 48 percent (just under 1.2 million tweets) of all assertions. Those statements showed a slight preference for SSM, with 23 percent in favor and 18 percent opposed. The two weeks after that, however, showed dramatic shifts in opinion, with 55 percent of assertions opposed, 32 percent in favor, and 13 percent neutral or mixed. After that, sentiment shifted back in support of marriage rights for same-sex couples.

The 2013 Pew Twitter data represented a departure from patterns the organization identified a year before in a May 2012 analysis of Twitter and blogs (Hitlin & Tan, 2012). In that study, statements supporting the right of LGB couples to marry outnumbered those opposed by more than two-to-one. Timing may explain the difference, given that the 2012 study period (May 7–11) included President Barack Obama's announcement that he was publicly supporting marriage equality. During that time, the president's statement was the most popular subject on blogs and No. 3 on Twitter, according to the New Media Index from the Pew Research Center's Project for Excellence in Journalism. On blogs, 40 percent of the conversation supported SSM, compared to 14 percent opposed, and 45 percent neutral. The Twitter numbers were very similar: 41 percent of assertions were positive, 16 percent negative, and 43 percent neutral. The blogosphere practically blew up after the president's statement, with the conversation about SSM growing by more than 60 percent. In the three days prior to Obama's revelation, blogs averaged about 2,500 statements about marriage equality a day, but from May 9 to 13, it jumped to more than 4,200 statements a day. Interestingly, in spite of increased chatter, levels of support did not shift much at all. Prior to Obama's statement, 40 percent of blog statements were in favor, compared to 16 percent opposed, and 44 percent neutral. Afterwards, those numbers were basically the same, with 40 percent in favor, 14 percent opposed, and 46 percent neutral. On Twitter, the increase in discussion was heftier after the president's statement, although the levels of support also remained constant. From May 6 to 8, there was an average of roughly 120,000 statements on Twitter, compared to more than 315,000 from May 9 to 13. In both periods, however, the tone was identical: 41 percent in favor, 16 percent opposed, and 43 percent neutral.

Pew has attributed the high levels of online support for SSM to the younger demographics of social media users (Hitlin & Tan, 2012). Sociologist Andrew Perrin (2015) prepared a report for Pew describing trends in social media usage from 2005 to 2015. He found that young adults were among the earliest social media adopters, dominating social media during some of the key court rulings and ballot initiatives in the late 2000s. In 2008, 63 percent of adults age 18–29 reported using social networking sites, compared to just 2 percent of those 65 or older. In 2012, the year President Obama publicly announced his support for SSM, those figures were 83 percent and 19 percent, respectively. Usage by older adults has increased in recent years, but the 18–29 age group is still the most active among adults online. At the same time, a May 2016 Pew Research Center study showed that younger people are more likely than any other age group to favor SSM. Millennials, people born in 1981 or later, are the generation most likely to support SSM (71 percent), compared to 56 percent of Generation X (born from 1965 to 1980), 46 percent of Baby Boomers (born from 1946 to 1964), and 38 percent of the Silent Generation (born from 1928 to 1945).

One reasonable argument, or two?

Now that we've taken a thorough look at how the news media have framed coverage of SSM, it's time to return to the question *BuzzFeed*'s Ben Smith raised when he defended his company's decision to publicly support marriage equality. That question is whether news coverage of the marriage issue has shifted from a "two-reasonable-arguments" model to one that suggests there is just one reasonable point of view. As you recall, many controversial issues such as abortion or immigration are treated by the media as having multiple reasonable "sides," and thus news coverage is expected to fairly represent those differing points of view. Other topics, however, are considered to be more one-sided, with a large majority of the public agreeing on that side and finding the opposite side morally untenable. This one-sided approach fits topics such as human trafficking and race-based civil rights. After all, it's unlikely that you'll see news reports that "balance" stories about these issues by quoting a source in favor of sex trafficking or racism. Smith has made it clear that he considers SSM to be a "one reasonable argument" issue, suggesting that public opinion and judicial action have shifted sufficiently to this point of view. He also argues that such a stance does not compromise a news outlet's ability to cover issues fairly, and that by being upfront, news personnel are adhering to journalistic norms related to transparency.

It may come as a surprise to learn that early media coverage of gay-related topics actually operated under a "one reasonable argument" perspective. Journalists working in the early- and mid-1900s framed homosexuality in the news just as it was classified by legal, medical, and religious experts of the time: as a mental illness that led individuals to deviant behavior. They didn't feel the need to seek out an opposite point of view. Indeed, it was rare that gay or lesbian sources were included in these news reports; instead straight officials were quoted as experts about the dangers of the homosexual lifestyle. By the time SSM moved onto the news agenda, however, public understanding had shifted somewhat. Homosexuality was no longer classified as a disease by the medical community, although there was still substantial public disapproval of LGBT+ individuals, as well as the prospect of SSM. Fast forward to post-2015, to an America in which the U.S. Supreme Court has declared that same-sex couples deserve the same access to marriage that heterosexual couples do and a majority of U.S. residents agree that LGB couples should be allowed to legally marry. What are the implications for news coverage of the issue? Does it mean that journalists should consider marriage equality to be the only "reasonable argument"?

It's clear from looking at contemporary media coverage patterns that news frames focused on equality and civil rights are more common than those focused on homosexuality or SSM as morally unacceptable. After examining scores of news reports over a span of several years, Leigh Moscowitz has concluded that one of the most significant shifts in coverage was "in the declining role of oppositional sources" (2013, p. 102). Journalists were no longer expected to seek out sources to express moral outrage at the idea of SSM. Moscowitz explains that "oppositional perspectives are acknowledged but appear more as journalistically obligated afterthoughts tacked on to the end of the story" (p. 103). However, it is still most common for news coverage about marriage-equality issues to feature both proponents and opponents as sources (although not necessarily in equal measure), a pattern that appears to be continuing as the news media shift their focus to efforts by conservatives to pass state-wide religious-freedom legislation. News coverage of religious-freedom laws has included assertions from gay rights advocates that such laws would allow opponents of SSM to legally discriminate against LGB couples, along with claims from conservative advocacy groups that such legislation is needed to protect individuals from being forced to participate in gay-marriage-related activities that go against their religious beliefs.

Interestingly, however, both sides may be overestimating the impact of state-wide religious-freedom laws, resulting in media coverage that has also misrepresented the issue. Back in 2015 when Indiana was considering its own religious-freedom law, attorney Hans Bader wrote an essay critical of media reports, which he said overstated the likely impact of such legislation. Bader, who works with the libertarian-leaning Competitive Enterprise Institute, specifically said that news accounts have falsely implied that state-level religious-freedom laws give faith-based businesses a broad right to discriminate against LGBT+ individuals, "when in fact no such right has ever been recognized under the similar legislation that already exists at the federal level and in many states" (Bader, 2015). Public debate and news coverage surrounding such laws intensified in the summer of 2017 when the U.S. Supreme Court announced that it would consider an appeal from a Colorado baker with religious objections to SSM who had lost a discrimination case for refusing to make a cake for a gay couple. Bader remains perplexed about claims by both proponents and opponents of gay rights that a court decision will substantially increase the ability of businesses or individuals opposed to gay marriage to refuse service to LGB couples. "The courts are much more sympathetic to the gay litigants than they are to the businesses," he explained (Bader, personal conversation, June 30, 2017). Bader speculates that advocacy groups, including those for and against SSM, have a stake in keeping the religious-freedom issue front and center in the news media. Both sides, he suggests, are able to use the contentious debate over the effect of RFRAs as a marketing and fundraising tool, regardless of the fact that their claims in the news media are overblown.

Effects of media coverage of SSM on individual attitudes and public opinion

Just as there are multiple ways to examine the processes through which news frames are produced, there are also different methods for measuring the effects of those news frames. Evidence from surveys, experiments, time-series analyses, and case studies shows that under certain circumstances media frames can influence attitudes and public opinion across a wide variety of issues. Taking a micro-level approach to framing influence, Druckman (2001) has explained that "a framing effect is said to occur when, in the course of describing an issue or event, a speaker's emphasis on a subset of potentially relevant considerations causes individuals to focus on these considerations when constructing their opinions" (p. 1042). This tradition of framing research, which often uses experiments to identify effects, generally assumes that exposure to a value frame within media reports will lead individuals to rely on the interpretation of the value as portrayed within that frame (Brewer, 2002). An example of this approach can be seen in the now classic study by Nelson, Clawson, and Oxley (1997) in which framing a Ku Klux Klan rally as a free speech event produced significantly more tolerance of and even support for the event compared to when it was framed as a public disruption. But not all researchers use this approach to measuring media effects. Other scholars have addressed the influence of news frames by examining the relationship between framing patterns and shifts in aggregate public opinion (Johnson, 2012), while still others are concerned with ways that news media help to set the frameworks of public debate, increasing the likelihood of policy change (Zaller, 1992).

In their book *The Rational Public*, Benjamin Page and Robert Shapiro (1992) provide evidence that the ways that media frame social issues, as well as the sources they use in news reports, can account for short-term shifts in public opinion. Engel (2013) explains that this big-picture cause-and-effect relationship may be even more likely for topics such as legal cases and court rulings, where individuals' direct experience and personal knowledge are limited and most of their exposure to the topic is mediated through news coverage. As such, not only can differences in knowledge about the judicial rulings be attributed to how news media framed the ruling, but also variations in how the public feels about the ruling (Clawson et al., 2003; Engel, 2013). Researchers have long been interested in the "opinion ingredients" that shape public opinion about political issues, including those related to LGBT+ rights (Brewer, 2003, p. 1209). Not surprisingly, an individual's value structure serves as an important ingredient. For example, individuals who believe strongly in equality and egalitarianism are more likely to favor gay rights policies, whereas those who place more importance on traditional moral standards will likely view gay rights initiatives as a threat to those standards (Wilcox & Wolpert, 2000). New information about the nature of sexual orientation, which is likely to be disseminated through the media, can also affect the ways that individuals view gay rights initiatives such as legalizing SSM. For example, Wilcox and Norrander (2002) suggest that media reports about scientific research in the 1990s showing that sexual orientation is fixed at birth may have led to more positive attitudes toward gays and lesbians. It is also possible that increasing visibility and awareness of sexual minorities – either through personal contact or through media exposure – have helped to shift public opinion in the direction of gay rights (Wilcox & Norrander, 2002).

Framing research grounded in cognitive and social psychology provides two possible explanations for the ability of value frames in the news to influence how people connect their personal values to social and political issues. Some researchers have concluded that exposure to values language in news frames primes those values in audiences' memories, subsequently making them easier to recall when individuals are in a situation to express their views (Kinder & Sanders, 1996; Zaller, 1992). Others suggest that framing effects occur because of changes in the level of importance that individuals attach to their values (Nelson et al., 1997). In this type of situation, exposure to a particular frame in the news can cause an individual to assign greater weight to that value. Regardless of the specific psychological mechanism behind the effect, both of these approaches suggest that exposure to a value-laden news frame will enhance the role of that value in individuals' subsequent thought processes.

University of Delaware political science professor Paul Brewer (2002) has conducted experimental research examining the effects of news framing on how people use value language to explain their views on issues related to gay rights. As noted earlier in this chapter, the news media have tended to cover the issue of SSM in terms of two primary frames: one focused on civil rights/equality and the other on traditional moral values. Even though Brewer's work wasn't specifically focused on the marriage issue, his study nonetheless provides understanding of how audiences might react to media coverage of marriage equality. In Brewer's experiment, participants were exposed either to news reports framing gay rights through an equality frame, morality frame, or both and then asked about their views. Results showed that participants who received an "equality" frame were particularly likely to explain their views on gay rights in terms of equality and that participants who received a "morality" frame were particularly likely to explain their opinions in the terms of morality. Brewer noted, however, that exposure to a given frame also led participants to use value-related language in ways that challenged that particular value. Thus, people were influenced by the value inherent in the news frame, but not necessarily convinced to mimic it. Furthermore, the study's findings indicated that exposure to the "morality" frame interfered with the impact of the "equality" frame, suggesting that the presence of alternative frames can limit framing effects. In a follow-up study, Brewer (2003) also discovered that an individual's existing values can moderate framing effects, specifically that prior attitudes about gay rights influence susceptibility to new frames.

Rather than focusing on individual psychological responses to news frame exposure, Price, Nir, and Capella (2005) used group conversations as the unit of analysis in experiments about news framing of SSM and civil unions. Their research was conducted during the 2000 presidential election campaign when the issue of SSM received extensive coverage. Vermont, which had passed a law recognizing civil unions, was the site of intense activity, with marriage equality advocates battling against the Take Back Vermont movement that opposed any type of legal recognition for same-sex couples. Price et al. used a total of 54 groups involving 241 randomly selected participants, with some of the groups designed to be homogeneously conservative, some homogeneously liberal, and some heterogeneous. Groups were assigned to one of two framing conditions: a "SSM/special rights" frame or a "civil union/equal rights" frame. Results indicated that subsequent group discussions differed both as a result of the ideological leanings of the group as well as the frame the group was exposed to. The "marriage" frame especially led to polarized group discussions along ideological lines.

The work discussed thus far has focused on the effects of news frames of gay rights issues, including SSM, on individual attitudes and small-group discussions. But what about the influence on larger public opinion? Johnson (2012) sought to answer that question by comparing news framing patterns and levels of public opposition to SSM over eight years (2004–2011). The study was designed with the assumption that one factor behind decreasing opposition to marriage equality might be changes in the ways that news coverage framed the issue. A model Johnson developed to measure influence indicated that media coverage framing SSM in terms of equality and civil rights drives opposition down both in short-term measures of public opinion, as well as in the longer term. In other words, the more that news reports on SSM and civil unions utilized language associated with equality, the more opposition declined. The model also provided some evidence that higher levels of morality framing drove opposition to SSM and civil unions upward as well, although the relationship between these two predictors over time was not as strong. Finally, another model Johnson designed to track the influence of media coverage that balanced equality and morality framing found that as the difference between equality framing and morality framing in media coverage increases (with equality receiving more attention), opposition to SSM and civil unions decreases.

Gordon, Tadlock, and Popp (2007) used survey research to determine which variables could best predict public opinion regarding SSM and civil unions. In a national survey with more than 1,000 respondents, 42.5 percent of respondents said they strongly oppose SSM, and 9.5 percent said they oppose it somewhat. SSM was strongly or somewhat favored by 25.7 percent of those surveyed. In spite of all the media attention and controversy surrounding the debate, about one-fifth of respondents indicated they did not know if they opposed or favored it. The survey found higher levels of support for civil unions than marriage, with 35.8 percent saying they strongly favor or somewhat favor them, and 43.6 percent saying they strongly or somewhat oppose them. As with SSM, about 20 percent said they did not know how they felt about civil unions. Respondents were also asked whether they consider SSM and civil unions to be matters of traditional moral values or equal rights. On the issue of marriage, 43 percent felt it was about moral values. Nearly the same number (42.4 percent) saw the issue as one of equal rights. Civil unions were somewhat more likely to be seen as a matter of equal rights (48.7 percent) compared to 36.1 percent who said it was about traditional moral values. The study identified key variables that were useful in predicting the values position an individual would take in casting his or her attitudes about marriage equality. Specifically, the more liberal and educated the respondent, the more supportive he or she was of marriage and civil unions for same-sex couples, although party affiliation and income had no impact. After considering multiple other variables, the researchers found in the end that the very best predictor of attitudes about the marriage issue was whether an individual attaches the value of morality or equality to the issue; those who think in terms of equality are more likely to favor both SSM and civil unions.

This chapter and the previous one have taken a detailed look at how decisions get made in newsrooms when journalists report on SSM and what the resulting media coverage looks like. But, of course, there are other information sources that contribute to public discourse over marriage rights. The next three chapters will focus on the advocacy organizations most influential within the marriage equality movement, looking at messaging strategies and output. We'll also take an in-depth look at the extent to which advocacy groups were able to successfully use social networking sites to spread their messages, grow their base, and influence public opinion and policy. Chapter 5 will start this process with a focus on two primary national LGBT+ rights organizations involved in the fight for marriage equality: the Human Rights Campaign and Freedom to Marry.

Note

1 According to the Pew report (Hitlin et al., 2013), a story was considered "supportive" of SSM if it included twice as many statements in favor than opposed. A story was coded as

"opposed" if there were twice as many statements in opposition. Stories were considered "neutral" if the 2:1 threshold was not met on either side. The statements could come from any source – journalists, quotes, experts, etc.

References

Adams, T. (2013). Frames of homosexuality: Comparing Los Angeles Times' coverage of California's Proposition 6(1978) and Proposition 8(2008). *Sexuality and Culture,* 17(2), 213–228. http://doi.org/10.1007/s12119-012-9145-2

Bader, H. (2015, April 2). Anti-business media myths preface reporting on RFRA laws. *CNSnews.com.* Retrieved from http://www.cnsnews.com/commentary/hans-bader/anti-business-media-myths-pervade-reporting-rfra-laws

Biskupic, J. (1993, May 7). Ruling by Hawaii's Supreme court opens the way to gay marriages. *The Washington Post,* p. A10.

Brewer, P. R. (2002). Framing, value words, and citizens' explanations of their issue opinions. *Political Communication,* 19(3), 303–316. http://doi.org/10.1080/01957470290055510

Brewer, P. R. (2003). Values, political knowledge, and public opinion about gay rights. *Public Opinion Quarterly,* 67(2), 173–201. http://doi.org/10.1086/374397

Bronstein, C. (2005). Representing the third wave: Mainstream priming media framing of a new feminist movement. *Journalism & Mass Communication Quarterly,* 82(4), 783–803. http://doi.org/10.1177/107769900508200403

Clawson, R. A., Strine, H. C., & Waltenburg, E. N. (2003). Framing Supreme Court decisions: The mainstream versus the black press. *Journal of Black Studies,* 33(6), 784–800. http://doi.org/10.1177/0021934703033006004

Druckman, J. N. (2001). On the limits of framing effects: Who can frame? *Journal of Politics,* 63(4), 1041–1066. http://doi.org/10.1111/0022-3816.00100

Engel, S. M. (2013). Frame spillover: Media framing and public opinion of a multifaceted LGBT rights agenda. *Law & Social Inquiry,* 38(2), 403–441. http://doi.org/10.1111/j.1747- 4469.2012.01319.x

Entman, R. (1993). Framing: Toward clarification of a fractured paradigm. *Journal of Communication,* 43(4), 51–58. http://doi.org/10.1111/j.1460-2466.1993.tb01304.x

Goffman, E. (1974). *Frame analysis: An essay on the organization of experience.* Boston: Northeastern University Press.

Gordon, C. A., Tadlock, B. L., & Popp, E. (2007). Framing the issue of same-sex marriage: Traditional values versus equal rights. In C. A. Rimmerman & C. Wilcox (Eds.), *The politics of same-sex marriage* (pp. 193–214). http://dx.doi.org/10.7208/chicago/9780226720029.001.0001

Haider-Markel, D.P. (2001). Defense, morality, civil rights, and family: The evolution of lesbian and gay issues in the U.S. Congress. In M. Bernstein & R. Reimann (Eds.), *Queer families, queer politics: Challenging culture and the state* (pp. 358–378). New York, NY: Columbia University Press.

Haider-Markel, D. P., & Joslyn, M. R. (2013). Politicizing biology: Social movements, parties, and the case of homosexuality. *Social Science Journal,* 50(4), 603–615. http://doi.org/10.1016/j.soscij.2013.06.001

Hitlin, P., Jurkowitz, M., & Mitchell, A. (2013, June 17). News coverage conveys strong momentum for same-sex marriage. Pew Research Center. Retrieved from http://www.journalism.org/2013/06/17/news-coverage-conveys-strong-momentum/

Hitlin, P., & Tan, S. (2012, May 17). In social media, support for same-sex marriage. Pew Research Center. Retrieved from http://www.journalism.org/2012/05/17/social-media-support-samesex-marriage/

Iyengar, S. (1991). *Is anyone responsible? How television frames political issues*. Chicago, IL: University of Chicago Press.

Johnson, T. (2012). Equality, morality, and the impact of media framing: Explaining opposition to same-sex marriage and civil unions. *Politics & Policy*, 40(6), 1053–1080. http://doi.org/10.1111/j.1747-1346.2012.00398.x

Kershaw, S. (July 7, 2003). Adversaries on gay rights vow state-by-state fight. *The New York Times*. Retrieved from http://www.nytimes.com/learning/teachers/featured_articles/20030707monday.html

Kinder, D. R., & Sanders, L. M. (1996). *Divided by color: Racial politics and democratic ideals*. Chicago, IL: University of Chicago Press.

Li, X., & Liu, X. (2010). Framing and coverage of same-sex marriage in U.S. newspapers. *Howard Journal of Communications*, 21(1), 72–91. http://doi.org/10.1080/10646170903501161

Liebler, C. M., Schwartz, J., & Harper, T. (2009). Queer tales of morality: The press, same-sex marriage, and hegemonic framing. *Journal of Communication*, 59(4), 653–675. http://doi.org/10.1111/j.1460-2466.2009.01451.x

Lippmann, W. (1922). *Public opinion*. New York: Harcourt, Brace and Company.

Lloyd, R. (1963, June). Let's push homophile marriage. *One*, 9(6), 5–10.

McFarland, K. (2011). Media influence and frame diversity in the debate over same-sex marriage. *The Communication Review*, 14(4), 255–278. http://doi.org/10.1080/10714421.2011.624002

Moscowitz, L. M. (2010). Gay marriage in television news: Voice and visual representation in the same-sex marriage debate. *Journal of Broadcasting & Electronic Media*, 54(1), 24–39. http://doi.org/10.1080/08838150903550360

Moscowitz, L. M. (2013). *The battle over marriage: Gay rights activism through the media*. http://dx.doi.org/10.5406/illinois/9780252038129.001.0001

Nelson, T. E., Clawson, R. A., & Oxley, Z. M. (1997). Media framing of a civil liberties conflict and its effect on tolerance. *American Political Science Review*, 91(3), 567–583. http://doi.org/10.2307/2952075

New York Times. (2004, March 7). The road to gay marriage. In R. M. Baird & S. E. Rosenbaum (Eds.), *Same-sex marriage: The moral and legal debate* (pp. 81–84). Amherst, NY: Prometheus Books.

Page, B. I., & Shapiro, R. Y. (1992). *The rational public: Fifty years of trends in Americans' policy preferences*. Chicago, IL: University of Chicago Press.

Pan, P.-L., Meng, J., & Zhou, S. (2010). Morality or equality? Ideological framing in news coverage of gay marriage legitimization. *The Social Science Journal*, 47(3), 630–645. http://doi.org/10.1016/j.soscij.2010.02.002

Perrin, A. (2015, Oct. 8). Social media usage: 2005–2015. Retrieved from Pew Research Center website: http://www.pewinternet.org/2015/10/08/social-networking-usage-2005-2015

Price, V., Nir, L., & Cappella, J. N. (2005, August). *Framing public discussion of gay civil unions*. Paper presented to the 2003 annual meeting of the American Political Science Association, Philadelphia, PA.

Rimmerman, C. A., Wald, K. D., & Wilcox, C. (Eds.). (2000). *The politics of gay rights*. Chicago, IL: University of Chicago Press.

Savage, D. G. (2015, January 11). Supreme Court faced gay rights decision in 1958 over "obscene" magazine. *The Los Angeles Times*. Retrieved from http://www.latimes.com/nation/la-na-court-gay-magazine-20150111-story.html

Scheufele, D. A. (1999). Framing as a theory of media effects. *Journal of Communication*, 49(1), 103–122. http://doi.org/10.1111/j.1460-2466.1999.tb02784.x

Schmalz, J. (1993, May 7). In Hawaii, step toward legalized gay marriage. *The New York Times*. Retrieved from http://www.nytimes.com/1993/05/07/us/in-hawaii-step-toward-legalized-gay-marriage.html

Semple, K. (2003, July 31). Vatican says lawmakers have duty to oppose gay marriage. *The New York Times*. Retrieved from http://www.nytimes.com/2003/07/31/international/europe/vatican-says-lawmakers-have-duty-to-oppose-gay-marria ge-2003073193578425896.html

Stewart-Winter, T. (2006). What was same-sex marriage? *The Gay and Lesbian Review Worldwide*, 13(1), 33–35.

Warren, D. M., & Bloch, K. R. (2014). Framing same-sex marriage: Media constructions of California's Proposition 8. *The Social Science Journal*, 51(4), 503–513. http://doi.org/10.1016/j.soscij.2014.06.011

Weinger, M. (2013, March 26). HuffPo officially comes out in support of gay marriage. *Politico*. Retrieved from http://www.politico.com/blogs/media/2013/03/huffpo-officia lly-comes-out-in-support-of-gay-marriage-160264

Wilcox, C., & Norrander, B. (2002). Of moods and morals: The dynamics of opinion on abortion and gay rights. *Understanding public opinion*, 2, 121–148.

Wilcox, C, & Wolpert, R. (2000). Gay rights in the public sphere: Public opinion on gay and lesbian equality. In C. A. Rimmerman, K. D. Wald, & C. Wilcox (Eds.), *The politics of gay rights* (pp. 409–432). Chicago, IL: University of Chicago Press.

Wildermuth, J. (2009, January 6). Prop. 8 proponents say Brown "profoundly wrong." *SFGate*. Retrieved from http://www.sfgate.com/news/article/Prop-8-proponents-say-Brown-profoundly-wrong-3177641.php

Zaller, J. (1992). The nature and origins of mass opinion. http://dx.doi.org/10.1017/CBO9780511818691

5

THE PROPONENTS: MAKING THE CASE FOR MARRIAGE EQUALITY

When the Human Rights Campaign was founded in 1980, the outlook was dim for same-sex couples who hoped some day they might get married. The 1970s may have witnessed the emergence of the gay liberation movement, but there was no indication that marriage rights were on the horizon. In 1972 the U.S. Supreme Court declined to consider *Baker v. Nelson*, a legal challenge to the state of Minnesota's refusal to issue a marriage license to a gay male couple, and the following year Maryland became the first state to pass a law explicitly banning marriage for gays and lesbians. It would take another 20 years before the LGBT+ movement would start to consider marriage as a realistic goal, and even then it wasn't a major priority.

From the beginning of the gay rights movement in the United States, the issue of marriage has been a contentious one. Individual activists, as well as advocacy groups, have disagreed about whether marriage should take priority over other concerns – indeed whether it should even be a goal at all for a movement devoted to challenging sexuality-based social norms. Some queer activists have vehemently opposed campaigns for marriage equality, arguing that marriage is an oppressive and patriarchal state-sanctioned institution that would suppress sexual diversity (Bernstein & Burke, 2013). Others have considered marriage rights to be a legitimate goal of the gay rights movement, but not one that should take priority over issues such as employment discrimination and hate crimes (D'Emilio, 2006). This chapter will examine how marriage rose from low on the list of goals for the LGBT+ rights movement to become its signature priority. We'll concentrate primarily on the messaging strategies used to rally support and fight opposition after the marriage movement gained steam in 2003. Although there were dozens of organizations involved in the SSM movement, we'll focus on two of the major players: the HRC, a large multi-issue organization known worldwide for its LGBT+ advocacy, and Freedom to Marry, an organization that was created with marriage equality as its sole purpose.

History of the Human Rights Campaign and Freedom to Marry

The HRC's mission is "to end discrimination against LGBTQ people and realize a world that achieves fundamental fairness and equality for all," and it claims more than 1.5 million members and supporters. Now arguably the nation's best known LGBT+ rights organization, HRC was launched in 1980 as the Human Rights Campaign Fund, a political action committee. Founder Stephen Endean had gotten his start with gay rights activism in his 20s in Minnesota and worked with the Gay Rights National Lobby before starting HRC. In 1985, the HRCF merged with the Gay Rights National Lobby, forming the largest LGBT+ political organization in the country. A decade later, after expanding its operations to include research, education, and media outreach, the HRC dropped "Fund" from its name and underwent a large-scale reorganization and rebranding. Among those changes was the adoption of its new logo, the now-famous yellow equal sign on a blue background.

The Washington, D.C.-based HRC has since been instrumental in a series of significant gay rights victories, having influenced passage of employment non-discrimination legislation, the repeal of the military's Don't Ask, Don't Tell policy, legislative and judicial rulings on marriage equality, and the election of many queer state and national public officials. In addition to its lobbying activities, HRC also consults with corporations to adopt fair employment policies and issues a well-publicized annual "Corporate Equality Index" that evaluates major companies in relation to LGBT+ employees and consumers. In spite of its celebrated successes – or maybe because of them – the HRC has also been a source of controversy, criticized by some for being elitist and lacking diversity. Its largely white, well-connected gay male staff has been accused of providing a less-than-welcoming atmosphere for racial minorities and lesbians and being too deferential to powerful political interests in Washington (Stone, 2012; Villarreal, 2015) and corporate interests nationwide (Meronek, 2015). HRC has also been accused of failing to sufficiently include transgender individuals in its push for antidiscrimination legislation (Juro, 2013) and for inflating its membership numbers (Queerty, 2009).

Although HRC may be the highest-profile gay rights organization, the individual most closely associated with the marriage equality movement worked elsewhere. During the 1990s, attorney Evan Wolfson directed the Marriage Project for the Lambda Legal Education and Defense Fund. Wolfson had been involved in the *Baehr v. Miike* case in Hawaii, as well as *Baker v. Vermont*, which resulted in the Vermont state legislature establishing civil unions for same-sex couples. In 2001 Lambda Legal announced that Wolfson would leave the organization with a grant from the Evelyn & Walter Haas Jr. Fund to focus solely on the fight for marriage equality. After months of planning, in 2003 Wolfson launched FTM with a dual purpose: to shift public opinion to favor marriage equality and to achieve legal relationship recognition nationwide. Wolfson became somewhat of a celebrity within the marriage movement, with numerous profiles appearing in national media, some referring to him in almost mythical terms as "the Paul Revere of gay marriage" (DeFore, 2017) and "Mr. Marriage" (Freiberg, 2001).

Why marriage?

Evan Wolfson may have always believed that marriage rights were the key to LGBT+ equality, but others disagreed. To understand how marriage emerged as the LGBT+ rights movement's signature priority, we need to address the "why marriage" question in two ways. First is the broader approach that asks why LGB couples should fight at all to have their relationships recognized by the state. To answer this, we need to consider the benefits – and costs – of inclusion within the institution of marriage. The second approach is more specific, asking "why marriage *now*?" Answering this question involves defending a choice in the 1990s and 2000s to dedicate LGBT+ movement resources to the marriage battle over other issues such as employment discrimination.

First of all, why marriage? The most obvious answer is that LGB couples want to marry for the same reasons straight couples do. They want to formalize their love for and commitment to each other in a public and legally sanctioned ceremony shared with friends and family. They want acceptance and respect from their communities and society at large, and some want to raise children within a structure that recognizes their rights as parents. Psychologist Gregory Herek (2006) argues that marriage can help to overcome stigma traditionally assigned to sexual minorities, which can also improve their mental and physical health. Wolfson, in his book *Why Marriage Matters*, sums up this "acceptance" argument for marriage, insisting that it is "a social statement, preeminently describing and defining a person's relationship and place in society" (2004, p. 4). And then, of course, there are the rights. Many LGB couples want to marry so that they may benefit from the more than 1,000 federal rights and protections that married couples enjoy but nonmarried individuals do not. These rights apply to just about every aspect of life, including real estate, health insurance, adoption, hospital visitation, survivorship benefits, and taxation.

In spite of all these advantages, marriage was not a major priority for the broader LGBT+ rights movement prior to the 1990s. Instead, the focus was on issues such as employment discrimination, AIDS and health care, hate crimes, access to the military, and the repeal of sodomy laws (Warner, 1999). The failure of early marriage-related lawsuits in the 1970s led many activists to believe that a focus on same-sex marriage "was not only dangerous, but also utterly inconceivable" because it was assumed that sexual minorities would never be accepted into such a culturally traditional institution (Moscowitz, 2013, p. 36). As a result, there were relatively few activists forcefully pushing for marriage as a priority. Based on a series of interviews with LGBT+ advocacy operatives in 2005, media scholar Leigh Moscowitz (2013) determined that most staffers at the larger gay rights organizations – even if they were not philosophically opposed to the idea of marriage – simply did not consider it a high priority. Interestingly, it was opponents of same-sex marriage who made it a priority for the LGBT+ movement (Moscowitz, 2013; Stone, 2012). Alarmed by gay-friendly court decisions in Hawaii in the early 1990s, these opponents went on the offensive, pushing state-wide constitutional amendments banning gay marriage and calling for federal legislation, resulting in the 1996 Defense of Marriage Act.

These initiatives of course drew significant media attention, including requests from journalists for LGBT+ rights organizations to present their side of the marriage debate. As a result, leaders of the gay advocacy groups were put on the defensive, playing catch-up in their efforts to articulate a stance.

But it was not until 2003 when the *Lawrence v. Texas* ruling decriminalized sodomy that queer advocacy organizations were forced to push all-in regarding same-sex marriage. Fearing that *Lawrence* would open the door to a host of additional gay rights, conservative groups ramped up their statewide efforts to ban same-sex marriage and also saw an opportunity to capitalize upon the issue for the upcoming presidential election. Republican strategist Karl Rove, a key architect of President George W. Bush's re-election campaign, viewed the *Lawrence* ruling and legalization of gay marriage in Massachusetts in spring 2004 as opportunities to get socially conservative voters to the polls (Solomon, 2014). The historic court ruling in Massachusetts, making it the first state to allow LGB couples full access to marriage, was especially galvanizing for Christian conservatives (Kowal, 2015). As Moscowitz (2013) notes, after Bush in February 2004 called for an amendment to the U.S. Constitution banning same-sex marriage, gay rights activists were forced to devote more organizational resources and attention to the issue. From that point, news media began to focus on same-sex marriage as *the* gay issue, furthering the impression that the movement was united behind marriage equality and marginalizing any internal disagreement over the importance of marriage (Moscowitz, 2013).

Social movements, identity, and communication strategies

Social movements are always faced with decisions about how to define themselves and communicate their goals to constituencies, policymakers, and the news media. In the early years of the LGBT+ movement, there was an uneasy tension between those who sought to disrupt social norms and those who preferred to alter social norms so as to gain access to institutions such as marriage (Armstrong, 2002; D'Emilio, 1983). Although the arguments take many forms, they boil down to an emphasis on opposition or assimilation. According to sociologist Mary Bernstein (1997), this dilemma is part of a larger issue faced by identity-based civil rights movements, which is whether to celebrate or suppress a minority group's differences from the majority.

This issue of how to publicly address gay–straight differences had been a source of contention since the early days of the homophile movement in the 1950s. Some members preferred an assimilationist approach that stressed similarities between heterosexual and homosexual individuals in terms of their shared desire to live happy and productive lives within a family structure, whereas others considered homosexuality to be a distinctive trait that should not be subsumed by mainstream culture (D'Emilio, 1983). For some, the decision was made for them, given the fact that openly celebrating sexuality-related differences might lead to a loss of employment or worse. As the gay rights movement gained prominence in the 1970s, however, the question shifted to one of strategy rather than survival. In discussing early

LGBT+ rights marches on Washington, Tarrow (1998) notes that marchers faced a common dilemma: "how to put forward a set of unsettling demands for unconventional people in ways that will not make enemies of potential allies" (p. 10). As with other movements, the lesbian and gay movement has shifted its emphasis over time. But by placing such a high priority on marriage – whether activists chose that route willingly or had it thrust upon them by the opposition – the movement seems to have signaled a purposeful shift away from cultural and sexual transformation toward the achievement of political rights through assimilation. This shift has been accompanied by a more moderate messaging approach that highlights similarities to the straight majority (Bernstein, 1997).

This assimilationist approach clearly influenced LGBT+ advocates' attempts to frame the marriage debate in the late 1990s, coincidentally a time when scholars began paying more attention to the framing processes of social movements. Framing studies experienced an "almost meteoric increase" within the fields of social psychology and political sociology during this period, with scholars beginning to regard identity message framing as key to understanding the nature and effectiveness of a movement (Benford & Snow, 2000, p. 612). Social movement leaders intentionally engage in the construction of meaning for their supporters and policymakers, and the result is what sociologists have labeled collective action frames (Polletta, & Ho, 2006). Similar to the role of news frames in helping audiences understand and interpret information provided in news reports, social movement collective action frames also perform an interpretive function, but in ways designed to mobilize supporters, attract those who are undecided, and demobilize opponents (Snow & Benford, 1988). In some instances, organizations draw their messaging strategies from broader "master" frames that allow connections with other movements, such as the master frames of injustice and rights, both of which had been deployed by the civil rights and women's movements prior to the emergence of gay liberation (Gamson, 1992; Tarrow, 1998).

Not surprisingly, a common tactic within social movements' framing efforts involves influencing the news and entertainment media to present an issue from a perspective that aligns with the movement's goals (Benford & Snow, 2000; Stone, 2012). Earlier models of the relationship between social movements and the news media (Gamson & Wolfsfeld, 1993) have described it as one of asymmetrical dependency in which social movements need the news media more than media need social movements. This model suggests that movements have few options other than mass media for widespread message dissemination. However, as we'll see in the next section, technological advances have provided LGBT+ advocacy groups with numerous options for creating and sharing messages – and for harnessing the power of their supporters to spread those messages in ways not possible in earlier campaigns.

A cautious approach: early messaging strategies

From his earliest work on marriage equality, Evan Wolfson seems to have instinctively understood the importance of message framing to social movement success.

Reflecting on a marriage rights paper he wrote in law school, Wolfson says that he has always believed that by focusing on the values of love, commitment, connectedness, and freedom, "we could transform non-gay people's understanding of who gay people are and why exclusion and discrimination are wrong" (FTM, 2015). But this very personal approach to marriage framing did not feature prominently in LGBT+ advocacy groups' early strategies.

After the Hawaii State Supreme Court's ruling on same-sex marriage pushed the issue onto the public agenda in the early 1990s, opponents took the fight to the state level, supporting legislation and ballot initiatives to ban gay marriage. National organizations such as the HRC provided support for state-wide campaigns designed to defeat the voter referendums, but with little success. In her historical examination of LGBT+-related state ballot initiatives, Stone concludes that funding same-sex marriage campaigns at the state level was "a losing gamble from the start" for national gay rights organizations because public opinion in the 1990s was clearly opposed to the extension of marriage rights (2012, p. 124). In spite of it being an uphill battle, HRC leaders were willing to work with selected state campaigns. One of its first was in Hawaii, where HRC joined with local groups to defeat Amendment 2. The measure asked voters a simple question: *Shall the Constitution of the state of Hawaii be amended to specify that the Legislature shall have the power to reserve marriage to opposite-sex couples?* After the earlier *Baehr v. Lewin* ruling from the Hawaii State Supreme Court that seemed to open the door to marriage equality, HRC leaders considered Hawaii a top priority. The group spent nearly a million dollars on the campaign, loaning staff and training local operatives. HRC campaign messages argued that Hawaiians should not tamper with their constitution and compared efforts to deny same-sex couples the right to marry to restrictions on Japanese Americans during World War II. But those messages apparently fell on deaf ears, as Amendment 2 passed in November 1998 with just under 70 percent of the vote (All Politics, 1998).

Early state-wide marriage campaigns struggled with decisions about how to frame their messages and counter the messages of opponents, which were primarily groups affiliated with the Religious Right (Stone, 2012). Many polls in the 1990s (and even in later years) indicated that messaging focused explicitly on marriage for same-sex couples would fail to attract voters – in fact, it could actually turn off some voters due to what is often referred to as the "ick" factor, referring to heterosexuals' discomfort with the notion of same-sex intimacy and sexuality (Moscowitz, 2013). There was significant debate within the movement about how visible LGBT+ lives should be within the campaign message strategy and whether strategy should serve a long-term goal such as education about the nature of sexuality or the short-term goal of winning an election (Stone, 2012, p. 71). Some state campaigns purposefully focused on other aspects of ballot initiatives such as unintended consequences for heterosexual families, the danger in amending state constitutions to take away rights, and the role of outsiders in campaigns – anything other than the desire of same-sex couples to have their relationships and love for each other recognized by the state. When these campaigns failed and same-sex marriage bans were written into state constitutions, national gay rights organizations such as the HRC were blamed. The HRC was criticized specifically for limiting LGBT+ visibility in its campaigns and letting the Religious Right frame the public conversation as one about "special rights" for gays. But HRC leadership soldiered on, learning from their losses and working to develop a set of "model campaign tactics" that relied on polling and could be useful for campaigns throughout the country. Stone (2012) refers to this approach as "preplanned hierarchical professionalism," noting that it was criticized by some for being too mainstream and focused on a "one-size-fits-all" approach (p. 81).

A close examination of HRC messaging and Internet use from 2004, an active yet inconsistent year for the marriage equality movement, indicated the organization was by then publicly committed to marriage as a movement priority. In 2004 Massachusetts became the first state to legalize same-sex marriage *and* President Bush publicly called for a national constitutional amendment limiting marriage to one man and one woman. Joseph Schwartz (2005), now a communication studies professor at Northeastern University, chose this time period to examine HRC's messaging activities and analyzed all materials on the group's website, including news releases, action alerts, informational pamphlets, print and video ads, and web-based movies, as well as electronic and traditional paper mailings. He identified four primary message frames within the content. The "road to legitimacy" frame stressed the similarities between heterosexual and same-sex couples, noting that they both want the best for their families and deserve the dignity that comes with having a state-recognized relationship. The "discrimination" frame compared the marriage equality fight to the earlier race-based civil rights movement and focused on the discriminatory nature of the proposed Federal Marriage Amendment. This frame was also used to cast opponents, who often referred to themselves as pro-family, as hypocritical for seeking to deny gay families fundamental protections such as visitation rights and health care benefits.

According to Schwartz's (2005) findings, the HRC also made use of an "exploitation" frame specific to the time period before the 2004 election. This frame accused President Bush of furthering his political career and drawing attention away from pressing topics (such as the failing economy and the war in Iraq) by pushing the Federal Marriage Amendment as a campaign priority. Lastly, HRC deployed what Schwartz (2005) referred to as an "agency" frame, which stressed the influence that ordinary people wield by sharing their personal stories of love and relationships and of family members and friends who deserved to be treated with dignity and fairness. This frame was the only one of the four that approached the marriage issue from a more intimate and emotional perspective. Within this frame, HRC asked supporters to tell their personal stories in a section of the website labeled "Defend Equality," a tactic that can now be viewed as a forerunner to its subsequent – and very successful – efforts to encourage supporters to share personal testimonies via social media. The goal of the agency frame, according to Schwartz, was to appeal to fair-minded straight individuals who would be moved by the personal accounts of same-sex couples and their families and friends. Based on his analysis, Schwartz (2005) concluded that HRC's communication materials gave the impression that marriage equality was its top priority and that gay men and lesbians' status in society depended on gaining the right to marry, a stance that seemed to be "tacitly privileging heterosexuality and reinforcing heteronormative ideals" (p. 24). From interviews in 2004–2005 with gay rights activists, including some from HRC, Moscowitz (2013) came to similar conclusions. She learned that there was a concerted effort to present to the public very palatable images of LGB couples and their families. Especially in key court cases in 2003–2004 in Vermont and Massachusetts, plaintiffs were carefully vetted and chosen with media suitability and savvy in mind. The lead plaintiffs in the Goodridge case in Massachusetts, Julie and Hillary Goodridge, were an attractive couple who had been together for several years and had a young daughter, and thus they were ideal to serve as the face of same-sex marriage (Koenig, 2014).

Still in its infancy, FTM was also heavily involved with the marriage fight in Massachusetts. The November 2003 *Goodridge* ruling had resulted in immediate and intense backlash, with the Catholic church and other religion-based opponents, members of the state legislature, Governor Mitt Romney, and even Democrat U.S. Sen. John Kerry stating their opposition to same-sex marriage and vowing to keep the court ruling from taking effect. Along with Evan Wolfson, Mark Solomon – who worked for marriage equality in a variety of positions, eventually serving as national campaign director for FTM – put in long hours during the early months of 2004 when the state legislature called a constitutional convention to start the lengthy process required in Massachusetts to amend the state constitution. Solomon's book *Winning Marriage* (2014) gives a detailed insider account of the post-*Goodridge* fight in Massachusetts. FTM had joined with the Boston-based group GLBTQ Legal Advocates & Defenders (GLAD) and other pro-gay organizations in a loose coalition called MassEquality. They had all initially celebrated the *Goodridge* decision but immediately afterwards were forced to go on the defensive to protect it (Solomon, 2014). Within a few weeks, religious and conservative groups sent national reinforcements to the state, coordinating with local clergy to begin a state-wide campaign to disparage the Supreme Judicial Court's ruling and rally the electorate to support its overturn. The conservative Focus on the Family launched a political action committee to raise money for candidates who supported a constitutional amendment to undo the ruling. According to *Winning Marriage,* MassEquality struggled in its response. As an umbrella organization comprising multiple sub-groups and with few full-time staff members, the constituent groups' leaders were often at odds with each other and could not agree initially on a course of action (Solomon, 2014). But additional staff were hired, and a strategy emerged to lobby individual legislators while also countering the messages of marriage opponents. The primary messaging frame used by FTM staffers working with MassEquality was simple: "no discrimination in the Constitution," an approach developed to counter the "One man, one woman – let the people vote" message of opponents who were calling for a state-wide vote on a constitutional amendment (Solomon,

2014). In spite of MassEquality's efforts, the amendment did pass the first of many steps involved in constitutional changes in Massachusetts, but was eventually defeated by the state legislature in 2007.

Although it was active in Massachusetts after the *Goodridge* decision in 2004, FTM's overall strategy in its early years was very internally focused, with emphasis on movement organization and fundraising rather than messaging. Like the HRC, Evan Wolfson and FTM lobbied (successfully) against the proposed Federal Marriage Amendment in 2004, spending significant amounts on traditional newspaper and television advertising, but with a limited digital presence (Bolcer, 2012). Meanwhile, as the post-*Goodridge* situation was unfolding on the East Coast, San Francisco Mayor Gavin Newsom took things into his own hands on the West Coast. While Massachusetts legislators were opening their constitutional convention to prevent the extension of marriage rights, Newsom announced that San Francisco officials would immediately begin issuing marriage licenses to same-sex couples. According to Solomon, the decision by Newsom to take action counter to a state law prohibiting same-sex marriage was considered unwise even by many gay activists. Solomon said he thought it strategic to "open up a second front in the marriage fight, taking a bit of the antigay wrath off of us in Massachusetts and showing that the demand for marriage was omnipresent" but noted that others thought it would only intensify national anti-gay backlash (2014, p. 36).

And there was indeed backlash. In spite of the efforts by the HRC, FTM, and other advocacy organizations in 2004, on November 2 of that year, George W. Bush was re-elected president and 11 states passed state initiatives banning same-sex marriage, more than in any previous election (Stone, 2012). The losses led to soul-searching among leadership of the marriage movement, who faced renewed criticism for focusing on the marriage issue at all. A November 2004 *New York Times* article described LGBT+ movement leaders as "embroiled in a bitter and increasingly public debate" over whether they should adjust priorities in the wake of such disappointing results (Broder, 2004). HRC, in particular, was the subject of media attention, with the press reporting conflict within leadership about how to proceed. The *NYT* article (Broder, 2004) went into great detail about intra-organization turmoil, noting that HRC had just accepted the resignation of its executive director and "adopted a new, more moderate strategy, with less emphasis on legalizing same-sex marriages and more on strengthening personal relationships." Some gay rights activists, including a few within the HRC, said they believed that aggressively pursuing same-sex marriage only played into the hand of Republicans and religious conservatives, who successfully capitalized upon the issue to energize their voters. Historian and activist John D'Emilio (2006) was more forceful in his criticism of national LGBT+ movement leaders. In an essay titled simply "The Marriage Fight is Setting Us Back," D'Emilio (2006) argued that "The battle to win marriage equality through the courts has done something that no other campaign or issue in our movement has done: it has created a vast body of new antigay law" (p. 10).

New strategies and coalitions

But the losses and criticism in 2004 did not keep marriage activists on the sideline for long. In November 2005, representatives from 10 advocacy groups, including HRC and FTM, met to devise a plan for moving forward. The result was "Winning marriage: What we need to do" (Carton, 2005), a strategy for achieving nationwide marriage equality first in the states and then nationwide. The document's introduction clearly put it into the assimilationist camp, insisting that to win, advocates would "need to show America that LGBT+ people have basically the same aspirations for a good life, the same dreams, hopes and fears that other Americans have" (Carton, 2005, p. 2). The plan also laid out messaging strategies and target audiences. It argued that, to be successful, a unified movement needed to achieve at least three messaging goals: to secure the support of the "movable middle" of voters who may still be undecided about same-sex marriage; to make those who already support gay rights care enough to get involved; and to explain to the LGBT+ community why the marriage fight is worthy of immediate action.

Over the next few years, the marriage equality movement experienced a series of victories (mostly in court rulings, with a few at the ballot box) and a series of setbacks, primarily in the passage of state bans on same-sex marriage. SSM was clearly advancing in terms of public opinion, however. In an analysis of attitudes toward SSM from 1988 to 2006, Baunach (2011) found that attitudes became more liberal over time; 71 percent opposed SSM in 1988, but by 2006, this figure dropped to 52 percent. Approximately two-thirds of the shift was because individuals modified their views over time, and one-third was due to younger cohorts replacing older ones. Baunach (2011) suggests that polling data indicate that the use of the equality/tolerance frame by SSM advocates may have convinced some people to change their minds.

One state that seemed to be constantly in the news in the 2000s, providing both wins and losses for proponents of marriage equality, was California. A flurry of judicial, legislative, and voter action there produced an unprecedented situation where the legality of same-sex marriages was constantly being revised. (A detailed look at the back-and-forth history of marriage in California can be found in Chapter 2.) The most prominent of the marriage milestones in California – and one of the most expensive ballot initiatives in U.S. history (Stone, 2012) – was the fight over Proposition 8 in November 2008. The ballot measure was only 14 words long, stating simply that "only marriage between a man and a woman is valid or recognized in California." But before the surprising outcome, in which the measure passed with 52 percent of the vote, more than $80 million had been spent and 50,000 individuals had volunteered to campaign either for or against the measure (Becker, 2014). The campaign, which drew an unprecedented amount of attention from out of state (Stone, 2012), has been called the largest LGBT+ field operation in history (Ehrenreich, 2008).

The HRC wasn't as heavily involved with Proposition 8 as it was in some of the ballot initiatives on the East Coast (Solomon, 2014). Nonetheless, HRC loaned staffers to the "No on Prop 8" campaign and contributed hundreds of thousands of dollars to Equality California, the state-wide LGBT+ group leading the effort (Hemmelgarn, 2008). Veteran LGBT+ political operative Mark Solomon (2014) recalls being concerned about No on Prop 8's strategy, especially the campaign's television spots. Equality California's messaging strategy focused on fairness, equality, and the unseemliness of changing a state constitution to deny rights to a group of people (Ehrenreich, 2008). Solomon described the TV spots as looking like typical political ads, highlighting the fact that high-profile leaders such as President Barack Obama, Senator Dianne Feinstein, and even Governor Arnold Schwarzenegger were against the amendment. The spots closed with a version of a tagline that seemed to Solomon to almost apologetically acknowledge that many California residents were still uncomfortable with the notion of marriage for gays and lesbians: "Regardless of how you feel about marriage, it's wrong to treat people differently under the law" (Solomon, 2014, p. 224). Looking back, it's clear that the arguments put forth by the No on Prop 8 campaign were rational ones that appealed to the intellect and a sense of fairness: the importance of protecting the constitution and fundamental rights. They were not designed to elicit emotions, and they did little to counter the emotion-inducing arguments of the "Yes on Prop 8" side, which painted dire pictures of a society in which gays were allowed to marry. Solomon recalled being dismayed at the lack of emotion in the ads against Prop 8. He understood why the marriage equality side might be downplaying the focus on actual marriage – after all, public support was below 50 percent – but given the fact that gay couples in California had already been marrying, Solomon (2014) said the detached approach made no sense.

According to a post-mortem article in *The Advocate* headlined "Anatomy of a Failed Campaign" (Ehrenreich, 2008), other gay rights advocates were also disappointed in Equality California's messaging strategy. Many criticized the No on Prop 8's early television ads, suggesting that they were too timid, minimizing the "gay angle" so as not to offend undecided straight voters (Jefferson, 2008). Ehrenreich notes that the first spot to air featured an elderly straight couple pleading on behalf of their unseen lesbian daughter. Another didn't use the word "gay," instead depicting two straight women having coffee together and discussing same-sex marriage in veiled terms. *The Advocate* quoted one political consultant as complaining, "They hid us in the closet. You cannot hide what you're fighting for" (Ehrenreich, 2008), an accusation that a member of the Equality California campaign staff defended by explaining that the ads were designed to be effective with undecided voters, even if they were not appealing to members of the LGBT+ community. HRC leaders, in a post-Prop 8 debrief session, identified another key shortcoming of the campaign: A failure to combat opponents' false assertions, as well as some inaccuracies reported in the news media, especially those dealing with race-related tensions (Stone, 2012). Others blame the loss, at least in part, on the lack of digital prowess on the part of the No on Prop 8 campaign. In a post-campaign interview with *The Bay Area Reporter* in San Francisco, No on Prop 8 campaign manager Steve Smith acknowledged that staffers initially failed to effectively utilize the Internet and other digital resources (Aiello, 2008). According to Smith, it wasn't until six weeks or so before the election that the campaign's website was upgraded by volunteers from Google, with immediate positive results. In the months prior to the website fix, the No on 8 campaign raised only about $1 million in Internet contributions, but in the last six weeks after the web fix, it raised approximately $22 million (Aiello, 2008).

In an essay on the FTM website (FTM, n.d.c.) titled "The movement's message problem," the group explains how a few political operatives actually experimented with different messaging in California and notes that it was successful, but deployed only in a limited area. In the months leading up to the Prop 8 campaign, a group of movement leaders – including FTM's Evan Wolfson – already sensed that an intellectual emphasis on rights and fairness wasn't going to work. They created a series of ads focused more on the emotional aspects of marriage and conducted a field experiment using the newer ads in the Santa Barbara media market. Voting results showed much higher support for marriage equality in Santa Barbara than others in Southern California. Wolfson expressed regret that the experimental campaign did not have sufficient funding to expand throughout the state.

Learning from loss

The unexpected loss in California devastated LGBT+ rights advocates, but it also helped to unite them. FTM's director of research and messaging, Thalia Zepatos, recalls that in an effort to develop a plan for moving forward, FTM launched an unprecedented attempt to collect and synthesize research data, analyzing every survey and focus group that staffers could get access to (Zepatos & Hatalsky, 2015). That involved the unenviable task of convincing multiple advocacy groups to share costly proprietary research. But many groups agreed, leading to what Zepatos described as a treasure trove of more than 85 studies. The data indicated that a shift in strategy was needed to persuade those whom Evan Wolfson has referred to as the "reachable, but not yet reached" segment of the population (E. Wolfson, personal communication, June 13, 2017). Wolfson doesn't consider this an indication that earlier strategies were ineffective; in fact, he insists that the previous mix of messages – ranging from personal and emotional appeals to those focused on rights, benefits, and legal principles – did a good job of growing support for marriage equality from about 27 percent in 1996 to a slight majority in 2010. But there remained a segment of the population that had yet to be convinced. These voters, according to Wolfson, were "the people who wanted to be fair and were willing to provide health benefits etc., but didn't understand why gay people needed marriage." To pull these voters into the marriage equality column, Wolfson said FTM and other groups adjusted and coordinated their messages to emphasize the importance of love and commitment and to show the public that same-sex couples shared their values (E. Wolfson, personal communication, June 13, 2017).

Wolfson believes that it's hard to overstate the importance of the collaboration that occurred in 2009–2010, with more than dozens of groups working together to synthesize research, recalibrate message framing and dissemination strategies, and essentially relaunch the campaign for marriage equality. Although it did not get a lot of public attention, Wolfson said an initiative called "Why Marriage Matters" was important to the success of the final phase of the movement. FTM staffers drafted a summary of what had been learned from the shared research and experience review and put it online in an open-source information portal. The site shared access to research findings, ready-made and tailorable messaging tools, graphics, and event kits to allow gay rights groups to educate the public – more strategically, efficiently, and effectively – about why LGB couples wanted full participation in the institution of marriage. According to the FTM website, more than 40 organizations joined the Why Marriage Matters partnership. In hindsight, Zepatos said FTM executives knew that these collaborative efforts had "cracked the code" on Election Day in 2012, when Maine, Maryland, Minnesota, and Washington were all victorious with pro marriage equality ballot measures (Zepatos & Hatalsky, 2015).

In addition to collaborating with other marriage equality partners in the key adjustment period after Prop 8, FTM also revisited its own internal structure and priorities, transitioning from an internal focus on movement strategy into a more outward-facing national campaign (E. Wolfson, personal communication, June 13, 2017). The outcome, branded publicly in 2009 as a "Roadmap to Victory," featured three big-picture goals: winning marriage rights in individual states, working to build a majority of support in terms of public opinion, and ending federal marriage discrimination. FTM made the details of Roadmap to Victory available on its website, encouraging marriage advocates to take advantage of it as a resource. Some of the reboot was not actually new, such as its focus on the personal stories of LGB couples and their families. But Wolfson, in a 2010 *Huffington Post* essay, made it clear that more emphasis was being put on messaging and that a revitalized campaign must take those personal stories "to kitchen tables, legislative corridors, Facebook, and Twitter, and personally make the case for marriage." The Roadmap to Victory's explicit focus on shifting public opinion reflected a recognition of the role American attitudes about an issue can play in judicial rulings, including those of the Supreme Court. Wolfson (2013) made this clear in yet another essay in the *Huffington Post*: "We must continue creating a climate demonstrating that America is ready for marriage, so that when the next case reaches the steps of the Supreme Court, the justices are encouraged to bring the country to national resolution, securing the freedom to marry and full respect for marriage nationwide."

A key component of the Roadmap to Victory was an increased emphasis on digital content and strategy. Working with the Blue State Digital agency and others, FTM launched a redesigned website in February 2010, created a robust email program, and developed a more aggressive approach to raising money online. Michael Crawford, who led the campaign for marriage equality in Washington, D.C. in 2009, was recruited by FTM in 2010 as part of its digital upgrade. Crawford helped to implement the new storytelling-centered strategy, producing videos and other multimedia content that featured emotionally powerful stories of same-sex couples and their families (M. Crawford, personal communication, June 22, 2017). Crawford was especially committed to showcasing the diversity within the LGBT+ community, a strategy he said had been invaluable to securing marriage rights in Washington, D.C. The D.C. campaign "made a concerted effort to put black gay families at the center of everything," and Crawford's team at FTM similarly worked to tell a diversity of stories, whether they be about Southern same-sex couples, those in the military, or those who were immigrants. Crawford was also tasked with improving FTM's message dissemination efforts by taking advantage of emerging social media platforms. One successful tactic his team developed involved identifying opportunities to insert marriage-related messages into popular culture. For example, FTM created visuals that featured pop superstar and marriage equality supporter Beyoncé Knowles and posted them to social media during high-profile events such as the Grammys. Another post featured country music singer and Christian Carrie Underwood explaining her support for same-sex marriage. In both cases, the singers' thousands of fans joined in the conversation, sharing the images and amplifying FTM's message.

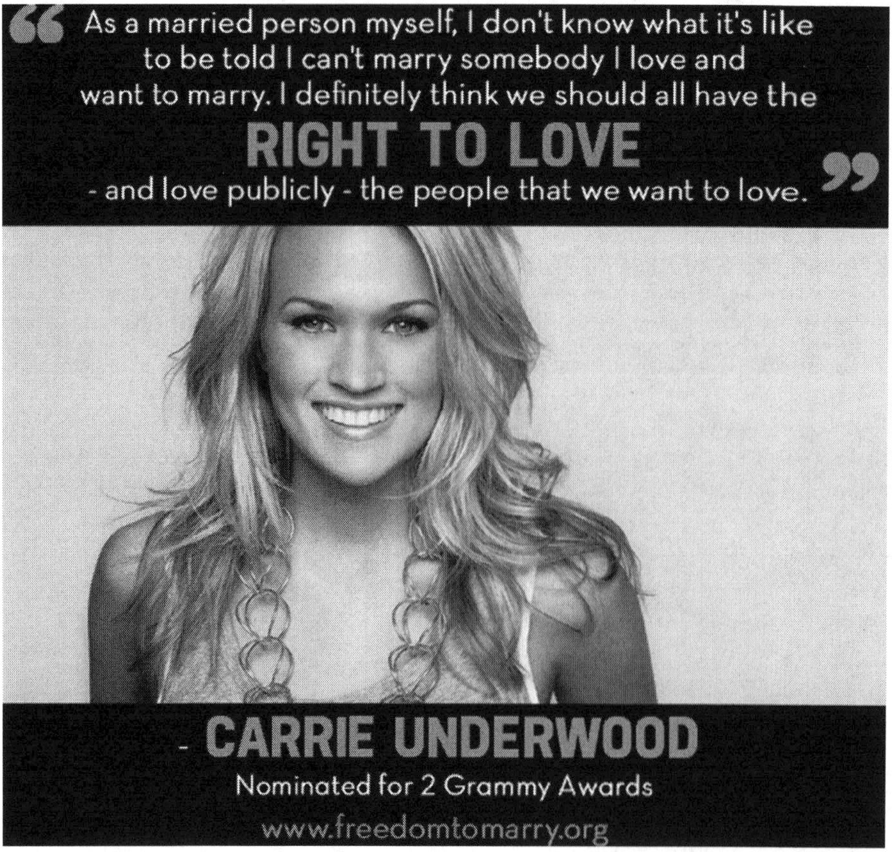

FIGURE 5.1 Freedom to Marry used celebrity endorsements to create buzz and increase visibility on social media. Country singer Carrie Underwood was among those who publicly stated support for same-sex marriage. (Image courtesy of Adam Polaski)

As new social media platforms emerged and existing ones were reconfigured to attract more users, FTM staffers adapted their message and delivery tactics. Adam Polaski, deputy digital director from 2012 to 2015, explains that soon after he was hired, Facebook made changes to its algorithm that resulted in visual content appearing more often in news feeds. In September 2012, Polaski designed a quote graphic of then First Lady Michelle Obama stating her support for marriage equality and posted it to Facebook, asking supporters to share the image. Even though it wasn't the most polished graphic he designed, Polaski recalls that it was wildly popular, becoming the group's most shared post up to that point. Polaski explains that the digital staff quickly learned to churn out visual content on the spot to take advantage of current events: "We started sharing those quote graphics and getting a lot of traction with them online, and our Facebook page really started to explode. I think it was like a perfect storm of Facebook's algorithm beginning to favor more visual content and us being able to jump on it fast" (A. Polaski, personal communication, May 25, 2017).

Another successful component of FTM's digital reboot involved a series of mini campaigns that focused on the stories of ordinary same-sex couples as told through videos posted to the group's website and shared through social media (Kowal, 2015). One of the first was the 2011 *Mr. President, Say 'I Do'* campaign designed to apply (gentle) pressure and help lay the groundwork for Barack Obama to publicly announce his support for marriage equality. The campaign began with an open letter to the president signed by public officials, business leaders, high-profile activists, and celebrities. FTM also invited members of the public to participate, running Facebook ads featuring celebrities who encouraged supporters to visit the group's website and sign the letter. FTM followed up in 2012 with *Democrats: Say 'I Do'*, a campaign designed to lobby the Democratic Party to formally include a position supporting marriage equality in the party platform. Both digital campaigns gained a lot of attention online and in traditional media, not-so-subtly signaling to Democratic leaders that the time was right to publicly support same-sex marriage (Wooledge, 2012).

Subsequent FTM mini campaigns focused on specific segments of the LGBT+ population, such as Southerners, young conservatives, and African Americans. One such campaign – *Freedom to Serve, Freedom to Marry* – featured videos of LGB military service members and their families. Michael Crawford explains that FTM needed a way to demonstrate the discriminatory impact of the Defense of Marriage Act that excluded same-sex couples from receiving federal benefits, and having military personnel tell their own stories was an effective strategy. Crawford recalls that those stories weren't always happy ones because of the harmful effects of discrimination, but he said they helped voters understand the very real effects of excluding same-sex couples from marriage (M. Crawford, personal communication, June 22, 2107). Another of FTM's targeted campaigns was *Southerners for the Freedom to Marry*. Lily Hiott-Willis, a part of the group's digital team who worked closely with that campaign, said the goal was to show that LGB couples were like other Southerners, with strong family connections and generally conservative values

(L. Hiott-Wills, personal communication, May 25, 2017). The campaign launched with a video focused on civil rights leader and Congressman John Lewis, who was unwavering in his support for marriage equality: "You cannot have rights for one segment of the population – for one group of people – and not for everybody." While opponents of same-sex marriage were using messages grounded in fear in Southern states, Hiott-Willis said FTM chose to focus on joy, love, and dignity.

FTM put substantial resources into these mini digital campaigns, and staffers credit them with shifting public opinion even more in favor of same-sex marriage. For each video released, there was a full distribution strategy that involved email and social media, paid advertising, and outreach to LGBT+ bloggers and traditional media. From 2010 to 2015, FTM created more than 40 online videos that generated millions of views across multiple social media platforms, relying in large part on supporters to share content. Old-fashioned email was also crucial for video distribution; the emails linked to individual video landing pages with social media sharing options built in. Facebook was quickly found to be a big driver of video views, especially beginning in 2014 when it shifted to more natively uploaded video (FTM, n.d.c). Facebook capabilities allowed FTM to target individuals more specifically, based on age, interests, location, and previous connection to LGBT+ advocacy organizations. In the strategy recap section of the FTM website,

FIGURE 5.2 Freedom to Marry distributed "explainer images" like this one through social media to help supporters keep track of progress in the same-sex marriage movement. (Image courtesy of Adam Polaski)

Facebook is described as the group's most effective platform, in large part because the visual and sharable nature of Facebook worked well with FTM's testimonial videos. Not surprisingly, YouTube was used primarily for distribution of video content, with FTM videos earning more than 3 million views between 2010 and 2015. Given its visual nature, Instagram was also a useful platform for sharing positive and powerful images of same-sex couples and their families. Twitter, on the other hand, was more effective for sharing breaking news such as court rulings or policy statements and the group's perspectives on current events, allowing FTM to help shape the public conversation and reach out to opinion leaders such as bloggers, reporters, and celebrities. The digital staff also used Twitter to monitor trends in public opinion and to determine where same-sex couples were receiving marriage licenses. All in all, FTM's digital presence on Twitter, Facebook, YouTube, Instagram, and Tumblr produced a combined total of more than 800,000 followers (FTM, n.d.a).

The HRC was also highly effective – and creative – in its use of social media to demonstrate the rapidly growing public support for same-sex marriage. Olivia Alair Dalton, senior vice president of communications and marketing, remains especially proud of an innovative way HRC allowed its supporters to participate in the complex legal process of 2015's *Obergefell v. Hodges* case. In advance of oral arguments, HRC created the "People's Brief," an actual amicus brief that anyone could sign through the HRC website. Dalton said that the point HRC wanted to make by producing an open amicus brief was that "every single American has an interest in marriage equality" (O. Dalton, personal communication, May 25, 2017). It required a herculean effort from HRC staffers to verify signatures and print the brief's thousands of pages, but when they were finished, a brief containing 207,551 signatories calling for nationwide marriage equality was delivered to the U.S. Supreme Court – the most of any amicus brief ever submitted. Dalton said it was worth the effort, resulting in significant social media buzz from individuals who were proud of their participation and wanted to share news of their part in the historic court case.

Turning the corner

As we've seen, the painful setback of Proposition 8 and the loss of ballot initiatives in 2008 and 2009 spurred soul-searching and strategy adjustments among advocates for same-sex marriage. Marriage proponents didn't have to wait long for more positive results in all three of the priority areas outlined in FTM's Roadmap to Victory: legalizing marriage at the state level, shifting public opinion, and federal court rulings/legislation. By the end of 2009, five states (Massachusetts, Connecticut, Iowa, Vermont, and New Hampshire) had legalized same-sex marriage, but only through court rulings and legislation, not at the ballot box. Marriage rights were also growing internationally, with Norway, Sweden, Iceland, Portugal, and Argentina allowing lesbian and gay couples to wed. Then, two key events in 2011 gave LGBT+ advocates hope that the U.S. marriage movement had turned a corner. First, in February, then President Barack Obama declared the Defense of Marriage Act unconstitutional and directed the Justice Department to stop defending it in court. Later that year, Governor Andrew Cuomo signed a bill giving same-sex couples in New York the right to marry – after the measure had been approved by a *Republican*-controlled Senate. At that point, it seemed as though the movement had gained momentum, and some advocates and pundits speculated that it might not be long until the fight was over.

Marketing expert John Hoffman was one such speculator. In a 2012 article for *Non-Profit Quarterly*, he suggested that nationwide marriage equality was inevitable, tying it specifically to the increased reliance by advocacy groups on social networking platforms to spread their message more broadly and effectively than traditional channels had previously allowed. Hoffman noted that despite the unavoidable struggles and setbacks that would likely lie ahead, the inherent qualities of social media would assure the passage of same-sex marriage and other rights for LGBT individuals and families. As he put it, "Social media is about storytelling, and so is the movement toward LGBT equality" (Hoffman, 2012). As already noted, both HRC and FTM had begun taking advantage of the newer social media platforms, with notable success. In two cases in particular, HRC and FTM put together social media campaigns that eventually involved tens of thousands of followers, drew significant media attention, and won numerous industry awards. These campaigns have been widely credited with helping to shift public opinion toward marriage equality, paving the way for U.S. Supreme Court decisions in 2013 and 2015 that resulted in nationwide legal same-sex marriage (Bakshy, 2013; Ball, 2015; Penney, 2015). The remainder of this chapter will examine these two campaigns.

What is that red equal sign all over Facebook?

On March 26, 2013, the U.S. Supreme Court began to hear oral arguments for two key marriage-related cases. The first, *Hollingsworth v. Perry*, regarded the constitutionality of Proposition 8, California's ban on same-sex marriage. The second, *U.S. v. Windsor*, dealt with the constitutionality of the Defense of Marriage Act, which limited the federal definition of marriage to a union between one man and one woman. The two cases had huge implications for the marriage equality movement, and activists on both sides were trying to sway public opinion in hopes of influencing the Supreme Court justices' reasoning.

HRC's digital communications team had planned for a big social media push to coincide with the U.S. Supreme Court cases. On March 25, HRC Marketing Director Anastasia Khoo started things off when she posted a specially designed version of the group's familiar yellow and blue equal sign logo to the HRC Facebook page. The symbolic marriage version of the logo used the colors of love and romance: a pink equal sign on a red background (Vie, 2014). On Facebook, Khoo asked HRC members to change their social media profile pictures to the new logo in a visible sign of support for marriage equality – and to encourage their friends, family, and colleagues to do the same. Facebook updates urged supporters to

"Share this image and ask your friends and family to join you!" and "Paint the town Red." The custom logo was one of many tactics the HRC included in its digital strategy (Khoo, 2013), and not one that was particularly innovative in terms of digital activism. Just the year before, the organization had been featured in *The Atlantic* in a glowing piece about the "social-network effect that is helping legalize gay marriage" (Scola, 2012). The story focused on HRC's use of a peer-to-peer networking app called Amicus, which organizations could tailor and rename to meet their specific networking needs. HRC used Amicus, branded for the marriage equality fight as "Call4Equality," for the November election in 2012 when Maryland, Maine, and Washington became the first states to legalize same-sex marriage by popular vote. Amicus allows supporters of a cause to harness their social connections to increase awareness of an issue, ask for votes, raise money, and motivate volunteers to get involved in offline activities. To use Amicus, an individual signs in through Facebook, and the software connects the user's list of friends with information about them from public records. The user can then pledge to make a certain number of contacts, ideally by phone, but also through email. The *Atlantic* article raved about the new tool and HRC's willingness to adopt digitally savvy data-infused campaigning tactics (Scola, 2012).

But it was the RES campaign, not Amicus, that made a big splash in 2013. A follow-up report that HRC (2013) compiled to showcase the success of its communication efforts described the RES campaign as the most successful use of social media to date for an LGBT+-related cause, and evidence supports that assertion. By the time activists were gathering outside the U.S. Supreme Court building the day after the specially designed logo was rolled out, the RES had created more than 10 million impressions across the U.S. and internationally, and millions of Facebook users had adopted it as their profile picture. According to Facebook, there was a 120 percent increase in profile photo updates on March 26, the day after Khoo's original post (Bakshy, 2013). HRC's Olivia Dalton suggests the RES, with its message of love, was successful because of its simplicity and directness: "You didn't have to understand what an amicus brief was or an Equal Protection Clause was or even what DOMA stood for. All you needed to understand about what was before the Supreme Court was in that image" (O.A. Dalton, personal communication, May 25, 2017). HRC staffers were shocked at how quickly the logo became a viral Internet phenomenon, and they were also excited by the boost to HRC's brand, especially the fact that many folks were learning about HRC for the first time. The news media jumped on the story, with a CNN report (Weisbrod & Merica, 2013) noting that as the U.S. Supreme Court justices prepared to consider same-sex marriage, "millions have taken to Facebook and Twitter to litigate the issue." The CNN story also mentioned social media campaigns that opponents of same-sex marriage had launched in advance of the Supreme Court hearings. For example, the Family Research Council asked its supporters to share a graphic featuring a man and a woman holding hands, but such efforts were hugely overshadowed by the HRC RES (Weisbrod & Merica, 2013).

FIGURE 5.3 Human Rights Campaign communication strategists encouraged same-sex marriage supporters to personalize the group's Red Equal Sign image, a tactic that magnified the Facebook campaign's reach. (Image used with permission of HRC)

Almost immediately, celebrities and politicians jumped on the bandwagon. One particularly influential early adopter was Star Trek actor and gay rights activist George Takei, known for his massive Facebook and Twitter following (Buchanan, 2013). Singing superstar Beyoncé joined in, posting the RES image on Instagram with an explanation cleverly connecting her *Single Ladies* hit to the marriage rights issue: "If you like it *you should be able* to put on a ring on it" (Henderson, 2013). The campaign even caught the attention of members of Congress, with more than a dozen switching their Twitter avatars to the RES (Milano, 2013). Within hours, variants and parodies of the logo, many of them quite funny, started popping up. One of the most popular overlaid the Internet meme "Grumpy Cat" on top of the red logo (explaining that marriage equality would make her less grumpy). The Associated Press (2013) reported that some Facebook users swapped matzoh for the pink lines as Passover began, others added Sesame Street's "best friends" Bert and Ernie, and some even got X-rated, swapping images of a penis for the bars in the equal sign. Within a few days, the RES had become Facebook's most viral campaign in its history (Khoo, 2014). Not everyone was thrilled with the campaign, of course. Some people were annoyed at the constant stream of RES posts in their news feeds, and others questioned how much good it could really do in terms of affecting the U.S. Supreme Court. An article on the online arts and culture news website *Vice* called the campaign "just another form of passive activism that isn't advancing the cause" and told participants to instead donate money or join those marching in support of marriage equality (Moylan, 2013). An ABC News story about the phenomenon quoted one skeptic who had tweeted, "Just got off the phone with #scotus Justice Scalia. Said he was going to vote no until he saw all the red profile pictures on FB. #pointless" (Milano, 2013). But it seemed that even those who didn't like the RES phenomenon couldn't stop talking about it.

Khoo explained that the campaign was specifically designed to draw young people into the national marriage discussion. In a commentary piece for *The Toronto Star* in April 2014, she explained the strategy behind the campaign: "Youth loom large in our work. All of us at HRC want to create a more welcoming world, and as the Supreme Court started to hear arguments about marriage equality, we wanted to send a message of hope to young people who might not feel accepted, or realize that there is a visible community of people out there who are supportive" (Khoo, 2014). Khoo said talking about how to reach a young audience gave her the idea for the RES initiative: "That's when I had an idea for a campaign that could harness the power of Facebook. We changed our logo to the colour of love, red, and asked people to adopt it as their profile picture in solidarity with the movement." Months after the RES campaign, HRC was still benefiting from buzz about its success. In 2014, the group received the top award at business and technology conference South by Southwest Interactive (SXSWI). The campaign also won two Hubbies for digital marketing in 2013 and 2014. Hosted by The Hub, the sister brand of *PR Week*, the Hubbies honor the best of digital innovation and brand achievement. HRC received the Best Social Media Presence award for the 2013 RES logo campaign, and Khoo won Digital Innovator of the Year. Even after many months, multiple awards, and countless media mentions, Khoo seemed surprised by the scope of her campaign's reach. Interviewed after winning the SXSWI awards, she explained that her team wanted to try something new to make sure they had a role in the public conversation about marriage equality. To do so, Khoo said they drew inspiration from longtime movement leaders' focus on the emotional aspects of marriage, but added a modern social media twist: "The major tenet was that people had an emotion attached to that logo. It was a way to show their support and a way that they could represent how they felt about something, and that's been key to our success and in winning these awards. You really have to make people feel strongly about something" (Soat, 2014).

A case study by the MIT Center for Civil Media (Vie, 2014) showed that the red logo campaign's reach was indeed significant. In addition to the already documented number of impressions on Facebook and Twitter, it drove a substantial amount of new traffic to the HRC website, which had more than 700,000 unique visitors in a 24-hour period around March 26. Even more important for the long-term success of HRC, almost 90 percent of those visitors were new to the site. Many of them signed and shared the HRC's "Majority Opinion" petition designed to illustrate the growing level of public support for marriage equality, drawing more than 67,000 new supporters. Vie (2014) referred to the social contagion phenomenon to explain the campaign's wide reach and domino effect. Users of SESs are most likely to adopt online content that is shared by friends, and those rates of adoption increase as additional friends adopt as well. Many of those who were previously unaware of HRC but adopted the RES logo because their friends did may feel inclined to visit the group's website so they can better understand the new phenomenon everyone is talking about. An article in *The Chronicle of Philanthropy* (Switzer, 2013) suggests an additional reason for the effectiveness of HRC's campaign: it promoted more than the organization. Technology allowed the group's supporters and others who adopted the avatar to customize the image to represent their own style or views. Some combined the logo with their own profile picture, while others did parodies as mentioned above. HRC capitalized upon this aspect of the campaign, creating a slide show of some of the variations for its website and putting them into a collage that was posted at the top of the group's Facebook page. Switzer (2013) also notes that other components of HRC's digital strategy in advance of the 2013 Supreme Court hearings got less buzz but were nonetheless successful. He praised the campaign for deploying new tools to call attention to the Supreme Court arguments, noting that HRC paid Twitter for "promoted Tweets" so that the group's messages would show up at the top of searches about the Supreme Court case. One of those messages was retweeted 14,000 times, the most retweets on a single message in HRC's history. They also paid so that ads on smartphones used within a half-mile of the Supreme Court building would display messages in support of same-sex marriage.

FTM did not reach the RES's level of viral success with any of its individual social media efforts, but its #LoveMustWin hashtag did help frame public discourse about same-sex marriage during the key first half of 2015. Everyone knows now that the *Obergefell v. Hodges* case that came before the U.S. Supreme Court in April 2015 was ultimately the most important one for the marriage movement. In that case, justices had to determine whether same-sex marriage is a right guaranteed by the U.S. Constitution and whether same-sex marriages performed in states where it has been legalized had to be recognized in states that banned the practice. Almost every gay rights organization in the United States worked to rally supporters and influence public opinion in the lead up to that case. FTM's digital team had multiple social media tactics to increase attention and support, but it was the Twitter hashtag #LoveMustWin that got the most buzz.

#LoveMustWin was clearly an appropriate wording choice for an organization run by Evan Wolfson, who for more than 30 years had argued that the key message of the marriage equality movement centers on love and family, not politics (Stewart, 2015). The #LoveMustWin campaign, created by FTM in conjunction with the Blue State Digital agency, focused on the importance of a nationwide ruling in favor of same-sex marriage and was active throughout the court's oral arguments and the announcement of the historic pro-marriage equality ruling in June 2015. In its website archives, FTM explains that it deployed #LoveMustWin across multiple social media platforms, asking for supporters to submit creative representations of the hashtag in whatever format they chose. Responses took the form of photos, songs, artwork, even baked goods. FTM recorded more than 50,000 uses of the hashtag, most of them on the day of the court's oral arguments, April 28. A number of well-known public officials and celebrities joined the campaign, which garnered a significant amount of earned media coverage. *The Washington Post* even reported on the day of oral arguments that (future) presidential candidate Hillary Clinton had used Twitter – and the hashtag #LoveMustWin – to make her first direct comments on the same-sex marriage issue before the court ruling (Gearan, 2015). As Michael Crawford, head of FTM's digital efforts put it, the #LoveMustWin campaign "helped send a message more powerfully than FTM could do itself because we empowered people to make their voices heard" (M. Crawford, personal communication, June 22, 2017).

After the Supreme Court's historic ruling in *Obergefell v. Hodges* was announced on June 26, 2015, #LoveMustWin was immediately replaced by the triumphant #LoveWins, featured prominently throughout all of FTM's social media presence and used by many other LGBT+ advocacy groups and individual supporters. At its peak, 35,000 tweets per minute were being posted using the hashtag (Stewart, 2015). Like the RES campaign two years before, #LoveMustWin won a Shorty Award for social media campaign excellence. Likewise, a *Brooklyn Magazine* story (Stewart, 2015) about the success of #LoveMustWin praised FTM's digital efforts for being a key component of a "central campaign that wasn't only devoted to win but was truly an authentic national campaign." A quote from FTM Deputy Digital Director Adam Polaski summed up the group's goal, as distilled into one very successful hashtag: "At the end of the day, what we're trying to get out is a love story and everyone getting married has a love story." The #LoveMustWin campaign, as the RES campaign did two years prior, was also strategically trying to sway public opinion as a conduit for influencing the Supreme Court, a point that Michael Crawford was very transparent about: "We showed the Supreme Court that America was ready to accept marriage. Whenever you are fighting for something that is trying to make people happy, then you're going to win. Love wins always, it might take some time but it wins and we had love on our side" (Stewart, 2015). Even though SCOTUS justices are not likely to decide a case based on a preponderance of Facebook images or tweets, there's still reason to think that widespread visible support for a social issue can influence how justices assess prevailing social norms and attitudes. In a piece in *Scientific American*, Tannenbaum (2013) argues that millions of people on Facebook or Twitter making their opinions on an issue "immediately, graphically, demonstrably obvious" can carry weight, creating "a widespread descriptive norm implying that it is socially acceptable to advocate for same-sex marriage" and leading to real change. And so, although justices might not be checking Twitter or Facebook to tally up the red avatars before rendering a decision, demonstration of solidarity through social media campaigns from advocacy groups such as the HRC or FTM could well have an impact.

Of course, there were also advocacy groups fighting just as hard in opposition to the extension of marriage rights to LGB couples. The next chapter will focus on these organizations, their leaders and strategies, and their use of social media to influence public opinion and policy.

References

Aiello, D. (2008, November 13). No on Prop 8 official grilled over campaign. *Bay Area Reporter*. Retrieved from http://www.ebar.com/news/article.php?sec=news&article=3475

All Politics. (1998, November 3). Hawaii gives legislature power to ban same-sex marriage. CNN. Retrieved from http://www.cnn.com/ALLPOLITICS/stories/1998/11/04/same.sex.ballot

Armstrong, E. A. (2002). *Forging gay identities: Organizing sexuality in San Francisco, 1950–1994*. Chicago, IL: University of Chicago Press.

Associated Press. (2013, March 27). Red equal signs: Gay marriage equality box spreads on social media. *Syracuse.com*. Retrieved from http://www.syracuse.com/news/index.ssf/2013/03/red_equal_signs_gay_marriage_equality_boxes.html

Bakshy, E. (2013, March 29). Showing support for marriage equality on Facebook [Facebook note]. Retrieved April 4, 2017, from https://www.facebook.com/notes/facebook-data-science/showing-support-for-marriage-equality-on-facebook/10151430548593859

Ball, M. (2015, July 1). How gay marriage became a constitutional right. *The Atlantic*. Retrieved from https://www.theatlantic.com/politics/archive/2015/07/gay-marriage-supreme-court-politics-activism/397052

Baunach, D. M. (2011). Decomposing trends in attitudes toward gay marriage, 1988–2006. *Social Science Quarterly*, 92(2), 346–363. http://doi.org/10.1111/j.1540-6237.2011.00772.x

Becker, J. (2014, April 16). How the President got to 'I Do' on same-sex marriage. *New York Times Magazine*. Retrieved from https://www.nytimes.com/2014/04/20/magazine/how- the-president-got-to-i-do-on-same-sex-marriage.html

Benford, R. D., & Snow, D. A. (2000). Framing processes and social movements: An overview and assessment. *Annual Review of Sociology*, 26, 611–639.

Bernstein, M. (1997). Celebration and suppression: The strategic uses of identity by the lesbian and gay movement. *American Journal of Sociology*, 103(3), 531–565. http://doi.org/10.1086/231250

Bernstein, M., & Burke, M.C. (2013). Normalization, queer discourse, and the marriage-equality movement in Vermont. In M. Bernstein & V. Taylor (Eds.), *The marrying kind* (pp. 319–343). Minneapolis: University of Minnesota Press.

Bolcer, J. (2012, August 13). Freedom to Marry pours $3 million into state marriage battles. *The Advocate*. Retrieved from http://www.advocate.com/politics/election/2012/08/13/freedom-marry-pours-3-million-state-marriage-battles

Broder, J. M. (2004, December 9). Groups debate slower strategy on gay rights. *The New York Times*. Retrieved from http://www.nytimes.com/2004/12/09/us/groups-debate-slower-strategy-on-gay-rights.html

Buchanan, M. (2013, March 27). Painting the Internet pink. *The New Yorker*. Retrieved from http://www.newyorker.com/news/news-desk/painting-the-internet-pink

Carton, E. (2005, June 21). Winning marriage: What we need to do. Retrieved from https://s3.amazonaws.com/s3.documentcloud.org/documents/2108219/final-marriage-concept-paper.pdf

D'Emilio, J. (1983). *Sexual politics, sexual communities: The making of a homosexual minority in the United States, 1940–1970*. Chicago, IL: University of Chicago Press.

D'Emilio, J. (2006). The marriage fight is setting us back. *Gay and Lesbian Review*, 13(6), 10–11.

DeFore, J. (2017, March 10). 'The Freedom to Marry': Film review. *The Hollywood Reporter*. Retrieved from http://www.hollywoodreporter.com/review/freedom-marry-985233

Ehrenreich, B. (2008, November 19). Anatomy of a failed campaign. *The Advocate*. Retrieved from http://www.advocate.com/news/2008/11/19/anatomy-failed-campaign

Freedom to Marry. (n.d.a). Lessons learned: Building the digital presence. Retrieved from http://www.freedomtomarry.org/lessons-learned/building-the-digital-presence

Freedom to Marry. (n.d.c). Messaging, messengers, and public support. Retrieved from http://www.freedomtomarry.org/pages/Messaging-Messengers-and-Public-Support.

Freedom to Marry. (2015, October 28). Evan Wolfson's 1983 thesis on the freedom to marry. [Blog post]. Retrieved from http://www.freedomtomarry.org/blog/entry/Evan-Wolfsons-1983-thesis-on-the-freedom-to-marry

Freiberg, P. (2001, March 30). Wolfson leaves Lambda to focus on freedom-to-marry work. *Washington Blade*. Retrieved from http://www.oocities.org/evanwolfson/ftm_washblade.htm

Gamson, W. A. (1992). *Talking politics*. New York, NY: Cambridge University Press.

Gamson, W. A., & Wolfsfeld, G. (1993). Movements and media as interacting systems. *Annals of the American Academy of Political and Social Science*, 528(1), 114–125. http://doi.org/10.1177/0002716293528001009

Gearan, A. (2015, April 28). Hillary Clinton goes all-in on gay marriage: "Love must win." *The Washington Post*. Retrieved from https://www.washingtonpost.com/news/post-politics/wp/2015/04/28/hillary-clinton-goes-all-in-on-gay-marriage-love-must-win/?utm_term=.0bb39601de44

Hemmelgarn, S. (2008, May 1). Big bucks seen in amendment battle. *The Bay Area Reporter*. Retrieved from http://www.ebar.com/news/article.php?sec=news&article=2929

Henderson, C. (2013, March 27). Red equal sign Facebook: Beyonce Instagrams sign, what's the red symbol all about? *EnStar*. Retrieved from http://www.enstarz.com/articles/15305/20130327/red-equal-sign-facebook-beyonce-instagrams-whats-symbol-about-twitter.htm

Herek, G. M. (2006). Legal recognition of same-sex relationships in the United States: A social science perspective. *American Psychologist*, 61(6), 607–621. http://doi.org10.1037/0003-066X.61.6.607

Hoffman, J. (2012, May 14). Sharing our way toward equality: Social media and gay rights. *Nonprofit Quarterly*. Retrieved from https://nonprofitquarterly.org/2012/05/14/sharing-our-way-toward-equality-social-media-and-gay-rights/

Human Rights Campaign. (2013). Marriage at the U.S. Supreme Court: A transformative moment for equality. Retrieved from http://hrc-assets.s3-website-us-east-1.amazonaws.com//files/assets/resources/SupremeCourt_Accomplishments-FINAL_1.pdf

Khoo, A. (2013, May 1). Painting the Internet red. *Stanford Social Innovation Review*. Retrieved from http://www.ssireview.org/blog/entry/painting_the_internet_red

Khoo, A. (2014, April 1). The power of social media in the gay rights movement. *The Star*. Retrieved from https://www.thestar.com/opinion/commentary/2014/04/01/the_power_of_social_media_in_the_gay_rights_movement.html

Koenig, K. (2014, May 16). Ten years ago, Massachusetts introduced us to gay marriage. MSNBC. Retrieved from http://www.msnbc.com/msnbc/ten-years-ago-massachusetts-introduced-us-gay-marriage

Kowal, J. F. (2015, September 29). The improbable victory of marriage equality. [Blog post]. Retrieved from https://www.brennancenter.org/print/15941

Jefferson, D. J. (2008, November 14). How my same-sex wedding made me an activist. *Newsweek*. Retrieved from http://www.newsweek.com/how-my-same-sex-wedding-made-me-activist-85409

Juro, R. (2013, April 1). Even after all these years, HRC still doesn't get it. [Blog post.] Retrieved from http://www.huffingtonpost.com/rebecca-juro/even-after-all-these-years-hrc-still-doesnt-get-it_b_2989826.html

Meronek, T. (2015, January 11). Human Rights Campaign under fire in LGBT community. *Truthout*. Retrieved from http://www.truth-out.org/news/item/28430-human-rights-campaign-under-fire-in-lgbt-community

Milano, D. (2013, March 26). What's that red equal-sign on Facebook all about? ABC News. Retrieved from http://abcnews.go.com/blogs/technology/2013/03/what-is-that-red-equal-sign-on-facebook-all-about

Moylan, B. (2013, March 26). The red marriage quality sign on your Facebook profile is completely useless. *Vice*. Retrieved from https://www.vice.com/en_us/article/4wq9nb/the-red-marriage-equality-sign-on-your-facebook-profile-is-completely-useless

Moscowitz, L. M. (2013). The battle over marriage: Gay rights activism through the media. http://dx.doi.org/10.5406/illinois/9780252038129.001.0001

Penney, J. (2015). Social media and symbolic action: Exploring participation in the Facebook Red Equal Sign profile picture campaign. *Journal of Computer Mediated Communication*, 20(1), 52–66. http://doi.org/10.1111/jcc4.12092

Polletta, F., & Ho, M.K. (2006). Frames and their consequences. In R.E. Gooden & C. Tilly (Eds.), *The Oxford handbook of contextual political studies*. http://doi.org/10.1093/oxfordhb/9780199270439.003.0010

Queerty. (2009, November 5). What do HRC + Scientology have in common? Inflating their memberships. [Blog post]. Retrieved from https://www.queerty.com/what-do-hrc-scientology-have-in-common-inflating-their-memberships-20091105

Schwartz, J. (2005, August). Framing gay marriage: The Human Rights Campaign's online campaign for marriage equality. Paper presented at the annual conference of the Association for Education in Journalism and Mass Communication, San Francisco, CA.

Scola, N. (2012, November 30). The social-network effect that is helping legalize gay marriage. *The Atlantic*. Retrieved from https://www.theatlantic.com/politics/archive/2012/11/the-social-network-effect-that-is-helping-legalize-gay-marriage/265793/

Snow, D. A., & Benford, R. D. (1988). Ideology, frame resonance, and participant mobilization. *International Social Movement Research*, 1(1), 197–217.

Soat, M. (2014, March 20). The Human Rights Campaign earns praise at SXSWI. *Marketing News Exclusives*. Retrieved from https://www.ama.org/publications/eNewsletters/MNE/Pages/The-Human-Rights-Campaign-Earns-Praise-at-SXSWI.aspx

Solomon, M. (2014). *Winning marriage: The inside story of how same-sex couples took on the politicians and pundits – and won*. Lebanon, NH: University Press of New England.

Stewart, D. (2015, September 14). #LOVEWINS: How a social media campaign promoting marriage equality swept the nation. *Brooklyn Magazine*. Retrieved from http://www.bkmag.com/2015/09/14/lovewins-how-a-social-media-campaign-promoting-marriage-equality-swept-the-nation

Stone, A. L. (2012). *Gay rights at the ballot box*. Minneapolis: University of Minnesota Press.

Switzer, C. (2013, April 8). Inside the Human Rights Campaign's social-media success. *The Chronicle of Philanthropy*. Retrieved from https://www.philanthropy.com/article/Inside-the-Human-Rights/155035

Tannenbaum, M. (2013, March 28). Will changing your Facebook profile picture do anything for marriage equality? *Scientific American*. Retrieved from http://blogs.scientificamerican.com/psysociety/2013/03/28/marriage-equality-and-social-proof

Tarrow, S. (1998). *Power in movement: Social movements, collective action and politics*. http://dx.doi.org/10.1017/CBO9780511813245

Vie, S. (2014). The Human Rights Campaign Facebook logo. Civic Media Project. Retrieved from http://civicmediaproject.org/works/civic-media-project/thehumanrightscampaignfacebooklogo

Villarreal, Y. (2015, June 4). 5 most disappointing things we learned about HRC's 'White Men's Club.' *The Advocate*. Retrieved from http://www.advocate.com/human-rights-campaign-hrc/2015/06/04/5-most-disappointing-things-we-learned-about-hrcs-white-mens-cl

Warner, M. (1999). *The trouble with normal: Sex, politics, and the ethics of queer life*. New York, NY: Harvard University Press.

Weisbrod, E., & Merica, D. (2013, March 26). Seeing red? Same-sex marriage debate goes viral. [Blog post]. Retrieved from http://politicalticker.blogs.cnn.com/2013/03/26/emblazoned-in-red-same-sex-marriage-dominates-social-media/comment-page-1

Wolfson, E. (2004). *Why marriage matters: America, equality, and gay people's right to marry.* New York, NY: Simon & Schuster.

Wolfson, E. (2010, August 5). After historic Prop 8 ruling, what's next for the Freedom to Marry [Blog Post]. Retrieved from http://www.huffingtonpost.com/evan-wolfson/after-historic-prop-8rul_b_671659.html

Wolfson, E. (2013, December 22). Top 10 Freedom to Marry moments in 2013. [Blog post]. Retrieved from http://www.huffingtonpost.com/evan-wolfson/the-top-10-marriage-equal_b_4467689.html

Wooledge, S. (2012, February 26). Will the Democrats say "I do" support marriage equality in 2012? *Daily Kos.* Retrieved from http://www.dailykos.com/story/2012/2/26/1068005/-Will-the-Democrats-say-I-do-support-marriage-equality-in-2012

Zepatos, T., & Hatalsky, L. E. (2015, June 26). The marriage movement's secret weapon: Radical cooperation. [Blog post]. Retrieved from http://www.huffingtonpost.com/thalia-zepatos/the-marriage-movements-se_b_7665696.html

6

THE OPPONENTS: THE RELIGIOUS RIGHT FIGHTS TO SAVE TRADITIONAL MARRIAGE

Social movement historians generally consider the June 1969 Stonewall riots in New York City as the start of the contemporary gay rights movement, but it's trickier to pinpoint the start of the *anti*-gay rights movement. Entertainer Anita Bryant often gets the credit for launching the organized fight against LGBT+ rights in the United States. Bryant had a lucrative singing career and was widely known in the 1970s as spokeswoman for the Florida Citrus Commission. But she was also an evangelical Christian who felt called to action when the Dade County (Fla.) Commission in 1977 began considering an ordinance to prohibit housing and employment discrimination against gays and lesbians. She wrote to the county commissioners, declaring that the proposed measure would infringe upon her right as a citizen to teach her children and to follow "God's moral code" (Clendinen & Nagourney, 2013, p. 296). In spite of protests by Bryant and other churchgoers, the ordinance passed and turned a local matter into a national debate about homosexuality (Wolraich, 2015). Disgusted by what she described as a law that condoned immorality, Bryant started Save Our Children, a coalition of Christian groups in South Florida. The organization collected the signatures needed to allow voters to consider the anti-discrimination ordinance, and when the repeal petition was voted on in June 1977, it easily passed.

And thus an organized movement opposed to gay rights was born. After their success in Florida, Bryant and her allies took the fight to other cities where they helped voters overturn similar pro-gay ordinances. Looking back, social movement scholars have identified the Save Our Children campaign against gay rights as a significant factor in the emergence of the conservative Christian movement – commonly known as the Religious Right – in the late 1970s and early 1980s (Fejes, 2008; Lane, 2006). It was from this broader cultural movement that organized opposition to SSM emerged, becoming what some in the Christian Right regard as "the defining battle in the cultural wars" (Wilcox et al., 2006, p. 57). This chapter will focus on the Religious Right and its efforts to prevent LGB couples from being able to legally marry. As with the previous chapter, we'll examine both large-scale, multi-issue national organizations (Focus on the Family and the Family Research Council), as well as one created specifically to fight against SSM (the National Organization for Marriage). We'll end with a look at how marriage equality opponents have pivoted after the 2015 *Obergefell v. Hodges* ruling to focus on the issue of religious freedom.

Emergence of the Religious Right and organized opposition to gay rights

Long before Anita Bryant, fundamentalist Christians played an influential role in American politics. Religious scholars (Marty, 1970; Williams, 2010) trace the origin of modern religious fundamentalism to a widening theological disagreement among U.S. Christians that intensified in the 1920s. On one side were theological modernists who favored adjusting church teachings to incorporate new scientific understandings such as the theory of evolution. On the other side were Christian fundamentalists who remained loyal to traditional Protestant doctrine such as the divinity and virgin birth of Christ (McVicar, 2016). As modernist influence grew, theological conservatives responded by starting their own religious and educational institutions.

Although much has been written about the Religious Right, there's no actual organization by that name. *The Oxford Research Encyclopedia of Religion* says the term *Religious Right* (also called the *Christian Right*) refers to individual leaders, religious organizations, and political advocacy groups that formed a loose coalition in the late 1970s in the United States (McVicar, 2016). Unlike earlier fundamentalists who considered politics distasteful, this newer coalition embraced a mix of theology and politics (Williams, 2010). They remained committed to the importance of traditional family values and Judeo-Christian teachings, but also advocated for free-market economic policy and a strong military. Much of the contemporary Religious Right's political motivation can be seen as a revolt against the secular humanism and changing sexual mores of the 1960s (Bull & Gallagher, 2001), and they were vehemently against LGBT+ rights. The Right considered it their mission to use political tactics to fight the increasingly bitter cultural wars over topics such as homosexuality and abortion (Lane, 2006). Prominent members of the emerging movement included psychologist and FOTF founder James Dobson and a Southern Baptist preacher and televangelist named Jerry Falwell. Falwell regularly preached against the evils of homosexuality and had supported Anita Bryant's efforts in South Florida. In 1978 Falwell publicly supported California State Senator John Briggs in sponsoring an ultimately unsuccessful ballot initiative allowing local school boards to ban gay teachers. Even though the Briggs initiative failed, Falwell's stature as a defender of conservative Christian beliefs grew.

Attempts by the federal government to deny tax-exempt status to private Christian colleges that did not allow African-Americans to enroll – combined with frustration over liberal cultural trends related to marriage and family – led Falwell in 1979 to create the political lobbying group Moral Majority to help elect conservative Christian candidates (Bull & Gallagher, 2001). High on the group's list of priorities was preventing efforts by the gay rights movement to normalize homosexuality, and Falwell routinely preached against gay liberation to galvanize supporters and raise money. Other Christian conservatives such as Pat Robertson followed Falwell into the public spotlight, with Robertson entering (and soon exiting) the 1988 presidential race, running largely on a platform in opposition to abortion and homosexuality and portraying evangelicals as victims of oppression and intolerance. Although both Falwell and Robertson had their struggles in the late 1980s, the influence of the Religious Right remained strong, especially in matters related to LGBT+ rights. For example, conservative Christians played a key role in the 1992 passage of Colorado's Amendment 2, which prevented towns or cities from taking action to recognize gay men or lesbians as a protected class. Advocacy groups that promoted Amendment 2 were successful in framing the campaign as one of "special rights," claiming that gays are already wealthy and politically powerful and do not need or deserve more rights than those of average citizens. During the Amendment 2 campaign, members of the Religious Right also juxtaposed gays and lesbians with African Americans, positioning blacks who had experienced discrimination as deserving of protection, unlike homosexuals (Stone, 2012).

The 1992 presidential campaign also saw the Religious Right and LGBT+ movements pitted against each other, each portraying the other as a threat to American society. The Right had far more resources and public supporters, but both groups received significant media coverage, especially after a shocking judicial ruling in Hawaii. After three same-sex couples sued in 1991 to force Hawaii to issue them marriage licenses, the Hawaii Supreme Court in 1993 surprised everyone by ruling that denying licenses to same-sex couples appeared to violate the state constitution's equal protection clause. But it was an especially big wake-up call for Christian organizations opposed to LGBT+ rights. Campaigns in multiple states, supported by national organizations such as FOTF, mobilized to ensure that the traditional definition of marriage as one man and one woman remained intact. Within months of the 1993 Hawaii court ruling, state legislatures across the country began considering proposals to amend their constitutions to override the "full faith and credit" provision that requires states to honor one another's contracts (Stone, 2012). Then in 1996 President Bill Clinton signed into law the Defense of Marriage Act, which defined marriage at the federal level as a union of one man and one woman, guaranteed that no state would be forced to recognize gay marriages performed in other states, and prevented same-sex couples from receiving federal benefits given to heterosexual married couples.

The next few years saw continued success for SSM opponents. Four states (Alaska, Hawaii, Nebraska, and Nevada) banned marriage rights for same-sex couples, while the only (small) step forward for marriage equality proponents occurred in Vermont, which in April 2000 became the first state to allow civil unions. In spite of their victories at the state level, many conservatives were concerned that DOMA would not be strong enough to head off potential pro-gay court decisions. And so, in the early 2000s they began pushing for an amendment to the U.S. Constitution that would ban SSM nationwide. Such a measure, labeled the Federal Marriage Amendment, was introduced into Congress in both 2002 and 2003, but when it came up for a vote in the House of Representatives in 2004, it fell short of the two-thirds required to pass it on to the Senate, a frustrating loss for conservative Christians.

Gay marriage opponents were also concerned about the June 2003 Supreme Court ruling in *Lawrence v. Texas* that had struck down statutes criminalizing sodomy. The court ruled that intimate consensual sexual conduct was protected by the Due Process Clause of the Fourteenth Amendment, an approach that both sides of the marriage debate realized could open the door to SSM if courts applied similar rationale to LGB relationships. The *Lawrence* decision mobilized conservative Christians across the country, many of whom felt that more aggressive action was needed at the state level (Stone, 2012) and were incensed that courts could unilaterally force gay marriage onto a public that did not support it (Goldbert, 2003). Indeed, at that time, more than half of Americans (52 percent) favored a law requiring that marriage be between a man and a woman, according to an Associated Press poll (Lester, 2003). Interestingly, however, polling also showed that Americans were reluctant to discriminate against gay men and lesbians in other areas even though they weren't comfortable with allowing gays to marry (Rimmerman & Wilcox, 2007).

Political scientists and sociologists who have studied the SSM movement point to 2003–2004 as a pivotal time for advocates on both sides of the marriage issue. In spite of all the legislative and judicial activity prior to 2003, most Americans outside of the few states that had passed initiatives or witnessed judicial rulings had not paid much attention to the SSM issue. As a result, the 2003 *Goodridge* decision legalizing gay marriage in Massachusetts and its subsequent media coverage presented an opportunity for advocacy groups – both pro and con – to define the issue for the public. Wilcox, Merolla, and Beer (2006) suggest that the Religious Right was much better prepared and willing than gay rights groups to mount a vigorous campaign. Many conservatives considered marriage to be the top priority in the culture wars, more important even than abortion in the lead up to the 2004 presidential election. Groups such as FOTF and FRC had conducted extensive message testing and already produced position papers on the subject. A policy analyst for the FRC, Peter Sprigg, had even written a full-length book titled *Outrage* (2004) to make the case for traditional marriage and counter opponents' arguments. The issue attracted individuals across religious traditions, including African American churches, a group that had previously been reluctant to work with the predominantly white Religious Right (Rimmerman & Wilcox, 2007).

One of the dilemmas the Christian Right movement faced going into 2004 was how to frame its message against SSM. The public was becoming increasingly supportive of general rights for sexual minorities (Baunach, 2011), but a majority still opposed marriage rights. Thus operatives had to develop messaging strategies that would sufficiently represent the threat to marriage posed by gays and lesbians without offending those who were more accepting of LGBT+ individuals. Ultimately, opponents coalesced behind a strategy that would frame the movement as protecting traditional marriage by focusing on the historic importance of the institution and the folly of changing something so time-honored and grounded in nature (Wilcox et al., 2006), an approach that did not explicitly demonize gays and lesbians. They also consistently warned about the dangers of activist judges whose rulings were often not in line with public opinion. FRC's Peter Sprigg (2004), for example, referred to the Massachusetts *Goodridge* decision as an example of "judicial tyranny at the behest of an activist minority group" (p. 21). Leaders of the anti-gay marriage movement used this activist judges frame to play up the importance of re-electing President George W. Bush over Democrat John Kerry in 2004 so that more conservative judges could be appointed to the bench.

Although efforts to pass the Federal Marriage Amendment were not successful, the Christian right was triumphant at the state level in 2004. Thirteen states passed constitutional amendments banning SSM, giving opponents of SSM a sense of momentum. But they also had reason to worry. Massachusetts had already started marrying same-sex couples, and there was concern that other New England states were moving in that direction. Before we examine in more detail how the remaining years of the marriage battle unfolded, let's take a look at the main arguments put forth to explain why Americans should reject legalized SSM.

The (conservative) case against same-sex marriage

We learned from the discussion in Chapter 4 of news coverage of the marriage debate that arguments against SSM have been presented primarily through the frames of morality, tradition, and family values. While this approach does not encompass all of the arguments against SSM, it does include those most commonly used in efforts to influence public opinion. From this point of view, which is often grounded in the teachings of Christianity and other religions, homosexuality is immoral and unnatural, representing either a state of sin or mental illness (or both). Likewise, opponents of SSM do not believe it is necessary or even wise to alter an institution that is the "fundamental building block of all human civilization" (Anderson, 2013). They stress the importance of marriage as a vehicle for procreation, the bearing and raising of children in a stable manner that is beneficial for society. This assertion helps to explain why government should be involved in marriage at all, because of the state's interest in what is best for society and continuation of the human species. Those who made this argument also consider a household with a mother and a father to be the optimal situation for childrearing. Because same-sex couples cannot bear children together and do not provide parents of different genders, their relationships do not contribute to society in a way that deserves the recognition or rights of marriage (Corvino & Gallagher, 2012).

Traditionalists have for years been concerned that marriage has become valued more for its ability to provide companionship and intimacy than its direct connection to procreation and the raising of children (Coontz, 2005). In an essay about the danger of loosening marriage restrictions, Ryan T. Anderson (2013) of The Heritage Foundation suggests that because of relaxed attitudes about sexuality and the introduction of no-fault divorce laws, marriage has become "an institution more about the desires of adults than the needs of children – an institution that need not even aspire to permanency." He argues that instead of liberation, changes in the way people view marriage have led to heartache. Anderson's essay also addresses another key argument that the Christian Right put forth in their opposition to SSM, that of religious freedom. Anderson suggests that any attempt to redefine marriage serves to marginalize those with traditional Judeo-Christian views and infringes upon religious liberty guaranteed by the U.S. Constitution. Those who oppose gay marriage also feel that they have inaccurately been portrayed as bigots because of their views (Sprigg, 2004).

One of the most controversial arguments against SSM is the idea that it could lead society down a "slippery slope," eventually resulting in the state sanctioning of polygamous and incestuous relationships. FOTF founder James Dobson famously predicted on his radio program several years ago that legalizing SSM would lead to "marriage between daddies and little girls," or "marriage between a man and his donkey" (Schweber-Koren, 2005). And then there are the more practical, less values-based arguments. For example, some have opposed SSM because of the cost that would be associated with extending marriage benefits to more people. Alternatively, some opponents argue that civil unions can provide the legal protections and benefits that LGB couples need without drastically changing the traditional definition of marriage. All of these arguments have been used at one point or another by conservative advocacy groups in their fight against SSM. Now we'll take a closer look at three such organizations. Two of them – Focus on the Family and the Family Research Council – are multi-issue national organizations whose histories are intertwined; in fact, for a few years the two groups were combined. The third is the National Organization for Marriage, which was founded more recently specifically to fight legalized SSM.

Focus on the Family and the Family Research Council

Psychologist James Dobson founded FOTF in 1977 as a radio program and ministry offering a conservative perspective on marriage and child-rearing. Dobson was an evangelical Christian already known for his controversial book *Dare to Discipline*, which defended and encouraged parents' use of corporal punishment in disciplining their children (Bull & Gallagher, 2001). FOTF eventually grew to include daily radio broadcasts, multiple magazines, a syndicated newspaper column, and a website, all produced out of a sprawling campus in Colorado Springs, Colorado. From its beginning, FOTF has considered homosexuality as a threat to families. The organization has consistently supported conversion therapy, a combination of psychological and spiritual counseling designed to help individuals who feel same-sex attractions to overcome their inclinations and convert to heterosexuality. Conversion therapy has been condemned by the medical and psychiatric communities, and FOTF and other religious groups have been widely criticized for their financial support of "ex-gay" organizations such as Exodus International (Schlanger & Wolfson, 2014).

FOTF is perhaps most famous for its media outreach – its popular radio show was inducted into the Radio Hall of Fame in 2008 – and earns a significant portion of its budget that way. The organization was founded as a 501(c)(3) non-profit, an Internal Revenue Service status that allows financial contributions to the group to be tax deductible but prohibits FOTF from overt political activity such as lobbying and supporting particular candidates. Within a decade of its founding, FOTF had grown significantly, allowing the group to briefly take over the FRC, a conservative Washington, D.C. based think tank. Both FOTF and FRC have consistently and strongly opposed LGBT+ rights, including – and especially – same-sex marriage (Bull & Gallagher, 2001).

The FRC, also a 501(c)(3) non-profit organization founded by Dobson, was involved with public policy from the start, as opposed to the more ministry-orientated nature of FOTF. FRC merged with FOTF for financial reasons in 1988, but separated four years later. FRC's leaders have been prominent within the Christian right movement, with Gary Bauer, Tony Perkins, and Peter Sprigg regularly quoted in the media, appearing before Congress, and hosting events to promote the group's conservative positions on marriage and family. Along with the rest of the Religious Right, FRC and FOTF were galvanized into action after the gay-friendly advances in 2003 in Vermont and Massachusetts, as well as the U.S. Supreme Court decision that year striking down Texas' sodomy law (Lochhead, 2003). FOTF was at its peak in terms of size in the early 2000s, employing more than 1,400 people at its Colorado Springs, Colorado, headquarters and hundreds of others across the country (Bull & Gallagher, 2001). Later budget deficits would lead to multiple years of layoffs that would cut the size of FOTF in half, but in 2003 the group had significant resources to invest in the fight against gay marriage.

The marriage issue quickly rose to the top of Christian advocacy groups' agenda, with both FRC and FOTF issuing policy papers, providing sample sermons to ministers, and asking candidates to sign a pledge in support for the proposed Federal Marriage Amendment (Wilcox et al., 2006). An FRC advertisement created to rally support for the amendment linked defense of traditional marriage to patriotism, arguing that voting for candidates who oppose SSM is a vote to protect America's future (Goldberg-Hiller, 2009). In an October 2004 rally called Mayday for Marriage in Washington, D.C., Dobson offered to get down on his knees to beg the thousands of marchers to go to the polls the following month to support President George W. Bush's re-election bid, and maybe even more importantly, to put pro-Federal Marriage Amendment candidates into office. A *New York Times* story suggested the rally "highlighted a new plunge into political activism" for FOTF and Dobson, whom it referred to as "perhaps the most influential public figure among evangelical Protestants because of his reputation as a source of advice on children and families" (Kirkpatrick, 2004, October 16).

Although the Federal Marriage Amendment ultimately failed, FOTF and FRC (along with the rest of the Religious Right) considered the elections of 2004 a victory in the fight to retain traditional marriage, and they were not shy about taking credit for their efforts to mobilize conservative voters. In an interview with *Christianity Today* after the elections, Dobson said there was no question that conservative Christians went to the polls because of the marriage issue, helping George W. Bush win re-election and multiple states pass SSM bans. A former staffer for the Bush campaign has debated such assertions, arguing that national security played a much larger role in voter turnout and Bush's win (Dowd, 2012). Nonetheless, Dobson has referred to the victories as a pivotal moment for the Religious Right, explaining "I have been critical in the past of the church's reluctance to 'dirty itself' in these so-called political battles, which are in reality profoundly moral in nature, but I believe this signals the dawn of a new day" (Rutledge, 2004). The FRC's Peter Sprigg was consistently on-message about the importance of traditional marriage to the essence of the United States. Regardless of the medium – be it through the group's website, direct mail, interviews with the media, or advertisements – the message was always the same: "Marriage is a public institution because it facilitates the union of men and women in reproducing the human race and the cooperation of mothers and fathers in raising and nurturing the children produced by their union" (Sprigg, 2004, p. 61).

The early anti-marriage-equality campaigns conducted by the FRC and FOTF were relatively traditional, with email blasts, pamphlets shared with religious congregations, and a significant amount of television and print advertising. An analysis by Michael Wilke, whose Commercial Closet website archives LGBT+-related advertising, shows that both sides of the marriage debate relied heavily on television and print advertising in the 2004 state ballot initiatives and individual political races. Altogether, politicians, pro- and anti-gay organizations, and corporate advertisers produced more than 100 different ads addressing SSM in 2004 alone (Wilke, 2005). Many of the ads, especially in Southern states, featured politicians proudly stating that they had voted against gay marriage or worked to defend traditional marriage. A number of the commercials included African-American couples stating their disapproval of SSM, with many worried that public schools would be forced to teach children that gay marriages are equal to heterosexual ones. A full-page 2004 newspaper advertisement run by FOTF implied that SSM would lead to children being raised without fathers, resulting in harmful physical and mental health consequences, poor performance in school, and increased criminal behavior (Cahill, 2004).

In addition to putting pressure on elected officials to publicly denounce SSM, FOTF also expected companies to do so. In 2004, the group called for a boycott of two of Procter & Gamble's best-selling products after learning that P&G had been critical of a Cincinnati, Ohio, ordinance that would exempt gays and lesbians from explicit civil rights protection. James Dobson said this was tantamount to supporting SSM, and he called on conservatives and Christians to boycott Tide laundry detergent and Crest toothpaste, two main moneymakers for the Cincinnati-based P&G (Kirkpatrick, 2004, September 17).

The National Organization for Marriage

The NOM is a non-profit organization founded in 2007 to help coordinate organized opposition to SSM in state legislatures – and to help pass California's Proposition 8 ban on SSM in 2008. The group's logo has two interlocking rings, one red and one blue, and its motto is simple enough: "protecting marriage and the faith communities that sustain it." Although it is younger than the other high-profile conservative groups involved in the battle over marriage, *The Washington Post* has referred to NOM as the "preeminent organization dedicated to preventing the legalization of same-sex marriage" (Hesse, 2009). Headquartered in Princeton, N.J., NOM is a political advocacy organization, first and foremost. In the *About Us* section of its website, NOM explains: "For decades, pro-family organizations have educated the public about the importance of marriage and the family, but have lacked the organized, national presence needed to impact state and local politics in a coordinated and sustained fashion. NOM seeks to fill that void, organizing as a 501(c)(4) nonprofit organization, giving it the flexibility to lobby and support marriage initiatives across the nation."

Just as it was difficult to separate the work of pro-gay Freedom to Marry from its founder Evan Wolfson, it is also difficult to think of NOM without envisioning its leader Brian Brown. He co-founded NOM with conservative activist Maggie Gallagher, who still consults for NOM but works primarily with other conservative organizations. Brown is clearly now the face and voice of NOM and has been the subject of numerous profiles in legacy media as well as Christian and conservative outlets. A 2009 profile of Brown in *The Washington Post* contrasted his style with that of Pat Robertson and James Dobson, the type of people "who specialize in whipping crowds into frothy frenzies, who say things like *Katrina was caused by the gays*" (Hesse, 2009). Brown, a married father of nine, is portrayed as intensely strategic but more measured in his rhetoric – described by *The Washington Post* as "pleasantly, ruthlessly sane" (Hesse, 2009). Although Brown himself has gotten a lot of positive press, NOM as an organization has its detractors. *Mother Jones* magazine wrote an exposé in 2010 about the group's lack of financial transparency and connection to the Mormon Church, which helped to fund the campaign for Proposition 8 in 2008. The article said that NOM "has engaged in a host of potentially illegal stealth campaign tactics" and waged legal battles to shield its supporters from public exposure (Mencimer, 2010). Indeed, the Maine Commission on Governmental Ethics and Election Practices did rule that NOM broke the law by not registering as a ballot question committee and not filing appropriate campaign finance reports. The Southern Poverty Law Center has criticized the group for hypocrisy, arguing that NOM claims to "keep its criticisms of homosexuality both civil and factual" while at the same time putting links on its website to "demonizing" and false documents from hate groups (Potok & Schlatter, 2012). The Human Rights Campaign even had a "NOM Exposed" section on its website, dedicated to tracking the organization's finances and debunking its claims.

One of NOM's first projects was to help pass a proposed constitutional amendment in Massachusetts in 2007 to override the *Goodridge* court decision that allowed gays to marry starting in 2004. The amendment failed, however, after the Massachusetts state legislature vote came up short of the 50 favorable votes needed to force a referendum. Although it had been in existence for only a short time, NOM came out of the gate swinging with its campaign tactics in Massachusetts. For example, after Democratic state Rep. Angelo Puppolo changed his position to vote no on the amendment, NOM paid for a billboard in the state capital of Springfield with the word "Betrayed" in large letters and a photo of Puppolo alongside illustrations of traitors Benedict Arnold and Judas Iscariot. But even though Massachusetts had disappointed NOM, the group was just getting started, already preparing for the biggest state ballot initiative of the entire marriage movement just over the horizon in California.

The campaign to pass Proposition 8

As noted previously, the status of SSM in California was in flux from March 2000, when voters passed a measure restricting marriage to heterosexual couples to May 2008, when the Supreme Court of California overturned the state's ban on SSM. An FRC press release issued after that 2008 ruling in favor of SSM depicted the decision as antidemocratic (Fisher, 2009), but the decision did not surprise most gay marriage opponents. They had already begun collecting signatures to place another measure on the ballot in November 2008 to amend the state constitution to ban SSM. That measure became the closely watched Proposition 8, which voters approved on November 4, 2008, sending shockwaves throughout a country that had just elected a decidedly liberal Barack Obama as its first African-American president.

In a post-mortem analysis of their victory in California (Schubert & Flint, 2009), the architects of the "Yes on Prop 8" campaign acknowledged that well-funded groups from across the country had joined together in an effort to stem the tide of pro-gay public opinion and political activity. Frank Schubert and Jeff Flint of Schubert Flint Public Affairs ran the campaign for the umbrella organization ProtectMarriage.com, a coalition of conservative groups, in addition to religious entities such as the Church of Jesus Christ of Latter Day Saints and the Catholic church. Much has been written about the influx of funding from the Mormon and Catholic churches – with significant amounts donated from outside the state of California – as well as the lack of transparency regarding donor influence (Messner, 2009; Stone, 2012). Regardless of the ethics or legality of that aspect of the Yes on Prop 8 campaign, it's difficult to argue with the success of its messaging strategy or use of new technology. The results were apparent at the ballot box, in addition to the multiple awards the campaign subsequently won for its digital strategy.

The Yes on Prop 8 campaign was not expected to win in a state known for its LGBT+-friendly brand of liberalism and where more than half of voters said they supported SSM. A mid-September 2008 poll showed support for the gay marriage ban at just 38 percent, and most activists on both sides of the issue thought Prop 8 was dead – yet in the end, it passed by 700,000 votes (Schubert & Flint, 2009). The campaign also astonished everyone, including the news media, with its technological prowess. People assumed the No on Prop 8 campaign opposing the gay marriage ban – whose leaders and supporters were younger and thus assumed to be more tech savvy – would have the upper hand in using digital technologies to energize and organize volunteers, target voters with precise messaging, raise money, and get out the vote (Stone, 2012). But it was ProtectMarriage.com, whose conservative leadership and members skewed older, that grabbed attention for their forward-thinking use of technology. Two tactics in particular may have allowed the Yes on Prop 8 campaign to overcome its initial low levels of support: online ads targeted using voter file data and a voter-turnout digital ad blitz in the 48 hours before the election (Kaye, 2009).

Schubert Flint Public Affairs, the conservative Sacramento-based firm hired to direct the Yes on Prop 8 campaign, worked with online political advertising pioneers Connell Donatelli to plan and execute its digital strategy. Frank Schubert, a former corporate PR executive who worked closely with NOM on multiple campaigns, has been described as the strategic mastermind behind Yes on Prop 8 (Eckholm, 2012). In the months following their victory, Schubert and his business partner Jeff Flint were very open about the campaign's carefully chosen message strategy, as well as its adoption of newly developed technology to enhance supporter engagement and precisely target different voter segments. They explained that an important early component of the campaign involved targeting online ads through the use of voter file data, a tactic designed to help identify volunteers, build the supporter e-mail list, and raise money (Schubert & Flint, 2009). Voter file matching allows campaigns to strategically target advertising by combining publicly available voter registration data with personal information drawn from subscriber databases of companies such as American Online, Microsoft, and Yahoo.

Yes on Prop 8 also spent thousands of dollars for Internet display ads to target voters based on online behavior and affiliation through various ad networks such as Advertising.com, the conservative Salem Web Network, and Google's AdSense content network (Kaye, 2009). Another tactic involved an advertising buy targeted to keyword searches related to themes such as family, religion, conservatism, marriage, and Proposition 8. All of these targeted advertisements directed individuals to the ProtectMarriage.org website for information about the campaign's views and events and to grow the campaign's email database. In addition to its massive Internet presence, the campaign also pumped money into television and radio advertising and ensured that radio and TV talk show guests promoting the Yes on Prop 8 initiative mentioned the ProtectMarriage.org site frequently. The digital team constantly updated and improved its website to deliver a steady stream of messages to update supporters, many of whom learned about the campaign through their churches, and to encourage them to act as ambassadors for the campaign. Schubert and Flint (2009) believe that the campaign's ability to organize a massive volunteer effort through religious denominations gave them a big advantage over proponents of SSM. They used a traditional grassroots church-based organization structure for volunteers, in addition to the latest web-based organizing tools. Online volunteer sign-ups were immediately sent electronically to the appropriate ZIP code supervisor for follow up, and staffers set up a state-wide voter file with remote access for regional volunteer leaders, allowing them to input results for canvassing efforts remotely, and then download and print updated voter lists (Schubert & Flint, 2009). The campaign also embraced the newly popular micro-blogging site Twitter, using it in conjunction with the ProtectMarriage.org website to counter claims by the opposition, notify supporters of rallies and other ways to be involved, and continue raising money.

In the final stage of the campaign, Yes on Prop 8 digital strategists prepared an onslaught of online advertising to generate last-minute buzz, get voters to the polls, and maintain positive momentum resulting from higher approval ratings coming out of state-wide surveys (Kaye, 2009). Flush from successful fundraising, the campaign launched what Schubert and Flint (2009) referred to as a "Google surge," a type of saturation buy. They spent more than $500,000 to place ads on every website that had advertising controlled by Google so that anyone logging in to the Internet in California during the final two days of the campaign saw one of the Yes on Prop 8 ads urging them to vote for traditional marriage and warning them of the consequences of doing otherwise. Working with Google to quickly determine how to reach the most voters (even on liberal and LGBT+ websites) allowed the ProtectMarriage.org strategists to optimize a last-minute surge in fundraising (Kaye, 2009).

In addition to its technological shrewdness, the Yes on Prop 8 campaign was very disciplined in its messaging. From the very beginning, Schubert and Flint (2009) decided on a broader strategy that would focus on the big-picture ramifications of SSM for all Californians. This approach meant that advertising did nothing to demonize the LGB couples who had gotten married since the California Supreme Court overturned the state's gay marriage ban. In fact, Proposition 8 supporters were asked to avoid demonstrations, protests, or rallies opposing those marriages. In interviews with news media, Frank Schubert says he made it clear: "Our fight was not with the gay couples getting married, our fight was with the flawed reasoning of a narrow majority of the California Supreme Court" that designated sexual minorities a special protected class whose rights might come into conflict with those who weren't gay (Schubert & Flint, 2009, p. 44). According to Schubert, strategists believed that a campaign focused solely on the value of traditional marriage would not be sufficient. Instead, the campaign "needed to convince voters that gay marriage was not simply 'live and let live' – that there would be consequences if gay marriage were to be permanently legalized" (Schubert & Flint, 2009, p. 45). To do this, Prop 8 proponents deployed tactics more commonly associated with "No" campaigns: raising doubts and pointing to potential problems with the court's ruling, which the campaign characterized as forcing gay marriage on the people of California.

Schubert recalls that pro-gay opponents of Proposition 8 began airing television ads before the Yes on Prop 8 campaign did, and he knew his side's first TV spot needed to make a splash. San Francisco Mayor Gavin Newsom, as it turns out, provided the Yes on Prop 8 campaign with great material for its ad. At a press conference following the gay-friendly court decision in May, Newsom "got increasingly excited the longer he addressed the crowd until, with a smirk on his face and his arms fully extended, he exclaimed, 'This door's wide open now. It's gonna happen – whether you like it or not'" (Schubert & Flint, 2009, p. 46). Schubert said that sound bite perfectly explained to voters why Prop 8 was needed: to put the will of the people before the will of four state judges. The spot, accompanied by a related radio ad, helped the group to solidify its base and begin to shift public sentiment.

Schubert said this messaging approach was devised after seeing survey results that indicated that Californians were increasingly tolerant of sexual minorities, but only to a certain extent – such tolerance would evaporate if individuals felt that gay rights would lead to negative consequences for other segments of the population. Messaging continually hit voters with warnings about what could happen because of LGBT+ individuals' new "protected class" legal status, focusing on three areas where this conflict of rights (gays vs. straights) might cause problems: religious freedom, individual freedom of expression, and how LGBT+ rights would be handled in public schools (Schubert & Flint, 2009). Taking a page from Anita Bryant's Save Our Children campaign from the 1970s, the Yes on Prop 8 campaign focused much of its advertising on ways that children could suffer from the court's ruling (Faderman, 2015). In one now-famous spot, the camera focused on upset and confused first-graders who had been taken to San Francisco City Hall, accompanied by members of the media, to watch their teacher's lesbian wedding. Schubert and Flint (2009) referred to the San Francisco City Hall incident as "the break of the election" (p. 47) because it provided evidence to support one of the Yes on Prop 8 campaign's main assertions: that young children in public schools would be forced to deal with the issue of gay marriage. Using that same theme, another ad showed an upset mother whose daughter had learned at school that day that "a prince could marry a prince, and I can marry a princess" (Faderman, 2015, p. 608).

In the weeks leading up to the November 4 election, Proposition 8 advocates steadily gained support, whereas approval for the No on Prop 8 pro-gay position was evaporating. Middle-aged Caucasians represented a large portion of voters who apparently changed their mind on the issue, eventually voting for Proposition 8. All five of California's most populous counties (Los Angeles, Orange, Riverside, San Bernadino, and San Diego) voted in favor of Prop 8 and against marriage equality even as Barack Obama was carrying four of the five in the presidential race. Likewise, many racial minorities voted to ban SSM, while also voting for Obama (Cillizza & Sullivan, 2013). Some suggest that gay marriage advocates suffered from having such a big lead to begin with because it made it difficult to rally supporters (Stone, 2012). But many believe that the better campaign won, in large part because of its ability to control the message through strategic use of newer digital technologies (Aiello, 2008; Kim, 2008; Schubert & Flint, 2009).

The three Christian advocacy organizations we've focused on in this chapter – the NOM, FRC, and FOTF – were all heavily involved in the Yes on Prop 8 campaign, contributing both cash and resources. Of the more than $80 million spent to pass Prop 8, California state records show that FOTF gave just over $727,000 in cash and services to ProtectMarriage.com (Lunig, 2009). In an e-mail blast to supporters after the successful election outcome, FOTF highlighted its contributions, which included paying for polling to determine messaging strategy, helping with fundraising, encouraging church leaders to get involved, airing broadcasts that called for prayer and financial support, and providing coverage of the campaign in FOTF media outlets (Morain, 2008). NOM co-founder Maggie Gallagher, a well-known conservative writer, was an active spokesperson for the anti-gay marriage coalition, helping to guide message framing (Pierceson, 2013). FRC also contributed just under $75,000 to the campaign. All three groups hosted pro-Prop 8 content on their websites and social media pages. FRC President Tony Perkins also gave media interviews and appeared in promotional videos warning Californians about what he perceived as negative effects on schoolchildren and families that had occurred in Massachusetts since SSM was legalized there (Leff, 2010).

Although Prop 8 got most of the national attention, voters in Florida and Arizona also approved constitutional bans on SSM in November 2008. After these victories, especially the one in California, anti-gay rights advocacy groups were emboldened, hoping to ride the momentum to more success. Next, we'll look at how they worked to build on the success of Proposition 8.

Post-Prop 8: the battle gets tougher

Seven U.S. states served as the primary battleground sites in the war over SSM, hosting more than two-thirds of all the ballot referendums and initiatives coordinated by the Religious Right through 2012 (Stone, 2012). Maine was one of those states, and it took centerstage early in 2009 when the state legislature there began to consider a bill to legalize gay marriage. In spite of intense lobbying from gay rights opponents, the measure passed and was signed by Maine's governor on May 6, 2009, setting it up to go into effect 90 days later. Undeterred, gay marriage opponents started the process to place a veto referendum on the ballot in November and began yet another state campaign to preserve traditional marriage. As had happened in California and other states, a coalition of religious and conservative groups formed a political action committee to coordinate the campaign, this one named Stand for Marriage Maine. The coalition easily secured the signatures needed to put Maine Question 1 on the ballot, and they hired the Schubert Flint Public Affairs group out of California to handle communications for the campaign. As an East coast-based organization, the NOM was heavily involved in the Maine campaign, contributing nearly $2 million, helping to raise additional funds, and consulting on campaign strategy. NOM came under fire for violating state law by refusing to reveal a list of its contributors, but that did not keep Brian Brown and other NOM staffers from continued fundraising. Eventually, NOM released its donor names from the Maine campaign, but only after a protracted legal fight and a $50,000 fine (Mistler, 2015).

Not surprisingly, the campaign pushing for approval of Maine Question 1 drew significantly from the strategy that had been so successful with Proposition 8 in California. Messaging focused heavily on the erosion of parental rights that could occur if public schoolchildren were taught about homosexuality and same-sex relationships. TV commercials produced by Schubert Flint featured parents worried that their young children were being taught in school that marriage between two women or two men is normal and good, even though their parents and community disagreed. The communications director for Stand for Marriage Maine, Scott Fish, in media interviews even referred to those TV spots as "sustainable advertising," implying that, regardless of which state they were used in, they would successfully turn people against gay marriage (Vick, 2009). Fish may have been right – Maine Question 1 passed 53 percent–47 percent on November 3, 2009, rejecting the state law passed earlier in the year that would have legalized SSM.

In addition to participating in the voter referendum in Maine, NOM also worked on a wider scale to promote traditional marriage in key states where legislatures were considering action. In April 2009, soon after Vermont legalized gay marriage, NOM began a "2 Million for Marriage" (2M4M) initiative with a goal of organizing at least two million activists nationwide by having them register at the nationformarriage.org website. The group also launched a $1.5 million ad campaign targeting states where additional marriage initiatives were likely to be considered in the coming months. The most prominent – and controversial – spot of the that campaign was a dramatic 60-second advertisement titled "Gathering Storm," in which a series of fearful-looking actors in front of a backdrop of dark clouds and lightning claimed that SSM would trample on religious freedom and parental rights. The actors warned that "there's a dark storm gathering" and urged viewers to visit the nationformarriage.org website to take action. The commercial drew significant criticism for being overwrought, but it also got a lot of press attention and more than 400,000 YouTube views and was even parodied by Stephen Colbert (Foust, 2009), drawing attention to the anti-gay-marriage campaign.

In 2010, NOM also launched a multi-city "Summer for Marriage" bus tour to host rallies against SSM. NOM President Brian Brown sent an email blast to supporters and posted an invitation on the group's blog asking traditional marriage supporters to bring friends and join him, his wife, and children at one of the rallies. Brown told NOM supporters it was urgent that they be vocal in their opposition to gay marriage and fight against activist justices who were forcing states to legalize SSM without allowing the people to vote. He argued passionately that "We have a right to vote for marriage. And we are going to fight for our rights – and, most importantly, for our children's right to grow up in a country where God's truth about marriage trumps political correctness and judicial tyranny!" (Brown, 2010). Brown said one goal of the bus tour was for proponents of traditional marriage to build their own communication networks to overcome unfavorable spin by the mainstream media, and he gave a shout out to FOTF news platforms for covering the tour. Brown urged supporters to stay connected to the tour by signing up at the NOM website, reading its blog, and following the group on Twitter to see first-hand stories from the tour (Brown, 2010).

In spite of the efforts of NOM and other conservative Christian groups, by the end of 2011, six states (Massachusetts, Connecticut, Iowa, Vermont, New Hampshire, and New York) had legalized SSM, and others were considering it. However, gay marriage opponents continued to fight and were able to celebrate a big win in May 2012. NOM, working with Frank Schubert under the auspices of Vote for Marriage NC, spent more than $425,000 on the campaign and was successful in passing North Carolina Amendment One by a startling 61 percent to 39 percent margin (Blumenthal, 2012). The amendment prohibited both SSMs and civil unions. In a message posted to its blog after the election results were announced in North Carolina, NOM's Brian Brown said the vote was a clear sign that gay marriage opponents were winning in the court of public opinion: "So much for the idea being promulgated by the media and the elite that same-sex marriage is inevitable. Just the other day, gay activists were predicting victory in North Carolina, but instead marriage won an overwhelming victory" (NOM, 2012, May 8). The euphoria didn't last for long, however. On November, 6, 2012, the state ballot winning streak for gay marriage opponents was broken as Maine, Maryland, and Washington became the first states to legalize SSM by popular vote. In Minnesota on the same day, voters rejected a proposal to ban gay marriage by amending the state constitution. Brian Brown acknowledged that NOM and its allies were disappointed, but insisted the election results did not represent a tipping point. He blamed the losses in part on finances: "Despite the fact that NOM was able to contribute a record amount to the campaigns (over $5.5 million), we were still heavily outspent, by a margin of at least four-to-one. We were fighting the entirety of the political establishment in most of the states, including sitting governors in three of the states who campaigned heavily for gay marriage" (Brown, 2012, November 7).

In spite of the setback, NOM did not back down. In fact, the group expanded its efforts in 2012 by adding boycotts to its anti-gay marriage arsenal. After Starbucks executives publicly expressed support for SSM, NOM announced an international "Dump Starbucks" protest campaign. Through press releases, blog posts, and social media, Brown pleaded with Christians worldwide to boycott Starbucks and contact local franchise managers to complain and make it clear that "corporations should not take sides in a culture war that pits a company against the majority of the American people, and nearly all its consumers in some international markets" (NOM, 2012, March 21). The boycott was announced after a Starbucks shareholders meeting in Seattle in which NOM staffers questioned the board about its policies promoting SSM and demanded protection for employees and customers who disagree. As part of its boycott, NOM also ran advertisements in local languages in the Middle East and Southeast Asia, as well as the United States, calling for customers to dump Starbucks and asking them to sign a petition. Within a month, almost 45,000 had signed (Brown, 2012, May 15). Later that year, NOM launched a similar campaign against General Mills because of its opposition to a Minnesota marriage ban amendment on the ballot in November 2012.

NOM may have been the most visible organization fighting to stop the spread of SSM after Proposition 8, but it was not the only one. FOTF was very much still active, covering traditional marriage-related events and issues in its multiple media outlets, holding rallies, and working to earn press coverage. But the message had softened significantly under new FOTF President Jim Daly (Freedman, 2013). James Dobson had served in that role from the group's founding in 1977 until 2003, when he stepped down as president and CEO but stayed on as chairman of FOFT's board. He resigned that position in 2009 because of what he referred to as philosophical differences with Daly, his chosen successor, "especially when it comes to confronting those who would weaken the family and undermine our faith" (Dobson, 2013). Daly was even more candid about his and Dobson's different approaches and the changes he thought were necessary for FOTF to stay relevant. In a book about his vision for FOTF's ministry, Daly (2012) calls on Christians to transcend political agendas and partisan battles and focus instead on outreach and building relationships that help spread the love of Christ. The book also warns against the Religious Right's efforts to single out homosexuality as a sin more serious than others. In an article for *The New York Times*, Daly explained that the organization had created a culture of animosity in its fight against gay rights. "We've said we hate the sin and love the sinner. But when you peel it back, sometimes we hated the sinner, too. And that's not the Gospel" (Freedman, 2013).

The FRC also adjusted its tone somewhat, although not its anti-gay-rights stance. In 2013 as the Supreme Court was about to consider two key marriage-related cases, Peter Sprigg, who a decade before had written an overtly anti-gay book titled *Outrage* to rally opponents of SSM, published a series of blog posts about the history of marriage and its significance throughout history and across cultures. In these posts, he took a softer approach, acknowledging that marriage as an institution had evolved over the years. But, he argued, the idea of marriage as being limited to one man and one woman had not changed: "Some aspects of marriage – particular rituals and traditions surrounding it, and particularly the roles played by the wife and the husband – have been subject to variation and change in different times and places. However, until the political correctness of the last decade or two pushed it underground, there was a virtually universal consensus that a male-female union was not an *optional* aspect of marriage, but was *essential* to it" (Sprigg, 2013).

All three groups – NOM, FRC, and FOTF – have active Twitter and Facebook accounts that keep supporters updated about legislation and policy changes, rallies, and other topics related to the ongoing discussion about SSM. NOM is by far the most involved, staying active even after SSM was legalized nationwide in 2015. Brian Brown regularly updates the group's blog and Twitter account with posts touting the work NOM has done for conservative issues and causes, such as supporting the nomination of Neil Gorsuch for the U.S. Supreme Court in 2017. The

FIGURE 6.1 Opponents of same-sex marriage also shared images on social media to make their viewpoints known. (Image courtesy of Joe Bob Hester, Jr.)

group was especially active on social media in the summer of 2017 to promote its annual March for Marriage in Washington, D.C. Brown's blog posts made it clear that the group wasn't backing down from its goal of overturning the Supreme Court's decision in *Obergefell v. Hodges*: "The March for Marriage is an important event to keep the fight to restore marriage in the public eye. NOM has pledged that we will never rest until this illegal, unjust ruling is reversed" (Brown, 2017, April 26).

Although all three groups continue to use social media to promote traditional marriage and oppose marriage rights for LGB couples, none of them launched any type of digital campaign comparable to those of Freedom to Marry and the Human Rights Campaign in the three years leading up to the 2015 Obergefell decision. A CNN story (Weisbrod & Merica, 2013) about the ubiquitous HRC red equal sign in 2013 noted that gay marriage opponents had asked followers of their Facebook page and Twitter account to use and share special images showing their support for traditional marriage. For example, an FRC image featuring a man and a woman holding hands received more than 10,000 likes and shares over the course of a few days. Likewise, organizers of a 2013 March for Marriage for opponents of SSM posted sharable graphics on their Facebook page, receiving almost 4,000 likes. Some high school students chose to download images of blue Christian crosses on Facebook to combat the red marriage equality logo in 2013 in what was described in the news as a "fierce Facebook confrontation" that resulted in some conservative students receiving angry responses from classmates

(Hansell, 2013). Lastly, in 2015 as a direct response to Facebook's "Celebrate Pride" rainbow filter that allowed users to show their support for the Supreme Court's legalization of SSM, rightwingnews.com developed a service that allowed people to add an American flag filter to their Facebook profile to show their displeasure with the court ruling (Plucinska, 2015). But none of these initiatives came close to the level of visibility enjoyed by the red equal sign and #LoveMustWin social media campaigns.

Joe Grabowski, NOM's director of communications, explains that after the success of California's Proposition 8 in 2008, organizations opposed to SSM were actually hampered in their ability to rally supporters and raise money through social media (J. Grabowski, personal communication, June 19, 2017). After their surprising loss, some pro-gay activists used California's campaign finance disclosure laws to identify and publicize the names of individuals who donated to the campaign against gay marriage. The tactic is known as "doxing," which involves publishing personal information about someone online in an attempt to embarrass or intimidate. Some Yes on Prop 8 donors received death threats and had their businesses boycotted after a controversial website, eightmaps.com, plotted their names and Zip codes onto a Google map (Stone, 2009). Website users could see markers indicating a contributor's name, general location, donation amount, and employer. The most high-profile example of Prop 8–related doxing was Mozilla CEO Brendan Eich, who eventually stepped down after an online dating service urged a boycott of the company's web browser because of a donation Eich made to support the measure. NOM's Grabowski said that doxing and other tactics such as flooding social media sites with negative messages – a form of Internet trolling – were designed to stigmatize and intimidate those who voice their disapproval of SSM. This presented a challenge for traditional marriage proponents who wanted to use social media to attract new supporters and galvanize existing ones because many like-minded individuals were reluctant to share their views for fear of retaliation (J. Grabowski, personal communication, June 19, 2017). As a result, NOM and other organizations opposed to SSM have found it difficult to maintain a vibrant social media presence.

Although conservative Christian advocacy organizations remain opposed to SSM, and some are calling for outright resistance to the Supreme Court's decision in *Obergefell v. Hodges* (Lerner, 2015), much of their energy has shifted to protecting the religious liberty of those individuals and organizations who do not support marriage rights for gays and lesbians. The closing section of this chapter will examine how gay marriage opponents have regrouped and are fighting to secure legislation that allows those who disagree with marriage equality to exercise their views without fear of retribution or discrimination.

In defense of religious freedom

Concern about the issue of religious freedom in relation to the SSM debate intensified after the passage of Prop 8 in California because of the significant backlash against gay marriage opponents. By the time he was interviewed by *The*

FIGURE 6.2 Even opponents of same-sex marriage adopted the Human Rights Campaign Red Equal Sign, but they altered the image to illustrate their belief that marriage laws should not be changed to include gay and lesbian couples. (Image courtesy of Joe Bob Hester, Jr.)

New York Times in 2013, FOTF president Jim Daly acknowledged that the Christian right was shifting its focus away from trying to win initiatives at the ballot box and toward preserving the religious freedom of those who oppose SSM (Freedman, 2013). Today, there is widespread consensus that the next crusade in the war over marriage is protecting religious liberty and the legitimacy of the view that marriage should be only between one man and one woman (Lerner, 2015; Lowry, 2015). Religious and conservative advocacy organizations have regrouped post-*Obergefell* to ensure that opponents of SSM aren't victimized for their beliefs, called out as bigots, or forced to participate in marriage-related activities that go against their religious beliefs. Joseph Grabowski of NOM said his organization continues to believe that a traditional view of marriage "ought to be a socially accepted one and part of a rigorous and healthy debate," instead of being characterized as bigoted (J. Grabowski, personal communication, June 19, 2017).

The Marriage Anti-Defamation Alliance (MADA), an offshoot of the NOM, has taken a big role in this new front of the marriage wars. Headed by NOM co-founder and conservative writer Maggie Gallagher, MADA's motto is simply "protecting & defending." The About section of the group's website (marriageada.org), which reflects an understanding that public opinion has shifted to favor marriage rights for LGB couples, demands room for those who disagree: "We recognize that marriage is an important issue, about which people of good will can and do disagree. We believe America should be a place where passionate moral disagreements are expressed with respect, thoughtfulness, and civility" (Marriage Anti-Defamation Alliance, n.d.). In a strategy reminiscent of Freedom to Marry's efforts to humanize the SSM issue through storytelling, MADA has called for individuals who feel they have been punished for their beliefs to make their stories known through the group's website: "If you have been threatened, harassed, or made to feel afraid because you believe in the great, foundational truth of Genesis – we are born male and female and called to come together in love to give children mothers and fathers – Marriage Anti-Defamation Alliance is here to help you: you are not alone" (Marriage Anti-Defamation Alliance, n.d.). The website features a series of short video stories, all of which carry the double-rings NOM logo. Some of the videos are hosted by Damian Goddard, MADA spokesman and a well-known former Canadian sportscaster who has produced a video telling his own story. In his MADA video and on his personal website (damiangoddard.com), Goddard tells of how he was fired in 2011 after 20 years in the broadcast business in Canada because of a Twitter message he posted defending heterosexual marriage. After significant public backlash, he was let go from his position as weekend anchor at Rogers Sportsnet, one of Canada's leading sports networks. Since then he has been involved in the fight to defend gay marriage opponents from discrimination and retribution. MADA's website also features a video from David Tyree, a former U.S. football wide receiver who played in the National Football League for seven seasons and later was named director of player development for the New York Giants. Others whose videos are featured on the MADA website are less prominent, but nonetheless have stories to tell about how their personal and professional lives suffered after they publicly stated or acted on their opposition to SSM.

Travis Weber, director of FRC's Center for Religious Liberty, suggests that this type of personal storytelling is exactly what opponents of SSM – and proponents of religious liberty legislation – must do. He says conservatives should take a page from the playbook of SSM advocates who successfully used social media to tell the stories of LGB couples who had been hurt by not being allowed to marry. Weber said conservatives should tell the stories of people of faith who had been harassed and demonized for their beliefs, losing friends, customers, and even their jobs (Lerner, 2015). MADA's website appears to be adopting that strategy, calling for those who have suffered to tell their stories and asking religious liberty supporters to share those stories widely.

MADA and NOM, along with other anti-gay-marriage advocacy organizations, are also working with conservative lawmakers in multiple states to craft and pass religious-freedom laws that will not run afoul of state constitutional provisions outlawing discrimination. After the 2015 U.S. Supreme Court decision in *Obergefell v. Hodges* that legalized SSM, many social conservatives turned to statehouses, working to pass state laws that would allow businesses, members of the clergy, and government workers to deny services to same-sex couples based on religious objections. Religious-freedom advocates have been walking a fine line, attempting to write laws that protect individuals and their beliefs but that don't violate constitutional anti-discrimination provisions. Exactly two years after the Obergefell decision, the U.S. Supreme Court agreed on June 26, 2017 to hear a case involving a Colorado baker, a born-again Christian who lost lower court fights over his refusal to make a wedding cake for a gay male couple because of his religious beliefs. The baker claimed that the First Amendment and Colorado's religious liberty law protect his freedom of expression, an argument that lower courts rejected. Religious conservatives are counting on the Supreme Court, with the recent addition of conservative justice Neil Gorsuch, to rule in favor of the baker and religious-freedom protections.

Although they were the public face of the SSM opposition movement, the Christian right was not the only segment of the population to disagree with LGBT+ advocacy groups who chose to prioritize the fight for marriage equality. Some within the gay rights movement have argued that other issues, such as employment discrimination, are more vital, while other gay activists oppose the institution of marriage altogether. In the next chapter, we'll look at the arguments and messaging strategies of the marriage opponents within the LGBT+ rights movement.

References

Aiello, D. (2008, November 13). No on Prop 8 official grilled over campaign. *Bay Area Reporter*. Retrieved from http://www.ebar.com/news/article.php?sec=news&article=3475

Anderson, R. T. (2013, March 11). Marriage: What it is, why it matters, and the consequences of redefining it [Backgrounder No. 2775]. The Heritage Foundation. Retrieved from http://s3.amazonaws.com/thf_media/2013/pdf/bg2775.pdf

Baunach, D. M. (2011). Decomposing trends in attitudes toward gay marriage, 1988–2006. *Social Science Quarterly*, 92(2), 346–363. http://doi.org/10.1111/j.1540-6237.2011.00772.x

Blumenthal, P. (2012, May 8). Amendment One N.C.: Anti-gay marriage donors (UPDATED). *The Huffington Post*. Retrieved from http://www.huffingtonpost.com/2012/05/08/amendment-one-nc-donors_n_1501265.html

Brown, B. (2010, July 1). NOM national marriage news. [Blog post]. NOM Blog. Retrieved from http://www.nomblog.com/1068

Brown, B. (2012, November 7). We are not defeated in our fight for traditional message. [Blog post]. NOM Blog. Retrieved at http://www.nomblog.com/30808

Brown, B. (2017, April 26). A major announcement. [Blog post]. NOM Blog. Retrieved from http://www.nomblog.com/41337

Brown, B. (2017, May 15). Take immediate action in support of religious liberty. [Blog post]. NOM Blog. Retrieved from http://www.nomblog.com/41345

Bull, C., & Gallagher, J. (2001). *Perfect enemies: The religious right, the gay movement, and the politics of the 1990s* (2nd ed.). New York, NY: Crown Publishers.

Cahill, S. (2004). *Same-sex marriage in the United States: Focus on the facts*. Oxford, UK: Lexington Books.

Cillizza, C., & Sullivan, S. (2013, March 26). How Proposition 8 passed in California – and why it wouldn't today. *The Washington Post*. Retrieved from https://www.washingtonpost.com/news/the-fix/wp/2013/03/26/how-proposition-8-passed-in-california-and-why-it-wouldnt-today/?utm_term=.f19faa068da0

Clendinen, D., & Nagourney, A. (2013). *Out for good: The struggle to build a gay rights movement in America*. New York, NY: Simon & Schuster.

Coontz, S. (2005). *Marriage, a history: From obedience to intimacy, or how love conquered marriage.* New York, NY: Viking.

Corvino, J., & Gallagher, M. (2012). *Debating same-sex marriage.* London: Oxford University Press.

Daly, J. (2012). *ReFocus: Living a life that reflects God's heart.* Grand Rapids, MI: Zondervan Publishing.

Dobson, J. (2013, August 17). The rest of the story. [Blog post]. Dr. James Dobson's family talk. Retrieved from https://web.archive.org/web/20130817203753/http://drjamesdobson.org/About/Commentaries/The-rest-of-the-story

Dowd, M. (2012, May 9). The facts: Gay marriage didn't tilt 2004 election. ABC News. Retrieved from http://abcnews.go.com/blogs/politics/2012/05/the-facts-gay-marriage-didnt-tilt-2004-election

Eckholm, E. (2012, October 9). One man guides the fight against gay marriage. *The New York Times.* Retrieved from http://www.nytimes.com/2012/10/10/us/politics/frank-schubert-mastermind-in-the-fight-against-gay-marriage.html

Faderman, L. (2015). *The gay revolution: The story of the struggle.* New York, NY: Simon and Schuster.

Fejes, F. (2008). *Gay rights and moral panic: The origins of America's debate on homosexuality.* http://dx.doi.org/10.1057/9780230614680

Fisher, S. (2009). It takes (at least) two to tango: Fighting with words in the conflict over same-sex marriage. In S. Barclay, M. Bernstein, & A. M. Marshall (Eds.), *Queer mobilizations: LGBT activists confront the law* (pp. 207–230). http://doi.org/10.1017/S153759271000232X

Foust, M. (2009, April 17). A winning strategy to stop 'gay marriage'? Baptist Press. Retrieved from https://web.archive.org/web/20120320070909/http://www.sbcbaptistpress.org/BPnews.asp?ID=30303

Freedman, S. G. (2013, March 8). Focus on the Family works to change its message. *The New York Times.* Retrieved from http://www.nytimes.com/2013/03/09/us/focus-on-the-family-transforms-its-message.html

Goldberg-Hiller, J. (2009). Do civil rights have a face? Reading the iconography of special rights. In S. Barclay, M. Bernstein, & A.-M. Marshall (Eds.), *Queer mobilizations: LGBT activists confront the law* (pp. 231–256). http://doi.org/10.1017/S153759271000232X

Goldbert, M. (2003, July 4). Confusion and outrage on the right. *Salon.* Retrieved from http://www.salon.com/2003/07/04/gay_marriage_11

Hansell, S. (2013, April 3). Facebook war: Blue crosses fight red equal sign. *The Huffington Post.* [Blog post]. Retrieved from http://www.huffingtonpost.com/sally-hansell/facebook-war-blue-crosses-fight-red-equal-signs_b_2996259.html

Hesse, M. (2009, August 28). Profile of Brian Brown, Executive Director of the National Organization for Marriage. *The Washington Post.* Retrieved from http://www.washingtonpost.com/wp-dyn/content/article/2009/08/27/AR2009082704139.html

Kaye, K. (2009, April 6). How "Yes on Prop 8" campaign took the web by storm. *ClickZ.* Retrieved from https://www.clickz.com/how-yes-on-prop-8-campaign-took-the-web-by-storm/83180

Kim, R. (2008, November 7). Why Proposition 8 won in California. ABC News. Retrieved from http://www.cbsnews.com/news/why-proposition-8-won-in-california

Kirkpatrick, D. D. (2004, September 17). Conservatives urge boycott of Procter & Gamble. *The New York Times.* Retrieved from http://www.nytimes.com/2004/09/17/us/conservatives-urge-boycott-of-procter-gamble.html

Kirkpatrick, D. D. (2004, October 16). Rally against gay marriage draws thousands to capital. *The New York Times.* Retrieved from http://www.nytimes.com/2004/10/16/us/rally-against-gay-marriage-draws-thousands-to-capital.html

Lane, F. S. (2006). *The decency wars: The campaign to cleanse American culture*. Amherst, NY: Prometheus Books.

Leff, L. (2010, January 25). Video: Pastor says Prop 8 could lead to polygamy. *The San Diego Union-Tribune*. Retrieved from http://www.sandiegouniontribune.com/sdut-video-pastor-says-prop-8-could-lead-to-polygamy-2010jan25-story,amp.html

Lerner, A. B. (2015, July 12). Conservatives regroup after gay marriage defeat. *Politico*. Retrieved from http://www.politico.com/story/2015/07/conservatives-regroup-after-gay-marriage-defeat-119984

Lester, W. (2003, August 18). Majority favors law against gay marriage. Associated Press. Retrieved from http://www.apnewsarchive.com/2003/Majority-Favors-Law-Against-Gay-Marriage/id-638c66aa583f78433e425977613d76f7

Lochhead, C. (2003, June 27). Gay rights affirmed in historic ruling. *San Francisco Chronicle*. Retrieved from http://www.sfgate.com/politics/article/Gay-rights-affirmed-in-historic-ruling-6-3-2577221.php

Lowry, R. (2015, June 30). The next gay-marriage battle. *National Review*. Retrieved from http://www.nationalreview.com/article/420508/next-gay-marriage-battle-rich-lowry

Lunig, E. (2009, February 12). Focus on the Family spent big on Proposition 8. *Rewire*. Retrieved from https://rewire.news/article/2009/02/12/focus-family-spent-big-proposition-8

Marriage Anti-Defamation Alliance. (n.d.). About. Retrieved from http://marriageada.org/about

Marty, M. E. (1970). *Righteous empire: The Protestant experience in America*. New York, NY: The Dial Press.

McVicar, M. J. (2016, March). The Religious Right in America. *Oxford Research Encyclopedia of Religion*. http://doi.org/10.1093/acrefore/9780199340378.013.97

Mencimer, S. (2010, March/April). Of Mormons and (gay) marriage. *Mother Jones*. Retrieved from http://www.motherjones.com/politics/2010/04/fred-karger-save-gay-marriage

Messner, T. (2009, October 22). The price of Prop 8 [Executive Summary Backgrounder No. 2328]. *The Heritage Foundation*. Retrieved from www.heritage.org/Research/Family/bg2328.cfm

Mistler, S. (2015, August 24). Ending long legal fight, group names donors who helped overturn Maine's same-sex marriage law in 2009. *The Press Herald*. Retrieved from http://www.pressherald.com/2015/08/24/national-organization-for-marriage-reveals-donors-from-2009-bid-to-overturn-maines-marriage-law

Morain, D. (2008, November 7). James Dobson's Focus on the Family praises Prop. 8 and passes the collection plate. *Los Angeles Times*. Retrieved from http://latimesblogs.latimes.com/washington/2008/11/james-dobsons-f.html

National Organization for Marriage. (2012, March 21). The National Organization for Marriage announces international "Dump Starbucks" protest campaign. [Blog post]. NOM Blog. Retrieved from http://www.nomblog.com/20812

National Organization for Marriage. (2012, May 8). NOM commends North Carolina voters for overwhelming vote in favor of marriage protection amendment. [Blog post]. NOM Blog. Retrieved from https://www.nomblog.com/22702

Pierceson, J. (2013). *Same-sex marriage in the United States: The road to the Supreme Court*. Lanham, MD: Rowman & Littlefield Publishers.

Plucinska, J. (2015, June 30). Americans are using a U.S. flag photo filter to protest the gay marriage ruling. *Time*. Retrieved from http://time.com/3941093/american-flag-filter-gay-marriage

Potok, M., & Schlatter, E. (2012, May 25). National Organization for Marriage continues to spread lies about gays. *SPLC Intelligence Report*. Retrieved from https://www.splcenter.org/fighting-hate/intelligence-report/2012/national-organization-marriage-continues-sp read-lies-about-gays

Rimmerman, C.A., & Wilcox, C. (Eds.) (2007). *The politics of same-sex marriage*. Chicago: University of Chicago Press.

Rutledge, K. K. (2004, December 30). Dobson on the gay marriage battle. *Christianity Today*, 49(1). Retrieved from http://www.christianitytoday.com/ct/2005/january/21.60.html

Schlanger, Z., & Wolfson, E. (2014, May 1). Ex-ex-gay pride. *Newsweek*. Retrieved from http://www.newsweek.com/ex-ex-gay-pride-249282

Schubert, F., & Flint, J. (2009, February 1). Passing Prop 8: Smart timing and messaging convinced California voters to support traditional marriage. *Politics*, pp. 44–47.

Schweber-Koren, R. (2005, October 7). Dobson: Same-sex marriage would lead to "marriage between daddies and little girls." *Media Matters*. Retrieved from https://www.mediamatters.org/video/2005/10/07/dobson-same-sex-marriage-would-lead-to-marriage/133967

Sprigg, P. (2004). *Outrage: How gay activists and liberal judges are trashing democracy to redefine marriage*. Washington, DC: Regnery Publishing.

Sprigg, P. (2013, March 15). Defining marriage: What marriage is. [Blog post]. FRC Blog. Retrieved from http://www.frcblog.com/2013/03/defining-marriage-what-marriage

Stone, A. L. (2012). *Gay rights at the ballot box*. Minneapolis: University of Minnesota Press.

Stone, B. (2009, February 7). Prop 8 donor web site shows disclosure law is 2-edged sword. *The New York Times*. Retrieved from http://www.nytimes.com/2009/02/08/business/08stream.html

Vick, K. (2009, November 2). Maine set to vote on gay marriage. *The Washington Post*. Retrieved from http://www.washingtonpost.com/wp-dyn/content/article/2009/11/02/AR2009110201107.html

Weisbrod, E., & Merica, D. (2013, March 26). Seeing red? Same-sex marriage debate goes viral. [Blog post]. Retrieved from http://politicalticker.blogs.cnn.com/2013/03/26/emblazoned-in-red-same-sex-marriage-dominates-social-media/comment-page-1

Wilcox, C., Merolla, L. M., & Beer, D. (2006). Saving marriage by banning marriage: The Christian Right finds a new issue in 2004. In J. C. Green, M. J. Rozell, & C. Wilcox (Eds.), *The values campaign? The Christian Right and the 2004 elections* (pp. 56–78). Washington, DC: Georgetown University Press.

Wilke, M. (2005). Same-sex marriage ads dominate 2004. *QNotes*. Retrieved from https://goqnotes.com/comercialcloset/comercialcloset_021205.html

Williams, D. K. (2010). *God's own party: The making of the Christian Right*. New York, NY: Oxford University Press.

Wolraich, M. (2015, April 4). Anita Bryant and the myth of the militant homosexual. *The Daily Beast*. Retrieved from http://www.thedailybeast.com/articles/2015/04/04/anita-bryant-and-the-myth-of-the-militant-homosexual

7

THE OPPONENTS WITHIN: QUEER RESISTANCE TO THE MARRIAGE MOVEMENT

Since the early 2000s, supporters of social movements have used social media images – avatars, memes, photo overlays, hashtags – to represent their affiliations and points of view, and the marriage equality movement was no exception. For a few weeks in 2013 and 2015 when the U.S. Supreme Court was considering key cases related to SSM, it seemed as though the movement's red equal sign and rainbow flag photo overlay were everywhere. Opponents of gay rights and SSM countered with their own visuals, sharing images of gold interlocked wedding rings, an American flag overlay, and the red equal sign logo altered to include a slash through it, signaling opposition to marriage rights for LGB couples. But these weren't the only two perspectives in the debate over SSM. Some activists *within* the LGBT+ community are strongly opposed to marriage, and they, too, have relied on social media to share their views. For example, the Against Equality collective, a loose coalition of radical queer writers and activists, adopted as its signature image a riff on the iconic Human Rights Campaign logo. In place of the HRC equal sign, the logo uses a greater-than sign, a visual statement of its disdain for an institution (marriage) that they believe requires assimilation into traditional hetero-centrist culture. The AE logo was not widely shared on social media; in fact, LGBT+ activists who oppose marriage have been far less likely than other factions of the SSM movement to disseminate their point of view through social networking platforms. Instead, they tended to rely on more traditional avenues of debate, including essays, media op-ed pieces, speeches, and books. This chapter will examine those materials and the arguments they contain to explain the perspective of LGBT+ activists who, for varying reasons, did not wholeheartedly endorse the fight for marriage.

As mentioned in Chapter 5, marriage has been a source of robust debate within the LGBT+ movement. Some activists consider it anathema to the goals of sexual liberation associated with queer resistance (Bernstein & Burke, 2013). Cult film director John Waters has jokingly said that one of the privileges of being gay "is that we don't have to get married or go in the Army" (Mead, 2007), but queer activists are serious in their concerns that allowing same-sex couples into the institution of marriage would force them into a restrictive and heteronormative state of "compulsory monogamy" (Emens, 2004). Others are not necessarily anti-marriage on principle, but they regard it a distraction that unnecessarily draws limited resources and attention away from higher priority issues such as employment discrimination and hate crimes (D'Emilio, 2006). This challenge from within their own community complicated the situation for LGBT+ rights organizations that opted to push forward on marriage, forcing them at least in the first few years of the movement to fight a battle on two fronts. Even now, after marriage rights have been extended to same-sex couples across the United States, there are those in the LGBT+ community who think the focus on marriage has damaged the larger LGBT+ rights movement, weakening its ability to secure resources for those in unconventional relationship structures and leading to political countermobilization of anti-gay forces (Buckley, 2013; Schacter, 2009; Vaid et al., 2013). In the end, however, even the strongest marriage skeptics within the LGBT+ community recognize that legalized SSM has provided access to rights, protection, and recognition for thousands of LGB couples. But they continue to push for legal recognition of alternative family and relationship types in addition to increased rights and protections for marginalized populations such as transgender individuals (J. D'Emilio, personal communication, June 9, 2017).

Before launching into discussion of the reasons that some LGBT+ activists have resisted the call for marriage, it is important to clarify the relationship between the "internal" and "external" critics of SSM. Far from being in agreement, they are actually polar opposites in their viewpoints. The *external* resistance, which was our focus in the previous chapter, was led by those who revere the traditional institution of marriage as the optimal structure for families and childrearing but are strongly opposed to gay rights and legal recognition of same-sex relationships. Simply put, they are pro-marriage but anti-queer. The *internal* resistance to marriage, on the other hand, emerged from some of the strongest advocates of LGBT+ rights, those who had worked tirelessly to end discrimination against gays and lesbians but were skeptical about the institution of marriage as a vehicle for transformation. This subset of the LGBT+ movement is pro-queer but anti-marriage, and they are the topic of this chapter.

Marriage as a distraction from higher priorities

Years before SSM was legal anywhere in the United States, thousands of LGBT+ rights advocates gathered in Washington., D.C. on October 10, 1987 to watch 2,000 LGB couples exchange symbolic wedding vows (Wheeler, 1987). The event, appropriately labeled "The Wedding," was part of a six-day March on Washington for Lesbian and Gay Rights. The happy couples and onlookers gathered behind the National Museum of Natural History and in front of the Internal Revenue Service building, a fitting location to protest the lack of recognition of same-sex domestic partners in U.S. law. Although it was obviously only a symbolic gesture, The Wedding was denounced by religious conservatives who lined the streets holding signs calling for participants to "repent or perish" (Wheeler, 1987). But members of the Christian right weren't the only ones opposed to the spectacle of hundreds of same-sex couples publicly demanding the right to marry; many within the LGBT+ movement were similarly distressed, albeit for different reasons (Ghaziani, 2008). Some argued that associating the queer rights movement with marriage would serve to undermine the radical nature of queer resistance, but others were concerned that it would detract from more pressing movement needs. Regardless of their views on the value of marriage, in 1987 most LGBT+ activists – even those participating in The Wedding – simply considered SSM a political impossibility (Bernstein & Taylor, 2013).

LGBT+ advocacy veterans Tom Stoddard and Paula Ettelbrick, both of whom worked in leadership positions for Lambda Legal, helped articulate the arguments for and against marriage in an influential intra-movement debate in 1989. Their arguments, summarized in two essays published in *Out/Look* magazine, help us understand the writers' very different visions about marriage and its proper place within the LGBT+ movement. In his essay titled "Why gay people should seek the right to marry," Stoddard (1997) pushed for tackling the marriage issue because of the practical benefits, political rights, and symbolic acceptance it could provide. He acknowledged the oppressive history of marriage but insisted that allowing LGB couples to participate could transform marriage, rendering it less patriarchal and restrictive. Stoddard considered marriage the centerpiece of society and suggested it should be the LGBT+ movement's top priority. For her essay, "Since when is marriage a path to liberation," Paula Ettelbrick (Ettelbrick & Stoddard, 1989) argued essentially the opposite. She dismissed the liberating potential of marriage, arguing that it would force gay men and lesbians to assimilate into the mainstream, reduce their cultural identity and distinctiveness, return them to invisibility, and undermine the goals of the LGBT+ liberation movement. Rather than devoting scarce movement resources to marriage, which historically has relegated women to second-class status, Ettelbrick urged LGBT+ advocates to seek support for diverse family forms, including those not headed by romantic partners.

Other LGBT+ activists in the 1980s–1990s felt that it was too soon to push for marriage because of widespread public disapproval of homosexuality. Three same-sex couples in Hawaii who decided to sue the state after being denied marriage licenses in 1991 were told their cause was essentially hopeless when they initially approached groups such as the American Civil Liberties Union and Lambda Legal Defense and Education Fund to take their case (Kowal, 2015). The pioneering couples moved forward nonetheless, hiring a private lawyer to take their case. It wasn't until after the surprising Hawaii Supreme Court ruling in 1993's *Baehr v. Lewin* that denying LGB couples the right to marry was a violation of the state constitution that the situation got the attention or support of the national LGBT+ movement. Even then some thought it unwise to fight for marriage rights, suggesting instead that resources be dedicated to more fundamental and universally agreed-upon gay movement objectives, such as decriminalizing sodomy. Sodomy statutes were considered the legal cornerstone that justified discriminatory treatment of gays and lesbians (Bernstein, 2003), and some activists felt those laws needed to be eradicated before any talk of marriage should proceed.

Others believed that by choosing marriage over other issues, movement leaders were catering to the elite within the LGBT+ movement. Activist Urvashi Vaid (1995) has criticized movement leaders and organizations for prioritizing the needs of its most privileged members – those who are white and well-off and thus have the resources to get married – at the expense of others. In a reflective essay about the marriage issue, LGBT+ historian and activist John D'Emilio (2007) echoed this concern. He asked, "Why are we seeking the sanction of the state for our intimate relationships? Why are we expending scarce movement resources so that couples can walk smilingly into the sunset? What about urgent issues like AIDS prevention, homophobia, violence, and the safety of queer youth, issues that legitimately might be termed matters of life and death?" (D'Emilio, 2007, p. 41). Similarly, New York University professor of social and cultural analysis Lisa Duggan (2012) has expressed disappointment that marriage equality has become the "singularly representative issue for the mainstream LGBT+ rights movement, often standing in for all the political aspirations of queer people." She argued that the queer movement was overly concerned with formal legal equality without sufficiently addressing the economic, racial, and gender-based inequities affecting low-income LGBT+ individuals, transgender people, and others in marginalized communities.

Although there is no way to know how big the anti-marriage faction of the LGBT+ rights movement was in the late 1980s when the marriage issue was starting to emerge, there is evidence that by 2013, marriage skeptics were a relatively small minority. Hull and Ortyl (2013) conducted focus groups and individual interviews with LGBT+ individuals to determine how well the LGT rights movement was representing the needs and interests of its constituents. The researchers were interested in the concept of "secondary marginalization" within social movements, which occurs when the more privileged members of a marginalized social group work to control the behavior and beliefs of the larger group in order to gain respect from and access to the dominant society. This often results in the marginalization of the needs of less privileged members of the group. Most constituents in Hull and Ortyl's study had either a positive or mixed opinion of the LGBT+ movement and its priorities, showing a relatively close alignment between the movement's priorities and what constituents thought they should be. Marriage and family were most often identified by study participants as the movement's main focus, as well as what the focus should be. Hull and Ortyl (2013) concluded that although some respondents indicated that the movement didn't fully represent them, it wasn't because of the focus on marriage rights.

In addition, a Pew Research Center online survey from 2013 asked a nationally representative sample of 1,197 self-identified LGBT+ adults about their views on marriage, in addition to other issues. Ninety-three percent of respondents said they favor SSM, although a significant minority (39 percent) thought the focus on marriage had drawn too much attention away from other issues more important to LGBT+ people. Interestingly, however, 58 percent said it should be the top priority even if it takes attention away from other issues. Survey results reported relatively low marriage rates among respondents; in 2013 when the poll was administered, 16 percent of LGBT+ adults were married, compared with about half the adults in the general public. A higher percentage aspired to marriage (Pew Research Center, 2013): a total of 60 percent of LGBT+ survey respondents were either married or said they would like to marry one day, still lower than the 76 percent of the general public who were either married or wanted to someday marry. LGBT+ survey respondents were twice as likely as those in the general public to say that obtaining legal rights and benefits is a very important reason to marry (46 percent versus 23 percent), but they were less likely (28 percent) to say that having children is a very important reason to marry than was the general public (49 percent).

It is clear that although some of the arguments addressed above have found fault with the institution of marriage, the concerns of those LGBT+ advocates we've discussed thus far are focused primarily on the issues of timing and prioritization. But there are those in the gay rights movement who oppose marriage outright, regardless of the timing or cultural context, and they are the subject of the next section of this chapter.

Beyond skepticism: rejection of marriage

A precursor to the modern LGBT+ rights movement, the early homophile movement of the 1950s in many ways was cautious in its approach to gay rights, adopting a relatively conservative and assimilationist strategy to gain public acceptance, in addition to legal rights and protections (Faderman, 1981; Peñaloza, 1996). In the late 1960s and 1970s, however, a more radical type of activist emerged, demanding freedom from sexuality-based oppression, judgment, and constraints (Marotta, 1981). Many of these activists did not hide their disdain for the institution of marriage and those LGB couples who desired access to it, as can be seen in the *Gay Manifesto*, one of the defining statements of the early gay liberation movement (Bernstein & Taylor, 2013). In the *Manifesto*, activist Carl Wittman (1970) described marriage as "a rotten, oppressive institution" and insisted that to believe "that happiness comes through finding a groovy spouse and settling down, showing the world that we're just the same as you" is an expression of self-hatred. This anti-marriage sentiment was also common among lesbian feminists, who viewed marriage as a historically patriarchal – and sometimes even violent – institution that required wives to be subservient physically and emotionally to their husbands, left them unable to own property, and relegated them to unpaid home-based labor (Echols, 1989; MacKinnon, 1989). These more radical LGBT+ activists called upon the gay rights movement to liberate queers from the constraints of heteronormative institutions such as marriage (Bernstein & Taylor, 2013) as part of a larger revolution that would challenge political, economic, and cultural norms related to gender and sexuality. As retired historian and LGBT+ activist John D'Emilio explained, members of the Stonewall generation thought queer life was subversive of marriage and family (D'Emilio, 2007).

Anti-marriage sentiment within the LGBT+ movement can take a variety of forms, but in general, arguments suggest that marriage is problematic for the gay community from cultural, political, and ethical perspectives (Badgett, 2009). On the cultural level, adopting marriage rights as a movement priority symbolically represents the acceptance of traditional heteronormative family structures and the rejection of distinctively queer family forms. On the political level, advocating for marriage leaves unchallenged the notion that the state should regulate relationships and/or privilege those couples who agree to seek a government-sanctioned license for their relationship. It also abandons any argument that noncouple family forms deserve rights and privileges. Ethically, seeking and exercising the option to marry means creating a "hierarchy of relationships" within the LGBT+ community that serve to marginalize families who are not headed by married couples (Badgett, 2009, p. 130). Some have also referred to a "homonormative critique" (Bernstein & Taylor, 2013; Duggan, 2002) that accuses marriage advocates of supporting "a politics that does not contest dominant heteronormative assumptions and institutions but upholds and sustains them while promising the possibility of a demobilized gay constituency" (Duggan, 2002, p. 179). Such a view envisions the outcome of marriage equality as simply a return to the status quo, removing any hope of a queer transformation.

In spite of queer activists' passionate rhetoric, however, there was little formal debate about the place of marriage within the LGBT+ rights movement in the 1970s-1980s. The lack of discourse did not indicate that gay rights advocates were in agreement about the issue, rather that widespread public disapproval of sexual minorities meant that it simply didn't matter whether gay rights activists wanted marriage equality. As Mary Bernstein and Verta Taylor explain in their book *The Marrying Kind: Debating Same-Sex Marriage Within the Lesbian and Gay Movement*, "Regardless of lesbian and gay feelings about marriage, during the 1970s LGBT+ people faced such a hostile climate that achieving the legal recognition of same-sex marriage was virtually unthinkable" (2013, p. 11).

After the marriage issue was forced onto the public agenda in the 1990s by the surprising turn of events in Hawaii, some LGBT+ movement leaders adjusted their thinking about marriage and began shifting resources to states where judicial and legislative action put marriage rights into play. This only further antagonized many queer activists and their academic counterparts, queer theorists, who felt a focus on marriage would do more damage than good to the movement (Halperin, 1997). Some of these individuals, such as Paula Ettelbrick, chose to make their case while working within existing LGBT+ advocacy organizations, whereas others formed their own collectives to pursue a more revolutionary approach. The Gay Shame collective, a movement formed in the 1990s in opposition to gay mainstreaming and the commercialization of Gay Pride events (hence their name), was one such group. Gay Shame derided the pro-marriage faction of the LGBT+ movement and compared them to religious conservatives, suggesting that "if you look at the rhetoric of the freedom to marry movement and the Republican Party, their similarities are frighteningly apparent. In their ideal world we would all be monogamously coupled, instead of rethinking the practice of coupling" (Boellstorff, 2007). Gay Shame promoted much of its ideology through AlterNet, a progressive activist news service launched in 1998, but the mainstream media paid almost no attention to the group outside of an occasional mention of their protests at gay pride parades. Historian John D'Emilio, who himself had written critically of the emphasis on marriage, notes that there were numerous anti-marriage essays and queer manifestos produced over the years. "The critiques were out there," he said, "but they had very little impact" (J. D'Emilio, personal communication, June 9, 2017).

A study by Bernstein and Burke (2013) of local news coverage of the marriage issue in two Vermont newspapers from 1996 to 2002 showed that queer arguments against marriage were present in news discourse, especially in an alternative newspaper for the LGBT+ community. They found that ebbs and flows in media inclusion of queer perspectives can be directly linked to movement-related activism and that news coverage of legislative and judicial activity generally does not displace queerer perspectives. In fact, the authors learned that discourse emerged to question the value of marriage specifically in response to the marriage equality movement, "providing an occasion to challenge an institution that had hitherto been uncontested" (Bernstein & Burke, 2013, p. 329). However, as John D'Emilio has suggested, queer arguments against marriage have for the most part been absent from national media coverage of the issue, which focused primarily on opposition to marriage from the Religious Right (Moscowitz, 2013). Others have proposed that marriage dissenters within the LGBT+ movement have censored themselves for fear of revealing division within the movement (Hartocollis, 2006).

A notable exception to this occurred in July 2006 when more than 200 pro-gay individuals – a prominent mix of LGBT+ and allied writers, scholars, educators, community organizers, journalists, and celebrities – grabbed national headlines by releasing a manifesto calling for movement leaders to think past the restrictions of marriage (Badgett, 2009). The statement titled "Beyond Same-Sex Marriage: A New Strategic Vision for All Our Families & Relationships" was posted by BeyondMarriage.org (a now defunct website) and signed by well-known activists such as Gloria Steinem, Armistead Maupin, and Cornel West (Hartocollis, 2006). It called for a new system of legal and institutional relationship recognition, one that would help secure government and private resources for individuals in various types of families, not just those headed by married couples. The signees did not suggest that LGB couples were undeserving of the right to marry, but they argued that a narrow focus on marriage ignored the needs of many queer individuals who chose not to marry. In place of marriage, the statement called for "access to a flexible set of economic benefits and options regardless of sexual orientation, race, gender/gender identity, class, or citizenship status" (BeyondMarriage.org, 2008).

The anti-marriage statement by itself likely would have gotten attention from the national press because of the prominence of its signers. But the timing – it was released on the same day that the Washington state Supreme Court upheld a ban on SSM – pushed it "above the fold" in news terms, shining the spotlight on intra-movement conflict between marriage advocates and marriage dissenters (Badgett, 2009). The result was a series of news stories showcasing claims by anti-marriage queer activists that the gay civil rights movement had been hijacked by a "distressingly conservative, politically correct part of the gay establishment" (Hartocollis, 2006). Those views were countered by pro-marriage advocates who assured reporters that marriage skeptics did not represent a large segment of the LGBT+ movement. Not surprisingly, marriage proponents such as Evan Wolfson of Freedom to Marry felt obliged to defend their focus on the marriage issue. In a *New York Times* story about the controversy, Wolfson pointedly said, "My organization is called 'Freedom to Marry' not 'Mandatory Marriage.' Gay people in America can't really say they've rejected marriage in favor of something else, because for most of us it hasn't been offered" (Hartocollis, 2006).

Not long after the Beyond Marriage statement caused a public stir, a separate group of authors, artists, and activists formed the all-volunteer AgainstEquality.org, an online archive, publishing, and arts collective dedicated to critiquing mainstream LGBT+ politics. AgainstEquality.org grew out of an angry blog post in 2009 by queer activist Ryan Conrad, who resented the millions of dollars being poured into a marriage-related ballot measure in his home state of Maine. In May of 2009, the Maine legislature had passed a law legalizing SSM, but gay marriage opponents collected enough signatures to force a state-wide vote on the issue in November of that year. Ryan said the campaign to keep the SSM law in place – which was ultimately unsuccessful – pulled vital resources from services for LGBT+ youth, the homeless, and those with AIDS and ignored the needs of marginalized LGBT+ residents of the state who had little interest in marriage (R. Conrad, personal communication, July 13, 2017). Well-off LGBT+ rights advocates from national groups such as the Human Rights Campaign and urban areas of Maine left the state without legal SSM, but with depleted resources and increased anti-gay sentiment, which Conrad said led him to publicly air his frustrations. Before long other like-minded writers and activists contacted him with their own essays, and eventually the Against Equality collective was born.

The group's website makes it clear that marriage is not the only institution it considers detrimental to LGBT+ populations: "As queer thinkers, writers and artists, we are committed to dislodging the centrality of equality rhetoric and challenging the demand for inclusion in the institution of marriage, the U.S. military, and the prison industrial complex via hate crimes legislation" (AgainstEquality.org, n.d.). As noted in the opening section of this chapter, Against Equality has adopted as its logo a version of the Human Rights Campaign's yellow and blue equal sign, but AE uses a greater-than sign in place of the equal sign and adds the tagline "queer challenges to the politics of inclusion." Conrad explains that the group's members feel they can do better than settle for inclusion within institutions that are inequitable to

FIGURE 7.1 Against Equality, a collective of queer writers and artists who oppose marriage as a hetero-centrist and mainstream institution, illustrates its point of view with a greater-than sign logo. (Image courtesy of Ryan Conrad)

begin with (R. Conrad, personal communication, July 13, 2017). AE has also created a set of postcards that creatively visualize its points of view and serve as resistance to the social media tactics of mainstream LGBT+ advocacy organizations. As Conrad explained in an interview with the *Seattle Gay News*: "There is a huge lack of visual culture reflecting more radical queer politics these days. So we thought we could help generate more through our digital archival project. How many times have you seen those vapid, pro-Gay marriage logos proliferating online and on social networking sites? We wanted to counter these" (Gairola, 2011).

In spite of the multiple pockets of marriage skeptics within the LGBT+ movement, the general public has likely remained unaware of the depth of the intra-movement division. After the marriage equality movement began to make real progress through the courts and state legislatures, much of the visible anti-marriage sentiment either receded or directed their efforts elsewhere (Schacter, 2009). Occasionally the news media would focus its attention on gay couples who weren't interested in marriage – for example, an October 2013 story in *The New York Times* was headlined "Gay Couples, Choosing to Say I Don't" and explained that some LGB couples consider marriage to be an archaic institution, whereas others identify as being in a "post-marriage" generation that doesn't need the external validation of a marriage license or ceremony (Buckley, 2013). Like marriage proponents within the LGBT+ movement, anti-marriage queer activists were faced with the question of "what next?" after the 2015 Supreme Court decision in *Obergefell v. Hodges* that legalized SSM nationwide.

A post-mortem: marriage skeptics post Obergefell

Now that marriage equality has been achieved across the United States, and the issue is no longer monopolizing the attention and resources of the gay rights movement, it's worth asking marriage skeptics whether they still resent its multi-year dominance. John D'Emilio, the historian and activist who in 2006 wrote an essay titled "The Marriage Fight is Setting Us Back," seems to be less pessimistic now. Reflecting on the effects of legalized SSM, he suggests that "marriage did more to reduce homophobia than probably any other issue" in the LGBT+ movement (J. D'Emilio, personal communication, June 9, 2017). In addition to providing access to important rights and benefits, D'Emilio said marriage served to normalize LGB couples and allowed non-gays to identify and empathize with them and their families. "It helped heterosexual people to understand, 'Oh, they love each other,'" he said (J. D'Emilio, personal communication, June 9, 2017). On the other hand, D'Emilio says the emphasis on marriage came at a price, especially for those lower-income and less-educated individuals who often do not have the resources to take advantage of marriage and its benefits. Another unintended consequence of legalized SSM, according to D'Emilio, was that "it helps to perpetuate and strengthen the stigma for the huge number of American children who do not live with two married parents."

In a 2013 essay on the state of the LGBT+ movement, a group of longtime gay rights advocates (Vaid et al., 2013) expressed many of the same sentiments about the effects of the marriage movement. They were disappointed that "the queer movement is focused on formal legal gay/lesbian equality only and still does not address the economic, racial and gender-based inequities affecting low-income LGBT folks, transgender people, people of color (POC), women and others in queer communities." The group, concerned about the religious liberty movement that has worked to create exemptions to LGBT+ civil rights laws, implored activists not to get complacent just because marriage had been legalized for LGB couples (Vaid et al., 2013). Gay activist, writer, and radio show host Michael Signorile (2015) has written an entire book on what he calls the risk of "victory blindness" (p. 3), warning activists that the post-marriage equality period is a treacherous one in which gay rights opponents will be galvanized to roll back LGBT+ advances. D'Emilio, too, predicts that the religious freedom movement will continue – and even increase – its efforts. He believes that marriage equality opponents will not be able to fully curtail marriage rights, but will "create a structure and culture of annoyance and insult" for same-sex couples who want to marry (J. D'Emilio, personal communication, June 9, 2017). Likewise, an important but often overlooked outcome of the battle over marriage, according to D'Emilio, is "the role that the marriage fight had in successfully mobilizing Republicans," leading to the election of Donald Trump as president and putting more state legislatures and governorships under the control of conservatives.

On the other hand, social movement and sexuality scholar Mary Bernstein, who in the past has challenged the goal of marriage equality and its potential homonormative effects, has adopted a more optimistic outlook. In a speech in 2015, she discussed the possibility that the marriage rights debate has created an expanded understanding of what it means to be a family, noting that children of same-sex parents (a topic too often overlooked) represent a future generation that will have extremely fluid notions of gender and sexuality norms. In her address, Bernstein humorously acknowledged a primary concern of the queer critique of marriage, asking "Are LGBT people truly marching en masse to the suburbs where they will be enclosed behind white picket fences, sipping homonormative Kool-Aid and failing to realize that heteronormativity and homophobia are alive and well?" (p. 322). She seems to think the answer is "no," suggesting that post-Obergefell activity provides evidence of a willingness on the part of gay rights advocates – even the less-radical national organizations such as the HRC – to address key areas that may have been neglected during the marriage fight, such as transgender rights, the intersection of issues related to race, sexuality, and gender, and a broader commitment to social justice.

Now that we've taken a look at the arguments and messaging strategies of both proponents and opponents of SSM, the last stakeholder we're going to examine is corporate America. A multitude of companies, especially in the final two years of the marriage battle, aligned themselves with marriage equality, using their stance as a marketing tool to position themselves as progressive and show their commitment to diversity. A smaller number publicly opposed gay marriage, taking a stand as defenders of traditional marriage and appealing to faith-based consumers. The next chapter will look at the messaging strategies of some of the key corporate players in the SSM debate.

References

AgainstEquality.org. (n.d.). Marriage. Retrieved from http://www.againstequality.org/about/marriage

Badgett, M. V. L. (2009). *When gay people get married: What happens when societies legalize same-sex marriage*. New York, NY: New York University Press.

Bernstein, M. (2003). Nothing ventured, nothing gained? Conceptualizing social movement "success" in the lesbian and gay movement. *Sociological Perspectives*, 46(3), 353–379.

Bernstein, M. (2015). Same-sex marriage and the future of the LGBT movement. *Gender & Society*, 29(3), 321–337.

Bernstein, M., & Burke, M.C. (2013). Normalization, queer discourse, and the marriage-equality movement in Vermont. In M. Bernstein & V. Taylor (Eds.), *The marrying kind* (pp. 319–343). Minneapolis: University of Minnesota Press.

Bernstein, M., & Taylor, V. (2013). Marital discord: Understanding the contested place of marriage in the lesbian and gay movement. In M. Bernstein & V. Taylor (Eds.), *The marrying kind* (pp. 1–35). Minneapolis: University of Minnesota Press.

BeyondMarriage.org. (2008). Beyond same-sex marriage: A new strategic vision. *Studies in Gender and Sexuality*, 9, 161–171. Retrieved from http://www.tandfonline.com/doi/abs/10.1080/15240650801935198

Boellstorff, T. (2007). When marriage falls: Queer coincidences in straight time. *GLQ*, 13 (2–3), 227–247.

Buckley, C. (2013, October 25). Gay couples, choosing to say "I don't." *The New York Times*. Retrieved from http://www.nytimes.com/2013/10/27/style/gay-couples-choosing-to-say-i-dont.html

D'Emilio, J. (2006). The marriage fight is setting us back. *Gay and Lesbian Review*, 13(6), 10–11.

D'Emilio, J. (2007). Will the courts set us free? Reflections on the campaign for same-sex marriage. In C. A. Rimmerman & C. Wilcox. *The politics of same-sex marriage* (pp. 39–64). Chicago, IL: University of Chicago Press.

Duggan, L. (2002). The new homonormativity: The sexual politics of neoliberalism. In R. Castronovo & D. Nelson (Eds.), *Materializing democracy: Toward a revitalized cultural politics* (pp. 175–194). Durham, NC: Duke University Press.

Duggan, L. (2012). Beyond marriage: Democracy, equality, and kinship for a new century. *Scholar & Feminist Online*, 10(1–2). Retrieved from http://sfonline.barnard.edu/a-new-queer-agenda/beyond-marriage-democracy-equality-and-kinship-for-a-new-century

Echols, A. (1989). *Daring to be bad: Radical feminism in America 1967–1975*. Minneapolis, MN: University of Minnesota Press.

Emens, E. (2004). Monogamy's law: Compulsory monogamy and polyamorous existence. *Public Law & Legal Theory*, 58. Retrieved from http://chicagounbound.uchicago.edu/cgi/viewcontent.cgi?article=1193&context=public_law_and_legal_theory

Ettelbrick, P., & Stoddard, T. (1989). Gay marriage: A must or a bust. *Out/Look*, 6, pp. 8–17.

Faderman, L. (1981). *Surpassing the love of men: Romantic friendship and love between women from the Renaissance to the present*. New York, NY: William Morrow.

Gairola, R. K. (2011, April 1). Equality beyond marriage: An interview with activist Ryan Conrad. *Seattle Gay News*. Retrieved from http://www.sgn.org/sgnnews39_13/page18.cfm

Ghaziani, A. (2008). *The dividends of dissent: How conflict and culture work in lesbian and gay marches on Washington*. Chicago, IL: University of Chicago Press.

Halperin, D. (1997). *Saint Foucault: Towards a gay hagiography*. New York: Oxford University Press.

Hartocollis, A. (2006, July 30). For some gays, a right they can forsake. *The New York Times*. Retrieved from http://www.nytimes.com/2006/07/30/fashion/sundaystyles/30MARRIAGE.html

Hull, K. E., & Ortyl, T.A. (2013). Same-sex marriage and constituent perceptions of the LGBT rights movement. In M. Bernstein & V. Taylor (Eds.), *The marrying kind? Debating same-sex marriage within the lesbian and gay movement* (pp. 67–102). Minneapolis: University of Minnesota Press.

Kowal, J. F. (2015, September 29). *The improbable victory of marriage equality*. Brennan Center for Justice. Retrieved from https://www.brennancenter.org/analysis/improbable-victory-marriage-equality

MacKinnon, C. (1989). *Toward a feminist theory of the state*. Cambridge, MA: Harvard University Press.

Marotta, T. (1981). *The politics of homosexuality*. Boston, MA: Houghton Mifflin.

Mead, R. (2007, March 26). The groom reaper. *The New Yorker*. Retrieved from http://www.newyorker.com/magazine/2007/03/26/the-groom-reaper

Moscowitz, L. M. (2013). The battle over marriage: Gay rights activism through the media. http://dx.doi.org/10.5406/illinois/9780252038129.001.0001

Pew Research Center. (2013, June 13). A survey of LGBT Americans: Attitudes, experiences and values in changing times. Retrieved from http://www.pewsocialtrends.org/2013/06/13/a-survey-of-lgbt-americans

Schacter, J.S. (2009). The other same-sex marriage debate. *Chicago-Kent Law Review*, 84(2), pp. 379–402.

Signorile, M. (2015). *It's not over: Getting beyond tolerance, defeating homophobia, and winning true equality*. Boston, MA: Houghton Mifflin Harcourt.

Stoddard, T. B. (1997). Why gay people should seek the right to marry. In Blasius, M. & Phelan, S. (Eds.), *We are everywhere: A historical sourcebook of gay and lesbian politics*. Routledge, pp. 753–756.

Vaid, U. (1995). *Virtual equality: The mainstreaming of gay and lesbian liberation*. New York, NY: Anchor Publishing.

Vaid, U., Duggan, L., Metz, T., & Hollibaugh, A. (2013, June 27). What's next for the LGBT movement. *The Nation*. Retrieved from https://www.thenation.com/article/whats-next-lgbt-movement

Wheeler, L. (1987, October 11). 2,000 gay couples exchange vows in ceremony of rights. *The Washington Post*. Retrieved from https://www.washingtonpost.com/archive/local/1987/10/11/2000-gay-couples-exchange-vows-in-ceremony-of-rights/b821006d-4b19-485b-94eb-d32f887c799d/?utm_term=.578b3452f5d1

Wittman, C. (1970). *Refugees from Amerika: A gay manifesto*. New York: Red Butterfly. Retrieved at http://library.gayhomeland.org/0006/EN/A_Gay_Manifesto.htm

8

FROM PARIAH TO CAUSE CÉLÈBRE: CORPORATE EVOLUTION ON THE ISSUE OF SAME-SEX MARRIAGE

Working for President Bill Clinton in the 1990s, political strategist Richard Socarides was assigned the difficult task of convincing corporate CEOs to publicly endorse the administration's gay rights initiatives. Socarides (2015) recalled that just getting executives to attend a meeting about gay rights back then was a challenge and that most businesses wanted nothing to do with LGBT+ issues for fear of consumer backlash. But the climate was vastly different in 2015 when political leaders and gay advocacy groups asked corporate America to show support for marriage equality in advance of an upcoming Supreme Court ruling. Instead of ducking meetings about gay rights, leaders of some of the largest corporations in the U.S. very publicly endorsed SSM. Prior to arguments before the U.S. Supreme Court in *Obergefell v. Hodges*, 379 companies signed an amicus brief in support of marriage equality, arguing that laws limiting marriage rights to heterosexual couples harmed businesses' ability to attract and retain top employees. As Socarides (2015) noted, the brief was signed by a broad cross-section of businesses from every region of the United States, "reflecting the commitment to the issue that has evolved, at first slowly and then forcefully, over the past decade."

This chapter will examine the evolution of corporate America's relationship with LGBT+ individuals and issues. We'll go back to the 1990s when gays and lesbians emerged as a coveted – but controversial – consumer market and then review efforts by both pro- and anti-gay advocacy organizations to influence corporate involvement with LGBT+ rights initiatives, especially SSM. We'll also consider the potential effects of collaboration with corporate interests on a social movement whose original purpose included liberating individuals from existing political, social, and economic norms.

The LGBT+ market is discovered

Tension between the corporate world and social movement activism is to be expected, and the gay liberation movement was no exception. Not long after the

1969 Stonewall riots, the first gay rights protest staged against a major corporation in the United States took place when queer activists picketed the ABC television network after a San Francisco ABC affiliate fired an employee who had joined the movement (Raeburn, 2004). LGBT+ activists used another economic protest tactic – a boycott – to push back against Anita Bryant, the Florida Citrus Commission spokeswoman who successfully lobbied in 1977 against a local anti-discrimination ordinance in Miami. The boycott of Florida oranges and juice drew national attention to the growing gay rights movement and demonstrated its willingness to take action against commercial entities that sought to marginalize LGBT+ individuals (Chasin, 2000).

Even as gay rights activists were fighting to change corporate attitudes and policies, businesses were starting to discover sexual minorities (particularly gay men) as a potentially lucrative consumer market segment. One of the earliest references to the notion of an LGBT+ market occurred in a 1976 *New York Times* article about gay-themed magazines that reached wide audiences but were struggling to attract national advertisers. The article (Dougherty, 1976) marveled at the efforts of publisher Donald Embinder, who had run a fullpage ad in the industry publication *Advertising Age* headlined, "Now you can reach America's most affluent minority… The Male Homosexual." Embinder was determined to sell corporate America on the untapped market potential of gay men who, he said, had money to spend and would be loyal to companies that advertised in LGBT+ media. In spite of Embinder's optimism, the gay and lesbian market would have to wait more than a decade to be fully "discovered." In the 1970s, marketing advice focused instead on strategies for targeting women and African Americans, with the Latino market emerging as its focal point in the 1980s (Peñaloza, 1996). There was one company, however, that began marketing to LGBT+ audiences before it became fashionable to do so. In 1981, Absolut Vodka started running ads in two magazines for gay men, the *Advocate* and *After Dark* (Elliott, 2011), and the company soon expanded beyond advertising, helping to sponsor LGBT-related charities and events. According to Michael Wilke, founder of the non-profit Commercial Closet Association, Absolut was the first continuously present major brand in gay media. Thirty years later, in 2011, Absolut proudly marked its three-decade relationship with the LGBT+ community with a yearlong anniversary campaign, "Absolut Outrageous," featuring the tagline: "Celebrating 30 years of going out and coming out" (Elliott, 2011).

Corporate interests eventually turned more of their attention and advertising dollars to the LGBT+ market segment in the early 1990s after marketing agencies began to trumpet gays and lesbians (but still mostly gay men) as a "dream market" with elevated socioeconomic status and large amounts of disposable income that was ripe for the taking (Johnson, 1993). In his book *Untold Millions: Positioning Your Business for the Gay and Lesbian Consumer Revolution*, Grant Luckenbill (1995) described increasingly visible and powerful LGBT+ consumers as "a marketplace revolution – serious, multifaceted, and destined to reorganize customer landscapes in consumer product and service industries across the country" (p. 1).

He predicted that political and societal achievements by the LGBT+ rights movement would not only lead gays and lesbians to be more conspicuous and purposeful consumers but would also affect the commercial buying habits of heterosexual Americans. Not wanting to miss out, major corporations in the 1990s began to actively target gay men – and occasionally lesbians – as consumers, and companies such as Miller, Subaru, American Express, The Gap, and Wyndham Hotels produced specifically tailored print advertising campaigns (Hester & Gibson, 2007). The Swedish furniture chain Ikea in 1994 produced the first mainstream U.S. television commercial that featured openly queer individuals, a gay male couple who was buying a dining room table (McMains, 2014). The spot ran in only three markets (New York, Philadelphia, and Washington, D.C.) and then only after 10 p.m. to ensure that it wouldn't be seen during "family hour" programming. Those restrictions, however, did little to lessen objections from conservative Christian groups, which called for boycotts of Ikea stores.

In spite of their influence on advertisers, the claims of LGB affluence that proliferated in the 1990s were extremely misleading. The inflated statistics were spread in part by gay-owned marketing agencies that created slick self-promotional materials boasting of a lucrative – and loyal – new market (Gluckman & Reed, 1997; Schulman, 1998). For example, Overlooked Opinions, a now-defunct U.S. gay marketing firm, in the early 1990s released a report showing that gay men and lesbians earned average incomes above those of straight men and women (Chasin, 2000). Many of the claims implied that all gays and lesbians were flush with disposable income, an inaccurate conclusion that was based on a narrow and non-random sample of periodical readers (Chasin, 2000). Even though the figures were eventually shown to be artificially inflated (Luckenbill, 1995), they were repeated often and perpetuated the "myth of the gay consumer" as a white male urban professional with excessive good taste and discretionary income (Bronski, 1984). Political conservatives jumped on the claims of LGBT+ prosperity and used the inaccurate data in attempts to repeal civil rights legislation (Gluckman & Reed, 1997). As Schulman (1998) notes, this dream consumer myth was especially off-target for lesbians. Women in the 1990s made significantly less than men, and lesbians made even less than straight women (Luckenbill, 1995). Thus, a lesbian household, especially if the heads of the household were women of color, would likely not have enjoyed much disposable income at all.

In addition to gaining clout as a potential consumer market, gays and lesbians were also starting to see advances in the corporate workplace, as larger numbers of LGBT+ employees organized to lobby for gay-friendly policies and protections. Sociologist Nicole Raeburn (2004), in her book about the corporate workplace movement for LGBT+ rights, says that after a fledgling start in the late 1970s, the movement gained power in the 1990s, and by the end of that decade there were more than 80 documented gay employee networks within *Fortune* magazine's top 1,000 U.S. companies. Raeburn found evidence that those networks were vital to improving workplace climates, noting that the majority of companies that agreed to equitable-benefits policies did so only after facing internal pressure from mobilized groups of LGBT+ employees. The 1990s also witnessed more corporations openly sponsoring LGBT+ events and charities, a philanthropic gesture that was also part of a deliberate marketing strategy (Chasin, 2000). For example, a 1996 advertisement in the *Advocate* for a rainbow-themed Visa credit card endorsed by openly lesbian tennis star Martina Navratilova touted that "Every time we use the rainbow card, we help fund organizations serving the lesbian and gay community" (Chasin, 2000, p. 200).

The double-edged sword of being a dream market

Being courted as a consumer market was met with mixed reactions by the LGBT+ community. Those who celebrated the increased visibility and influence of gay consumers hoped that economic power would pave the way for other political and social gains. Marketing professor Lisa Peñaloza explains that being acknowledged as a valuable market in a capitalist society resulted in a "profound sense of social validation and legitimation" for individual gays and lesbians, as well as queer communities (1996, p. 15). Lesbian activist Alexandra Chasin (2000) has reacted more cynically, suggesting that promises of equality grounded in levels of personal consumption fail to acknowledge the systematic nature of discrimination. But Peñaloza is not as quick to dismiss the value of marketplace inclusion, noting that "many civil rights gains were and continue to be manifest in the marketplace – at the lunch counters, in bus and retail service, in hotel accommodations, and in socially acceptable standards of dress" (p. 16). In this sense, Peñaloza argues, the marketplace serves as an important locale for disenfranchised groups to fight for social and political inclusion. Grant Luckenbill (1995), whose book touts the benefits of consumer-based respect, also argues that courting the gay market forces corporations to demonstrate an awareness of issues important to the LGBT+ community.

Others have suggested that economic validation would facilitate the assimilation of gays into the cultural mainstream, a phenomenon that some find worrisome (Gluckman & Reed, 1997). Chasin (2000), for example, is concerned that in order to gain recognition as a viable market segment, "gay men and lesbians had to persuade mainstream advertisers that they pursue happiness in the market, just as other Americans do" (p. 47). She suggests that the assimilationist nature of gay consumerism only serves to weaken a movement grounded in sexual radicalism. Chasin argues that gay marketing pitches lure queer consumers with the seductive implication that as long as they can consume like heterosexuals, they will have the same rights and social standing as heterosexuals. Likewise, media and sexuality scholar Katherine Sender worries that "only the most sanitized, privileged, accomodationist, apolitical aspects of gay existence are made visible at great cost for the real diversity and necessary offensiveness" of a movement that rejects the goal of being just like everyone else (2004, p. 10). In a related critique, Chasin (2000) also suggests that, in their efforts to attract corporate advertising and sponsorship deals, national gay rights groups have adjusted their political agendas to favor the most economically and politically palatable issues – such as SSM – that fit in with a consumerist culture.

Advocacy organization efforts to influence corporate approaches to LGBT+ issues

By the early 2000s, the corporate world regarded gays and lesbians as a large and profitable enough consumer bloc that it was no longer considered out of the mainstream to market to them. In 2004, the Commercial Closet reported that more than one-third of Fortune 100 companies had produced advertising directly aimed at the LGBT+ market (Commercial Closet Association, 2011). Less worried about the risk of alienating non-gay consumers, CEOs regularly explained that it was just a matter of business – not politics – to market to sexual minorities (Sender, 2004). In other words, although companies were willing to create marketing campaigns to appeal specifically to the underserved LGB market and even to adjust workplace policies to meet the needs of LGBT+ employees, most of them avoided taking a stand on issues related to gay rights.

The Human Rights Campaign for years has worked to capitalize upon this "business-first" attitude, encouraging corporate executives to improve their bottom lines by catering to gay customers, employees, and investors. HRC's efforts have been buoyed by research documenting the loyalty of LGBT+ consumers (Luckenbill, 1995) and their willingness to participate in "buycotts" to promote equality (Becker & Copeland, 2016), as well as positive links between LGBT+-supportive workplace climates and outcomes beneficial for employers (Badgett et al., 2013). In 2002, HRC launched one of its most successful initiatives, the Corporate Equality Index, which scores companies based on a survey that assesses their policies and practices related to sexual orientation and gender identity and expression. CEI criteria continually evolve to address emerging issues, but in general, the criteria include assessments of advertising and marketing to the LGBT+ community, workplace policies and benefits, and company stances on policies that are considered harmful to LGBT+ rights.

The CEI has grown in size and popularity each year, and the HRC now has a fully searchable database and mobile app, in addition to an annual Buying for Workplace Equality guide (McBride, 2017). According to HRC President Chad Griffin, 2017 represented the largest increase in top-rated businesses in the history of the CEI survey, with 515 employers earning perfect scores, up from 23 during the index's first year (HRC, 2017; Socarides, 2015). A *Time* magazine article about growth in corporate support for LGBT+ rights credits HRC for much of the progress, noting that businesses now seek out HRC guidance on how to improve their workplace policies and public image (Steinmetz, 2016). Although there was some early speculation that scoring high on the CEI might hurt a company with its conservative consumers, an analysis of stock market reaction to the release of the inaugural CEI in 2002 suggests that firms were not penalized for supporting workforce diversity (Johnston & Malina, 2008). In addition, more recent research has found evidence of positive links between LGBT-supportive workplace climates and greater job commitment, improved workplace relationships, increased job satisfaction, and improved health outcomes among LGBT+ employees (Badgett et al., 2013).

This is not to say there wasn't backlash against companies that openly supported gay rights initiatives, including SSM. In summer 2015 for example, evangelical pastor Franklin Graham used Facebook to call for a boycott of gay-friendly businesses "to fight the tide of moral decay that is being crammed down our throats by big business, the media, and the gay & lesbian community" (Timm, 2015). Graham announced that he was pulling his ministry's financial accounts from Wells Fargo after it ran an advertisement featuring a gay couple, and he also criticized Tiffany's, which advertised wedding rings for same-sex couples. That same year, the organization Faith Driven Consumer took a page from the HRC playbook and formed its own corporate assessment index, this one designed to support companies whose actions are compatible with Christian views. The group claims to represent 41 million Christian consumers who spend $2 trillion annually (FDC, 2015), and it sponsors "buycotts" to support businesses that are openly welcoming to Christians (Bedard, 2015). The launch of its Faith Equality Index was meant to remind corporations that not all consumers are pleased with corporate support for issues such as SSM, and it encourages equal protections for all groups "in order to create parity, at minimum, between Faith Driven Consumers and other groups that are embraced in the rainbow of employment, philanthropy, and marketing diversity" (FDC, n.d.). The Faith Equality Index rewards companies for actions such as use of the word "Christmas" in seasonal advertising, philanthropic support of faith-based charities, and proactive public support for religious liberty protections. Notably, the FEI also awards points for "respect for, acknowledgement of, and compatibility with biblical teaching on sexuality, gender, marriage and family" (FDC, 2015). Not surprisingly, the top two companies in the inaugural FEI rankings were Chick-fil-A and Hobby Lobby (Bedard, 2015), both of which are known for their conservative stances and policies. The Hobby Lobby chain of craft stores was involved in a legal challenge that went all the way to the U.S. Supreme Court, which ruled in 2014 that the company's owners had a religious-liberty right to refuse to offer contraception coverage for its employees. And famously, fast food chain Chick-fil-A had made the news in 2012 for its CEO's public statements against SSM. In the next section, we'll take a look at the actions of Chick-fil-A and other companies that participated in the marriage debate during the movement's closing years, 2012–2015.

Corporate involvement in the marriage movement homestretch

In the final four years of the marriage equality fight, scores of companies publicly demonstrated their support for SSM either through traditional methods such as press releases and speeches or through social media. You'll recall from Chapter 5 that HRC's pink and red marriage equality logo essentially took over Facebook in the spring of 2013, with individuals and companies customizing the logo to show their support. Bud Light, for instance, replaced the bars of the equal sign with two beer cans. Companies opposed to marriage equality were less vocal, likely in part because of the backlash they feared (Aarons-Mele, 2013; Wallace, 2015). A well-publicized example of such backlash occurred in 2012, when Chick-fil-A CEO

Dan Cathy told a Christian news organization that his company supported "the biblical definition of the family unit" and added in a later interview "I think we are inviting God's judgment on our nation when we shake our fist at him and say, 'We know better than you as to what constitutes a marriage'" (Sverson, 2012). The Cathy family had always been upfront about wanting to incorporate Christian principles into the workplace and had donated to groups supporting the traditional definition of marriage. But Cathy's comments nonetheless caused a ruckus, with gay rights supporters calling for a Chick-fil-A boycott and staging kiss-ins at its restaurants (Sverson, 2012). In response, former Arkansas governor Mike Huckabee announced he was celebrating Chick-fil-A Appreciation Day and invited conservatives nationwide to join in. Conservative advocacy groups, able to publicly take a stance without fearing the loss of customers, were quick to defend Dan Cathy. For example, to show its support the National Organization for Marriage started a "Thank Chick-fil-A" campaign where supporters could go to the group's website to join a roster of Chick-fil-A and traditional marriage advocates. Cathy did not back down from his stance and the following year took to Twitter to express his disappointment with the Supreme Court's pro-marriage equality decisions in June 2013. The tweet was deleted soon afterward, but not before Twitter users took a screen shot of it, which read: "Sad day for our nation; founding fathers would be ashamed of our gen. to abandon wisdom of the ages re: cornerstone of strong societies" (Lobosco, 2013). Company officials said the tweet was removed because Cathy had realized his views did not represent those of all Chick-fil-A employees, and Cathy himself eventually admitted his stance was not a wise business decision, saying that in hindsight, he regretted "making the company a symbol in the marriage debate" (O'Connor, 2014).

Although some pro-SSM companies were also criticized for their public stance – as noted with Wells Fargo and Tiffany's above – many were undaunted by challenges from LGBT+ rights opponents (Broderick, 2015). One such company was the Starbucks coffee chain, which in 2012 had supported a pro-SSM referendum in Washington state, making it the target of a boycott by the National Organization for Marriage and criticism from some customers and investors. During an annual shareholder meeting in March 2013, one attendee who was involved in the traditional marriage movement publicly complained to Executive Chairman Howard Schultz that Starbucks had lost customers because of its support for SSM (Allen, 2013). Schultz unapologetically explained that the decision to back marriage equality was not based solely on economics, but instead was meant to acknowledge the diversity within the company's 200,000+ employees. Schultz's straightforward response to continued criticism from the complainer – "You can sell your shares in Starbucks and buy shares in another company" – quickly spread through social media, garnering Starbucks many more positive than negative comments on social media (Allen, 2013).

During the lead-up to the key *Obergefell v. Hodges* U.S. Supreme Court case in 2015, corporate support for SSM was strong. More than 370 companies signed an amicus brief telling the court that "Allowing same-sex couples to marry improves employee morale and productivity, reduces uncertainty, and removes the wasteful administrative burdens imposed by the current disparity of state law treatment" (Kaufman, 2015). In addition, hundreds of companies used social media to demonstrate their support prior to the court's decision and again after the ruling was released. Corporate Twitter accounts posted supportive messages using #LoveWins and #LoveWon, company logos featuring rainbow flag colors appeared on Facebook, and a growing number of ad spots began to include same-sex couples. Some brands cleverly connected the marriage equality ruling to their existing brand messaging; for example, MasterCard tweeted "True love: Priceless. #AcceptanceMatters," and JELL-O posted "J-E-L-L-O is for everyone. So is L-O-V-E. #DecisionDay #Pride" (Johnson, 2015). These responses themselves made the news, with media outlets compiling lists of "brands that love LGBT the most" (Wallace, 2015) and the "best brand tweets celebrating marriage equality" (Lee, 2015). A CNBC story (Castillo, 2015) about companies that used Twitter to celebrate the court ruling said the most successful brand tweets, based on analytics from social marketing software company Spredfast, were Starbucks, The Sims, and American Airlines. The news report indicated that Spredfast hadn't detected any brand that had immediately spoken out negatively against the *Obergefell* decision through Twitter.

Although it is impossible to describe all of the ways that businesses demonstrated their support for marriage equality, one brand's marketing efforts in the year between the key Supreme Court rulings of 2013 and 2015 show just how far corporate America has come from its initial reluctance to embrace the gay rights movement. Honey Maid graham crackers, a subsidiary of Mondelēz International, in 2014 launched its "This is Wholesome" portfolio campaign that included images of non-traditional families enjoying its crackers. Although advertising experts called the campaign "brilliant" for its progressive repositioning of an old-fashioned brand (Garber, 2016), "This is Wholesome" wasn't Honey Maid's first foray into the debate over marriage equality. In 2013, the brand had joined the chorus of companies adopting the HRC red equal sign logo; Honey Maid's version, of course, used graham cracker rectangles in place of the equal sign bars. But it was an advertisement released in March 2014 that received the most attention for its message about diversity and inclusivity. The 30-second spot featured a montage of different families: two fathers, a single dad, a punk rock family, and an interracial one. As viewers watched images of these happy families enjoying graham crackers, the voiceover said "No matter how things change, what makes us wholesome never will. Honey Maid. Everyday wholesome snacks for every wholesome family. This is wholesome." The reaction was swift and generally positive. A story in *The New Yorker* said the advertisement had captured society's shifting notion of what makes a family in "the most radical and moving way of any national campaign so far" (Solomon, 2014). *The New Yorker* piece also praised Honey Maid for unabashedly describing families headed by same-sex couples as wholesome, noting that "people have long suggested that the new structures of the American family are 'unwholesome' as a way of rationalizing intolerance."

Honey Maid executives knew that not everyone would embrace their expansive view of family, and indeed, there was social media backlash from angry individuals, most of whom objected to the depiction of a same-sex couple as parents. Instead of letting it lie or issuing a statement in defense of the ad, Honey Maid turned its response into a continuation of the "This is Wholesome" campaign. The company released a follow-up spot on social media that earned more than 1.5 million views on its first day online (Solomon, 2014). The video, simply titled "Love," features no voices, only title cards and video. It opens with explanation of reaction to the original ad: "On March 10th, 2014, Honey Maid launched 'This is wholesome,' a commercial that celebrates all families. Some people didn't agree with our message." Viewers then see emails and tweets with comments such as *Horrible, NOT WHOLESOME*, and *Disgusting!* The next title card explains, "So we asked two artists to take the negative comments and turn them into something else." The video then shows two women in a large room, rolling printouts of the negative comments into tubes, which are then arranged visually to spell out a script version of the word "love." That at first seems like the end of the spot, but another title card appears: "But the best part was all the positive messages we received. Over ten times as many." The video switches to close-ups of comments such as *family is family* and *love the Honey Maid ad*. The viewer watches as the room fills up with tubes made from the positive messages, clearly superior in number to the negative ones. The last title card continues "Proving that only one thing really matters when it comes to family …" and the closing shot shows the original script "love" surrounded by the multitude of tubes made from the positive comments.

The Digital Training Academy (2014) praised the "This is Wholesome" campaign for its content, as well as its digital strategy, describing it as "a great example of social media amplification and how a campaign can expand into a video series for maximum impact and reach." Honey Maid was also praised for the success of its #thisiswholesome hashtag and its use of Thunderclap, a social media platform that allows a company to magnify its message's impact by collecting posts and tweets about a certain topic and publishing them simultaneously, causing a bigger splash than messages would individually. Although it was only one of many brands that creatively harnessed social media to support SSM, Honey Maid's good-natured but unapologetic approach nicely illustrates how newer technologies have allowed corporations to take a public stance in a more playful manner that makes the most of user-generated content.

Even though SSM is now legal nationwide, some companies continue to publicly push for expanded rights for LGBT+ individuals. The latest battlefield has focused on so-called "bathroom bills" in states such as North Carolina and Texas that restrict bathroom options for transgender people and curtail anti-discrimination rules. Multiple companies have announced boycotts of states that pass such legislation, demanding that political leaders understand the negative impact that it has on corporations' ability to attract employees and do business. A *Washington Post* article (McGregor, 2016) suggests that "Corporate America's evolution on gay rights appears to have reached a tipping point" where the risk of speaking out is less than the risk of not doing so, indicating success on the part of HRC and others to help corporate leaders understand the value of gay-friendly policies. A *Time* article also acknowledged the changing public climate regarding gay rights, suggesting that "the more businesses and cultural institutions that speak out, the more pressure and permission there is for others to do the same" (Steinmetz, 2016). And that brings us to the final chapter of this book, where we'll examine in detail the notion of "permission" to support marriage equality. We'll look at how gay activists and advocacy organizations, the news media, and corporate America helped to create conditions in 2015 that helped the U.S. Supreme Court find its way to a marriage equality ruling.

References

Aarons-Mele, M. (2013, July 2). What made same-sex marriage go viral? *Harvard Business Review*. Retrieved at https://hbr.org/2013/07/what-made-same-sex-marriage-go-viral

Allen, F. E. (2013, March 22). Howard Schultz to anti-gay-marriage Starbucks shareholder: "You can sell your shares." *Forbes*. Retrieved from https://www.forbes.com/sites/frederickallen/2013/03/22/howard-schultz-to-anti-gay-marriage-starbucks-shareholder-you-can-sell-your-shares/#625b8bab43fa

Badgett, M. V. L., Durso, L. E., Kastanis, A., & Mallory, C. (2013, May). The business impact of LGBT-supportive workplace policies. The Williams Institute. Retrieved from https://williamsinstitute.law.ucla.edu/wp-content/uploads/Business-Impact-of-LGBT-Policies-May-2013.pdf

Becker, A. B., & Copeland, L. (2016). Networked publics: How connective social media use facilitates political consumerism among LGBT Americans. *Journal of Information Technology & Politics*, 13(1), 22–36. http://dx.doi.org/10.1080/19331681.2015.1131655

Bedard, P. (2015, November 3). Christmas "buycott" to back Christian friendly businesses. *The Washington Examiner*. Retrieved from http://www.washingtonexaminer.com/christmas-buycott-to-back-christian-friendly-businesses/article/2575256

Broderick, R. (2015, June 15). This is how American Airlines responded when a passenger got upset over their new rainbow flag logo. *BuzzFeed*. Retrieved from https://www.buzzfeed.com/ryanhatesthis/this-is-how-american-airlines-responded-when-a-passenger-got?utm_term=.ueBPPbYwD7#.nm6aaXOlgV

Bronski, M. (1984). *Culture clash: the making of gay sensibility*. Boston, MA: South End Press.

Castillo, M. (2015, June 26). Brands use social media to back same-sex marriage. CNBC. Retrieved from http://www.cnbc.com/2015/06/26/brands-use-social-media-to-back-same-sex-marriage.html

Chasin, A. (2000). *Selling out: The gay and lesbian movement goes to market*. New York: St. Martin's Press.

Commercial Closet Association. (2011). Overview and history of the global gay and lesbian market. Retrieved from http://commercialcloset.com/common/news/reports/detail.cfm?Classification=report&QID=4784&ClientID=11064&TopicID=384&subsection=resources&subnav=resources

Digital Training Academy. (2014). Food case study: Honey Maid turns social media hate into love with diverse family campaign. Retrieved from http://www.digitaltrainingacademy.com/casestudies/2014/09/honey_maid_turns_social_media_hate_into_love_with_diverse_family_campaign.php

Dougherty, P. H. (1976, July 13). Homosexual magazines in bids. *The New York Times*, p. 66.

Elliott, S. (2011, October 26). Absolut celebrates 30 years of marketing to gay consumers. *The New York Times*. Retrieved from http://www.nytimes.com/2011/10/27/business/media/absolut-heralds-its-marketing-to-gay-consumers.html

Faith Driven Consumer. (n.d.). FEI criteria. Retrieved from http://www.faithdrivenconsumer.com/fei_criteria

Faith Driven Consumer. (2015, November 2). Faith Equality Index debuts, seven brands rise to the top. Retrieved from http://www.faithdrivenconsumer.com/faith_equality_index_debuts_seven_brands_rise_to_the_top

Garber, M. (2016, April 5). Honey Maid, moral compass for us all. *The Atlantic*. Retrieved from https://www.theatlantic.com/entertainment/archive/2016/04/the-paternalism-of-brands/476946/

Gluckman, A., & Reed, B. (Eds.). (1997). *Homo economics: capitalism community, and gay and lesbian life*. New York: Routledge.

Hester, J. B., & Gibson, R. (2007). Consumer responses to gay-themed imagery in advertising. *Advertising and Society Review*, 8(2). Retrieved from https://muse.jhu.edu/article/216980

Human Rights Campaign. (2017). Corporate Equality Index 2017. Retrieved from http://assets.hrc.org//files/assets/resources/CEI-2017-Final.pdf?_ga=2.257653067.1111253426.1498125397-1368281798.1493029402

Johnson, B. (1993, January 18). The gay quandary: Advertising's most elusive, yet lucrative target market proves difficult to measure. *Advertising Age*, 64(18), pp. 29 & 35.

Johnson, L. (2015, June 26). 12 winning brand tweets that followed the Supreme court's same-sex marriage ruling. *AdWeek*. Retrieved from http://www.adweek.com/digital/12-winning-brand-tweets-after-supreme-courts-ruling-same-sex-marriage-165600/

Johnston, D., & Malina, M. A. (2008). Managing sexual orientation diversity: The impact on firm value. *Group & Organization Management*, 33(5), 602–625. DOI: 10.1177/1059601108321833

Kaufman, A. C. (2015, March 5). Here are the 379 companies urging the Supreme Court to support same-sex marriage. *The Huffington Post*. Retrieved from http://www.huffingtonpost.com/2015/03/05/marriage-equality-amicus_n_6808260.html

Lee, J. (2015, June 26). 32 of the best brand tweets celebrating marriage equality. *BuzzFeed*. Retrieved from https://www.buzzfeed.com/jarrylee/love-wins?utm_term=.boVppgnAJ1#.qk0ZZYDVEp

Lobosco, K. (2013, June 27). Chick-fil-A president deletes anti-gay marriage tweet. CNN. Retrieved from http://money.cnn.com/2013/06/27/technology/social/chick-fil-a-gay-marriage-tweet/index.html

Luckenbill, G. (1995). *Untold millions: Positioning your business for the gay and lesbian consumer revolution*. New York: HarperCollins Publishers.

McBride, S. (2017, February 8). HRC releases 2017 Buying Guide for equality-minded shoppers. [Blog post]. Retrieved from http://www.hrc.org/blog/hrc-releases-2017-buying-guide-for-equality-minded-shoppers

McGregor, J. (2016, April 5). Corporate America's embrace of gay rights has reached a stunning tipping point. *The Washington Post*. Retrieved from https://www.washingtonpost.com/news/on-leadership/wp/2016/04/05/corporate-americas-embrace-of-gay-rights-has-reached-a-stunning-tipping-point/?utm_term=.76665fa9de57

McMains, A. (2014, October 30). 20 years before it was cool to cast gay couples, Ikea made this pioneering ad. *AdWeek*. Retrieved from http://www.adweek.com/creativity/20-years-it-was-cool-cast-gay-couples-ikea-made-pioneering-ad-161054/

O'Connor, C. (2014, March 19). Chick-fil-A CEO Cathy: Gay marriage still wrong, but I'll shut up about it and sell chicken. *Forbes*. Retrieved from https://www.forbes.com/sites/

clareoconnor/2014/03/19/chick-fil-a-ceo-cathy-gay-marriage-still-wrong-but-ill-shut-up-about-it-and-sell-chicken/#e4ff0ec2fcbf

Peñaloza, L. (1996). We're here, we're queer, and we're going shopping! *Journal of Homosexuality*, 31(1–2), 9–41. DOI: 10.1300/J082v31n01_02

Raeburn, N. C. (2004). *Changing corporate America from inside out: Lesbian and gay workplace rights*. Minneapolis, MN: University of Minnesota Press.

Schulman, S. (1998). The making of a market niche. *The Harvard Gay & Lesbian Review*, 5(1), 17–20.

Sender, K. (2004). *Business, not politics: The making of the gay market*. New York: Columbia University Press.

Socarides, R. (2015, April 27). Corporate America's evolution on LGBT rights. *The New Yorker*. Retrieved from http://www.newyorker.com/business/currency/corporate-americas-evolution-on-l-g-b-t-rights

Solomon, A. (2014, April 5). Honey Maid and the business of love. *The New Yorker*. Retrieved from http://www.newyorker.com/business/currency/honey-maid-and-the-business-of-love

Steinmetz, K. (2016, April 13). How corporate America became LGBT movement's key ally. *Time*. Retrieved from http://time.com/4292758/business-support-lgbt-rights-north-carolina/

Sverson, K. (2012, July 25). Chick-fil-A thrust back into spotlight on gay rights. *The New York Times*. Retrieved from http://www.nytimes.com/2012/07/26/us/gay-rights-uproar-over-chick-fil-a-widens.html

Timm, J.C. (2015, June 9). Evangelical pastor Franklin Graham: Boycott gay-friendly businesses. MSNBC. Retrieved from http://www.msnbc.com/msnbc/evangelical-pastor-franklin-graham-boycott-gay-friendly-businesses

Wallace, G. (2015, January 12). Brands that love LGBT the most. CNN Money. Retrieved from http://money.cnn.com/2015/01/12/news/companies/lgbt-brands/index.html

9

SOCIAL MEDIA AND THE INEVITABILITY OF SAME-SEX MARRIAGE

Historians will almost certainly look to the *Obergefell v. Hodges* decision on June 26, 2015 as the day marriage equality was achieved in the United States. But, of course, years of work by thousands of SSM advocates paved the way for the Court's decision. Other scholars have already analyzed the marriage-related legal cases and state-wide ballot initiatives fought over the years, efforts of the LGBT+ rights movement to coalesce around marriage as a priority, and news media coverage of the issue. *Social Media and Same-Sex Marriage* has touched on these areas, but our primary focus has been messaging. More specifically, this book has been concerned with how communication related to SSM helped produce a social climate that by 2015 indicated that America's citizens, celebrities, corporate executives, and political leaders were ready for legalized SSM. We've already discussed the frames news media used in their coverage of the battle over marriage and the effects of those frames on audiences. And we've examined the messaging strategies of proponents and opponents of SSM, in addition to the ways that companies used marketing techniques to connect their brands to the issue of marriage.

Our focus now turns to consideration of the effects of persuasive discourse found on social media and shared through social networks. The introduction to this book asked why people adjusted their views about SSM and what role social media messages had in the rapid shift in public opinion. This chapter will return to those questions and apply two theoretical frameworks – spiral of silence and the theory of dissonant identity priming – to help answer them. Ultimately, this closing chapter should help us understand (1) why so many people, including those who were not otherwise engaged with the movement itself, were willing to associate with the issue of SSM through social media, (2) how support for SSM seemed to explode in online social networks, spreading at a rapid pace and overshadowing the opposition, (3) how advocacy groups' micro-campaigns that tapped into unconvinced voters' racial, geographic, and ideological identities were able to sway opinions, and (4) how the simplicity and visual nature of the movement's key message made it uniquely suitable for digital platforms that excel at storytelling and are populated in large part by young people. We'll end with a look at the newest battle in the fight over marriage – the issue of religious freedom – and the conflict that arises when LGB couples' right to marry is weighed against individuals' faith-based opposition to participating in SSM-related activities.

Before moving forward, it's important to understand just how unusual the shift in attitude change about SSM has been. Changes in public opinion regarding LGBT+ rights in general represent one of the quickest evolutions in the history of American moral values (Morini, 2017). According to the Pew Research Center (2013, March 20), the growth in support for the more specific issue of SSM was also among the largest changes in opinion for any policy issue. A Pew survey in 2003 showed just 33 percent of adult respondents in favor of marriage rights for LGB couples, with 58 percent opposed. Starting in 2004, there was steady growth in approval, with about a two-percentage-point increase each year until 2013 (Silver, 2013). The most recent data from Pew (2017) and Gallup (2017) indicate a more rapid increase since 2013, with 62 percent of survey respondents in the Pew survey and 64 percent in the Gallup survey indicating in 2017 that LGB couples should be legally allowed to marry.

Much of the shift in public opinion about SSM can be attributed to what is called cohort replacement, in which conservative older individuals die and are replaced by progressive younger ones (Hart-Brinson, 2014). Pew (2013, March 20) notes that the coming of age of Millennials – who were born from about 1980 to about 2000 and who support LGBT+ rights in higher numbers than any previous generation – explains a large part of the shift. But birth and death rates do not account for all of the growth in approval for SSM, suggesting that some of those who were previously opposed have changed their minds (Baunach, 2011). Indeed, Pew survey results from 2013 showed that 28 percent of marriage equality supporters reported having shifted their position on the issue in favor of SSM. When asked why they changed their minds, respondents most often said it was because they know someone who is gay or lesbian (32 percent), because they have grown more open as they aged (25 percent), because SSM is inevitable (18 percent), and because government shouldn't regulate whom people love (18 percent).

Viral politics: who participates and why

Networked digital media have been conceptualized by some as an effective forum for citizens who are interested in the public deliberation of issues (Castells, 2007; Chadwick, 2008; Dahlgren, 2009) and want to publicly display their political identities (Penney, 2015). However, coercive practices by members of the majority can hamper meaningful online social interaction, potentially resulting in the reluctance of minority members to speak out for fear of social isolation (Ho & McLeod, 2008; Gearhart & Zhang, 2015). Practices such as trolling, doxing, and general harassment can drive people from SNSs, or at a minimum, severely limit their perceived freedom of expression. Even the perception that an opinion one holds is in the minority can reduce the chances that it will be shared, which is a basic tenet of Elisabeth Noelle-Neumann's spiral of silence theory (1974). These social psychological tendencies related to public expression of views can help us to understand why social media campaigns in support of SSM were so popular in the final years of the marriage equality movement and how LGBT+ advocacy groups were able to use their supporters as "nodal distribution agents" to magnify the impact of the movement's message within social networks (Penney, 2015, p. 55). They can also help us understand why opponents of SSM were limited in their ability to maintain a robust digital presence.

A study of LGBT+ individuals' use of Facebook for political self-expression by Fox and Warber (2015) can help us understand why some queer individuals may not have felt comfortable participating in social media campaigns but why others went out of their way to share images and messages in support of SSM. The extent to which LGBT+ individuals feel comfortable posting information about their identity or support for gay-related issues on Facebook depends in large part upon how out they are to members of their networks. In Fox and Warber's study, those who were not out felt compelled to stay silent for fear of exposure. Those who were partially out felt comfortable in voicing some support of LGBT+ issues but were more likely to conceal their sexual identity from some network members. Participants who were fully out to their networks, however, were found to actively work to make Facebook a supportive place. Rather than being silenced, these out individuals actively promoted their identity and went out of their way to "like" causes, share relevant content with their network, and post support for LGBT+ issues.

Multiple scholars have examined why members of SNSs choose to change their profile photo to a politically themed image. Penney (2015) focused specifically on the HRC's RES promotion in 2013, conducting interviews with 22 adult Facebook users who changed their profile photo. Penney wanted to know whether participants adopted the HRC image in order to sway public opinion, as a way to build a collective identity around support for SSM, or simply to show social support for LGBT+ individuals. Many of the interviewees said they participated in the symbolic action to encourage opponents of marriage equality to reconsider their stance, although very few explicitly said they were attempting to influence the U.S. Supreme Court justices. These respondents saw the collective visibility of the RES as potentially persuasive on a macro level, signaling to others with the same view that their opinions were not in the minority. Likewise, respondents hoped that fair-minded people who were against SSM might change their minds after seeing so much support for marriage equality.

LGBT+-identified participants in the study (4 of 22) were motivated to adopt the RES by a desire to increase their own queer visibility online in hopes of "putting a (virtual) human face on the issue of LGBT legal rights" and creating empathy in SSM opponents (Penney, 2015, p. 59). Other study respondents described a type of agenda-setting goal, hoping to draw public attention to the issue of SSM without necessarily advocating for one side or the other. Another objective of participants was to show support for LGBT+ youth who were struggling with their sexuality, a type of mental health outreach effort. This public show of support had actually been a goal for HRC strategists who designed the RES campaign. In addition to rallying political support for SSM, HRC marketing director Anastasia Khoo explained that the organization also "wanted to send a message of hope to young people who might not feel accepted or realize that there is a visible community of people out there who are supportive" (Khoo, 2013, June 22). A small number of respondents in Penney's (2015) study indicated concern about the issue of slactivism, specifically that RES campaign participants would not make any other effort to support LGBT+ rights. But other interviewees were more optimistic, predicting that the symbolic action would inspire more concrete activities and recruit more people to the cause. Indeed, HRC strategists had hoped for that particular outcome, raising awareness of the HRC brand and converting casual allies into more committed ones. Khoo said the organization purposefully decided to allow – and even encourage – social media users to alter the RES logo as they wanted. As she explained, HRC could have tried to control the campaign more tightly, "but success relied on allowing people to make our logo their own and feel like they were part of something bigger. In the end, doing so now gives us greater brand recognition and the opportunity to engage millions more, moving them up the ladder of engagement to take even bigger actions" (Khoo, 2013, May 1).

An international survey of Facebook users (Chapman & Coffé, 2016) also found that a desire to call attention to an issue drives most people who decide to adopt a politically related profile photo. Data from a 2013 online survey of 267 Facebook users age 14–35 found that marriage equality was the most popular campaign for those who changed their profile photos. In addition to high levels of SNS use, offline engagement in protests and political parties made it more likely that a person would engage in this type of symbolic political action. Among those who changed their profile picture, raising awareness was the primary goal. Identity formation was also cited as a motivating factor, especially for those who showed their support for marriage equality by adopting the RES as their profile picture.

The effects of online symbolic action

The studies described thus far focus on the individual motivations social media users have for participating in symbolic actions. But there is still the question of whether these campaigns have any influence on public opinion, public officials, or institutions such as the U.S. Supreme Court. More than 3 million people around the world changed their profile picture to support SSM in 2013 (Vie, 2014), but what good did it do? Research suggests a variety of answers. For one thing, the HRC profile picture campaign drove a significant amount of new traffic to the organization's website, with more than 700,000 unique visitors in a 24-hour period in March 2013, and almost 90 percent of those visitors were new to the site (Vie,

2014). In addition, results from a large-scale Facebook experiment in 2010 indicate that persuasive messaging on SNSs can influence civic behavior and information sharing (Bond et al., 2012). The study involved more than 60 million Facebook users who accessed the site on Election Day in November 2010. Individuals who logged into Facebook that day were randomly assigned to a "social message" group, an "informational message" group, or a control group. Those in the social message group (*n*=60,055,176) saw a statement at the top of their news feed. This message encouraged the user to vote, provided a link to identify polling sites, included a clickable button saying "I Voted," displayed a counter showing how many other Facebook users had reported voting, and showed up to six randomly selected profile pictures of the user's Facebook friends who had already clicked the "I Voted" button (Bond et al., 2012). Individuals in the informational message group (*n*=611,044) were shown the message, poll information, counter, and "I Voted" button but not any faces of friends. Those in the control group (*n*=613,096) were not shown any message at the top of their news feed.

Results of the study indicate that online political mobilization messages can influence political self-expression, information seeking and sharing, and actual voter turnout. Specifically, data suggest modest effect sizes, but nonetheless provide evidence that the presence of a Facebook social message "increased voting behavior directly by about 60,000 voters and indirectly through social contagion by another 280,000 voters, for a total of 340,000 additional votes" (Bond et al., 2012, p. 297). Further, messages involving images of close friends were found to be more influential, dramatically increasing the effectiveness of the mobilization message. The researchers concluded that "online mobilization works because it primarily spreads through strong-tie networks that probably exist offline but have an online representation" (Bond et al., 2012, p. 298).

The spiral of silence

The spiral of silence theory is concerned with the growth and spread of public opinion, particularly in relation to controversial and value-laden issues. It was developed by German researcher Elisabeth Noelle-Neumann (1974), who considered public opinion to be a powerful force on people's evaluation of their beliefs and their willingness to express those beliefs. SOS suggests that, in face-to-face communication settings, individuals will be less willing to divulge their opinions when they believe those opinions are unpopular, primarily because they fear social isolation or some other type of negative social judgment. Based on decades of survey research experience, Noelle-Neumann (1993) asserted that people inherently possess a quasi-statistical sense of public opinion and are generally able to discern public sentiment even without access to any formal type of polling data. The more similar people think their own opinions are to the perceived majority opinion, the more willing they will be to openly reveal their views. Likewise, the farther from public opinion people perceive their own views, the less likely they will express them. SOS also suggests that people react to perceived changes in majority opinions. If people perceive that public opinion has shifted and their views now match those held by the majority, they will likely express themselves freely in public. However, if people find that their views are losing supporters, then they become concerned and are more likely to remain silent (Noelle-Neumann, 1974). Because members of the perceived majority group tend to express themselves with self-confidence, whereas members of the perceived minority remain silent, the former appear to be strong in public and the latter weaker than their actual numbers suggest. According to Noelle-Neumann, this pattern encourages others to either express themselves or to fall silent – depending on whether their views match up with the perceived majority or minority – and a spiral process is initiated.

Noelle-Neumann (1993) did acknowledge the presence of resistant and committed minorities who are willing to risk social isolation and public criticism to make their viewpoints known. Likewise, subsequent SOS research has developed the concept of an individual's willingness to self-censor, which is defined as "the withholding of one's true opinion from an audience perceived to disagree with that opinion" (Hayes et al., 2005, p. 298) in an effort to control one's public image. Individual differences within this variable have been found to influence an individual's willingness to speak out in the face of opposition (Gearhart & Zhang, 2014). Research has also shown that the media, which "constitute the major source of reference for information about the distribution of opinion" (Katz, 1983, p. 89), can accelerate the muting of the minority in the spiral of silence. Indeed, the media's ability to shape opinion climate perceptions is at the core of the SOS's spiraling process.

Research support for SOS has not been universal. More than three decades of empirical testing has provided support for its basic tenets but has also shown that multiple variables influence opinion expression in public settings (Hayes, 2007). More recent studies that have tested SOS within the context of social media have shown that SNSs serve as a useful mechanism for people to scan their environment for estimates of public opinion. Researchers have speculated that some online settings, particularly those that permit user anonymity, would allow individuals with minority views to more freely express their opinions (Ho & McLeod, 2008). Metzger (2009), however, suggests that because SNS relationships usually mirror offline relationships, SNS users may be *more* concerned about social isolation because of its effect on their social standing within offline relationships. This appears to be the case. Research testing SOS effects within a social networking setting generally indicates that social media users are less likely to express and share their views if those views are perceived to be unpopular within their social networks.

Specifically, two studies by Gearhart and Zhang found evidence of the SOS effect in a social media setting specifically involving LGBT-related topics. One study (Gearhart & Zhang, 2015) involved a nationwide survey of more than 1,000 Facebook users and dealt with the issue of SSM. Results showed that Facebook users who perceived their opinions on SSM to be similar with the predicted future opinion of the nation were more likely to post their true opinions and less likely to refrain from commenting in hostile situations. In another study (Gearhart & Zhang, 2014), an online experiment, more than 750 individuals were presented with either a friendly or hostile hypothetical gay bullying scenario presented in a Facebook context with the ability to read and post comments. Willingness to self-censor and congruency with the national opinion climate were significant predictors of the degree to which respondents revealed their opinions and responded to others, indicating the presence of the spiral of silence phenomenon.

Pew researchers have also examined whether offline tendencies to downplay viewpoints that are considered unpopular are found in social media. Because of previous research investigating SOS effects in an online (but not social media) setting, the Pew research team wondered whether SNSs could provide a setting in which those with minority views might feel freer to express their opinions (Hampton et al., 2014). One previous study is of particular interest, given the focus of this book. Ho and McLeod (2008) used the subject of SSM to compare SOS effects in face-to-face and online chat room communication settings. Results of their experiment showed evidence for SOS effects, specifically that fear of isolation had a negative effect on opinion expression. However, participants were more reluctant to divulge their opinions in a face-to-face setting than in the online chat room. The researchers concluded that "unique features such as anonymity and reduced social cues in computer-mediated discussion may be able to abate some of the dysfunctional social-psychological influence on opinion expression and create an environment conducive for public deliberation" (Ho & McLeod, 2008, p. 201).

And so, Pew staffers and researchers from Rutgers University decided to test SOS in a social media setting, vastly different from an anonymous chat room. The group selected the contentious issue of security contractor Edward Snowden's 2013 revelations of government surveillance of citizens' phone and email records. At the time, Americans were divided over whether the leaks, and even the government's surveillance efforts, were justified. Pew sent a survey to 1,801 adults asking their opinions about the Snowden leaks, their willingness to talk about the revelations in various in-person and online settings, and their perceptions of the views of those around them. Their findings, as with the other studies already described, provided evidence that SOS effects do indeed occur in social media. In both in-person and online settings, people were more willing to divulge their opinions if they thought their audience agreed with them. Specifically, if people believed that those in their Facebook network agreed with their opinion about the Snowden issue, they were almost twice as likely to join a Facebook discussion about the issue. The researchers found no evidence to support the speculation that social media might provide a more welcoming forum for those who might otherwise remain silent; in fact, results showed that survey respondents were less willing to discuss the controversial issue in social media than they were in person. Furthermore, if people thought those in their social media networks disagreed with them, they were less likely to say they would state their views on the Snowden-NSA story online *and* in other contexts, such as gatherings of friends. This suggests silencing effects might spill over from online contexts to in-person contexts.

So, how might we apply SOS theory to explain the success of the SSM movement? First of all, SSM as an issue is a prime candidate for SOS effects – it is controversial and has moral components. And looking back, we can identify key events that influenced both proponents' and opponents' willingness to publicly share their views, setting off a spiral in favor of pro-marriage equality views. In 2008, SSM opponents were surprisingly successful in passing California's Proposition 8, a victory that devastated marriage equality advocates but also got their attention. In the aftermath of their defeat, some gay activists used campaign finance disclosure laws to identify individuals who had given money to the Yes on Prop 8 campaign and took to the Internet to publicize those individuals' names and personal information. A number of anti-SSM donors faced protests at their homes and places of employment, and Mozilla CEO Brendan Eich was even forced out of his job because of a boycott against his company. The result was a chilling effect for traditional marriage supporters, according to media accounts and an interview with Joe Grabowski, director of communication for the National Organization for Marriage (J. Grabowski, personal communication, June 19, 2017). After that, Grabowski said it was more difficult to get supporters to participate in social media campaigns and publicly state their opposition to SSM. At the same time, marriage equality advocates were regrouping, fine-tuning their message and putting substantially more resources into digital and social media. The result was a series of highly successful digital mini-campaigns focused on the personal stories of LGB couples and including simple yet meaningful visual images and hashtags that allowed SSM supporters to easily display and share their public support.

Simultaneously in the Proposition 8 aftermath, SNSs were growing in popularity, attracting young users who were more supportive of LGBT+ rights than any previous generation. The ability of SSM advocacy organizations to get a few key celebrities and public officials with huge social media followings – Beyoncé, Barack Obama, and George Takei, for example – on board helped even further. Although public opinion polls at the time were barely showing half the country in favor of SSM, the message coming from social media – and news media reports of the activity on social media – was overwhelmingly pro-marriage equality. Taken together, these factors produced a classic SOS pattern: a point of view (in this case, SSM marriage opposition) that was held by almost half the country and powerful enough to pass an anti-SSM ballot initiative in liberal California was unable to match its popularity in public opinion polls with visibility online. The anti-SSM message, which was grounded in fear of the effects of SSM on traditional morals and the institution of marriage – coupled with the intimidation likely felt by many traditional marriage supporters who dared share their views in SNSs – limited the anti-SSM movement's ability to get traction online. As marketing expert John Hoffman (2012) notes, stories of righteous indignation in defense of traditional marriage may invoke strong emotions, but they lack the opportunity for emotional connection embodied in stories of personal transformation.

On the other hand, pro-gay advocacy groups and individual SSM supporters flooded social networks with visual, upbeat, simple messages of love and commitment. Those messages were joined by similar ones from brands such as Honey Maid, Absolut vodka, and Apple that focused on the joy associated with marriage and featured company logos and products redesigned to include colors of the rainbow flag. Research shows that content that elicits an emotional reaction tends to be more widely shared, and content that stimulates positive emotions is more widely shared than content eliciting negative feelings (Berger & Milkman, 2012: Rees-Jones & Milkman, 2015). Likewise, SNS users are more likely to adopt online content that is shared by friends, and those rates of adoption increase as additional friends adopt the material (Bakshy et al., 2009). These tendencies clearly worked in SSM's favor, with the marriage equality's social media campaigns contributing to the creating of "a widespread descriptive norm implying that it is socially acceptable to advocate for same-sex marriage" (Tannenbaum, 2013). And public opinion polls show this was indeed the case. In 2013, 72 percent of Americans – including 59 percent of those opposed to SSM – believed that legal recognition of SSM was inevitable, according to the Pew Research Center (2013, June 6). A poll conducted in May of that year was the first Pew poll to register more than half (51 percent) of Americans favoring SSM, with 42 percent opposed. Conservatives were clearly frustrated at the changing public climate surrounding the issue of SSM. In 2010, a staffer at the conservative Witherspoon Institute suggested that "Americans appear to accept same-sex marriage more than they really do, perhaps because they believe it to be more widely accepted than it really is" (Franck, 2010). Specifically referencing SOS theory, he blamed the news and entertainment media, who he said had for years worked to frame the question of SSM in ways that favored its advocates.

The theory of dissonant priming

Thus far, we've looked at reasons why millions of people were willing to participate in pro-SSM social media campaigns by downloading personal profile images or using hashtags such as #LoveMustWin. And we've applied the spiral of silence theory to explain how the outsized visibility of the marriage equality movement on social media and in the news may have contributed to public sentiment that legal SSM was inevitable even before a large majority of the public was actually in favor of it. We've seen how this may have put in motion a downward spiral that led SSM opponents to stay silent about their views – in social media but also in face-to-face settings – which would leave others with the impression that fewer people opposed SSM than was actually the case. But we've yet to explain how social media campaigns from the marriage equality movement were able to change the minds of those citizens who were originally undecided about or even opposed to marriage rights for LGB couples.

As noted earlier, replacement of older, conservative voters by younger and more progressive ones cannot account for all of the shift in public opinion about SSM. Some citizens who were originally opposed to SSM have changed their minds. Political science professors Brian Harrison and Melissa Michelson (2017) have developed a theory that helps to explain the rapid rate of attitude change regarding SSM. Their theory of dissonant identity priming (TDIP) is concerned primarily with the effects of communication about contentious social issues, making it especially useful for those interested in SSM. Likewise, the theory relies heavily on the concept of social identity – which suggests that our sense of self is determined in large part by our perceived and real group memberships (Tajfel, 1982) – an approach that is fitting for an identity-based social movement such as LGBT+ rights.

The TDIP predicts that a persuasive message in support of a particular position that is able to prime an individual's sense of social identity can lead to attitude change, particularly if the message recipient is surprised in some way by the position taken by the source of the message. Thus, people will be more likely to support SSM upon learning that others within a shared identity group are also supporters, particularly if they find that support surprising. So, for example, country music fans would be more likely to favor SSM after hearing that Carrie Underwood, a committed Christian, was in favor of SSM. And African Americans would be more likely to support SSM when told that President Barack Obama was supportive. In both cases, the individuals publicly supporting SSM are members of the same shared-identity group as the message recipients. And in both cases, it is somewhat unexpected for the spokespeople – a country music singer who openly discusses her Christian faith and a U.S. president who had previously stated he was against marriage rights for LGB couples – to publicly support SSM.

How exactly does the TDIP work? First of all, as Harrison and Michelson (2017) explain, with controversial issues such as SSM, people often have strong opinions that may be especially resistant to persuasive attempts. Individuals tend to avoid communication – news, social media, interpersonal conversations – that might challenge their existing views, as well as settings where they might be called on to defend their views. But, if through a persuasive message, an advocacy group can get people to understand that the message is coming from someone in a salient shared-identity group, message recipients should be more open to hearing a message, thinking and conversing about it, and maybe even changing their minds. This happens because priming a shared in-group identity can help to reduce the perceived social distance between the message's source and its receiver, and it's most effective when the primed identity is especially important to the message recipient's sense of self. And, as mentioned before, counter-stereotypical messages, because they are unexpected, likely draw attention to the message even more.

Harrison and Michelson developed their theory based on evidence from a series of public opinion experiments related to four types of identities: religion, race, partisanship, and sports fanship. Much of their research was directly related to SSM, and they worked with LGBT+ advocacy groups to test their theories of attitude change within the context of SSM. Their findings lead to the conclusion that, "When nudged to consider advocates for LGBT rights as 'just like me' in some way – because of shared race or ethnicity, shared partisanship, shared religious faith or shared support for a sport or professional sports team – individuals in our experiments were often moved to be more supportive in their expressed attitudes and observed behaviors" (Harrison & Michelson, 2017, p. 42). In hindsight, the research findings validate the strategies of groups such as Freedom to Marry, which put significant resources into developing micro-campaigns that used unexpected spokespeople to target segments of the population one wouldn't normally think of as ripe for attitude change in relation to SSM. For example, FTM's Southerners for the Freedom to Marry campaign featured civil rights icon Rep. John Lewis and former George W. Bush advisor Mark McKinnon from Texas. The group's Young Conservatives for the Freedom to Marry campaign involved participants such as Craig Stowell, a non-gay ex-Marine. And there were multiple other personal story-based campaigns, each distributed widely through email, social media, paid advertising, and traditional media outreach. In their book about how to change attitudes about LGBT+ rights, Harrison and Michelson (2017) suggest that to be most successful, messaging strategies should help people think about queer individuals and their allies as members of a mutual in-group, not as members of an out-group. They explain that, "Marriage equality is not personally relevant to most individuals with straight sexual orientations, but triggering a sense of shared identity not related to sexual orientation will nevertheless lead targets to consider changing their attitudes on the issue" (p. 19). It's clear now that the micro-campaigns from FTM and efforts by HRC to bring popular celebrities and public officials on board as social issue leaders were able to capitalize upon the power of perceived shared identity.

Public opinion and the U.S. Supreme Court

Our discussion thus far has addressed reasons for the rapid shift in public opinion about SSM. But SSM was not legalized in the United States based on public opinion polls. It took a five–four vote of the U.S. Supreme Court in *Obergefell v. Hodges* for that to occur. There has been much speculation but little agreement about the relationship between U.S. Supreme Court decisions and public opinion. Does the court drive public opinion or is it driven by public opinion? Or do justices simply respond to the same social forces that simultaneously shape public attitudes? New York University law professor Barry Friedman's (2009) history of the relationship between the U.S. Supreme Court and public opinion suggests that justices prefer not to stray too far from the will of the people. A separate analysis found little evidence that justices respond strategically to public opinion but supports the idea that justices' preferences shift in response to the same social forces that shape the opinions of the general public (Giles et al., 2008). However, a more recent study that controlled for the influences of these social forces (Casillas et al., 2011) found that public opinion does have an influence on the Court's decisions. Specifically, as prevailing public opinion shifts in a liberal direction, the court responds by issuing a greater proportion of liberal judgments.

Two essays written by political scientists in 2013 specifically addressed the influence of public opinion about SSM on the U.S. Supreme Court. After the court's rulings in *U.S. v. Windsor* and *Hollingsworth v. Perry* failed to make SSM legal nationwide, NYU professor Patrick Egan (2013) speculated that it was related to public opinion, in that justices may have decided to moderate their intervention because they were sensitive to the possibility of backlash. Egan explains that the justices supportive of marriage equality may be haunted by the aftermath of decisions such as *Roe v. Wade*, which legalized abortion in 1973. Justice Ruth Bader Ginsburg publicly stated as much in 2013, suggesting that although public opinion was trending toward reproductive freedom at the time of the court's ruling, the *Roe* decision was too sweeping and gave abortion opponents a symbol to target (Associated Press, 2013), swinging the momentum to the anti-abortion side. A different perspective can be seen in an essay from Georgetown University professor Erik Voeten (2013), who wanted to explain why SSM was advancing in the courts while support for affirmative action was receding. Voeten suggested that gay rights are advancing because that's what the American public wants, and justices believe that ignoring public sentiment may compromise confidence in the court. He argued that moderate justices are especially concerned with the will of the people, and thus increases in public approval and the success of pro-SSM ballot initiatives in 2012 "may have been as important as any legal argument in shaping the outcome of the gay-rights cases" (Voeten, 2013). Harvard Law School professor Michael Klarman concurs. In an op-ed piece in *The New York Times*, Klarman (2015) says that rulings such as *Brown v. Board of Education* and *Obergefell v. Hodges* were inconceivable until enormous changes in the surrounding social and political context had first occurred.

It is not the goal of this book to document the role of public opinion in U.S. Supreme Court decisions. Our objective here has been to show how SSM advocates successfully capitalized upon social media–related phenomena – among them changing user demographics, the nature of viral content, the power of shared identity, and the public support of celebrities, political officials, and business leaders – to create a climate suggesting that a large part of the country was ready for marriage equality. So, the fact that someone's cousin replaced her Facebook profile photo with a red equal sign, or Hillary Clinton tweeted using #LoveMustWin, or Oreo created an ad with a rainbow-colored cookie likely did not directly cause the U.S. Supreme Court to vote in favor of marriage equality. But it did help to create an atmosphere in which it was socially acceptable to support SSM and sometimes socially risky to oppose it, a scenario that may have given the court permission to rule as it did.

Looking forward: the issue of religious freedom

Although the legality of SSM was settled by the U.S. Supreme Court in 2015, the battle over marriage continues. As explained in Chapter 6, the newest fight features a showdown between two basic American values: freedom from discrimination and freedom of religion. Faith-based opponents of SSM who provide wedding-related services argue that the U.S. Constitution protects them from having to provide service to same-sex couples, and their cause has been taken up by many of the advocacy organizations that previously fought to prevent the legalization of gay marriage. SSM supporters, however, argue that refusal to provide services to same-sex couples amounts to discrimination based on sexual orientation. The U.S.

Supreme Court has agreed to consider the issue, announcing in summer 2017 that it would hear a case – *Masterpiece Cakeshop, Ltd. v. Colorado Civil Rights Commission* – that involves a Colorado baker who lost lower court fights over his refusal to make a wedding cake for a gay male couple because of his religious beliefs. The legal issue before the Supreme Court will be whether applying Colorado's public accommodations law to compel the baker to create expression (in the form of a wedding cake) that goes against his religious beliefs about marriage violates the free speech or free exercise clauses of the First Amendment. Religious conservatives are counting on the Supreme Court, with the recent addition of conservative justice Neil Gorsuch, to rule in favor of the baker and religious freedom protections. SSM advocates hope that Justice Anthony Kennedy will again be a swing vote in favor of LGBT+ rights.

Conservative groups opposed to SSM have ramped up their fund-raising and messaging efforts in advance of the upcoming Supreme Court case. For example, National Organization for Marriage President Brian Brown in July 2017 sent supporters a fund-raising email detailing the group's strategy to strengthen religious freedom protections and eventually eliminate the legal right for LGB couples to marry. He said NOM's efforts involve working with conservative congressmen to pass the First Amendment Defense Act, which would prohibit the federal government from taking action against a person who acts in accordance with his or her faith-based beliefs about marriage. NOM also plans to file amicus briefs with the U.S. Supreme Court in the *Masterpiece Cakeshop* case (Montgomery, 2017). NOM regularly updates its blog with appeals to supporters to donate money and sign petitions to hold President Donald Trump's administration accountable for its campaign pledge to support traditional marriage and religious freedom. Likewise, the Marriage Anti-Defamation Alliance website features a call for individuals who feel they have been discriminated against because of their religious views to tell their stories through videos posted to the site.

As of the close of 2017, the religious freedom vs. anti-gay discrimination issue has not yet taken over social media the way SSM did. However, that may change once the case is before the U.S. Supreme Court in 2018. Based on what we know about public opinion regarding the issue, as well as the likely messaging strategies that will be used by advocacy organizations to argue their positions, SSM advocates may find it more difficult to dominate social media this time around. Although polling shows that, as of summer 2017, 64 percent of Americans support SSM (Gallup, 2017), public opinion about religious freedom and SSM is more closely divided. A Pew Research Center survey from September 2016 found that 49 percent of respondents said businesses that provide wedding services should be required to provide those services for same-sex couples, whereas 48 percent thought they should be allowed to refuse service based on religious objections to homosexuality.

It's also important to understand how the topic of religious freedom will allow faith-based SSM opponents to deploy a different messaging strategy that will have a better chance of gaining traction on social media. SSM advocates showed us how tapping into social media's affinity for simple and affirmative messages that tell personal stories can be a winning strategy. Religious freedom is one of the most basic of American moral and legal values. Regardless of whether a requirement that marriage service providers treat gay and straight couples the same is an actual violation of religious protections, religious freedom advocates will capitalize upon the affirmative concepts of freedom and liberty. We've already seen that groups such as the Marriage Anti-Defamation Alliance have learned the power of personal storytelling with their emotional videos of individuals who feel they have been harassed because of their religious beliefs. These types of stories may not provide the same upbeat visual appeal as wedding-based stories, but they can harness images related to patriotism, Christianity, and freedom – concepts that can easily be visualized in a manner suitable for social media. SSM advocates, on the other hand, will likely be focused on the issue of discrimination, a less positive message that is also less visual. Based on what we know about attributes that make it likely that a message will go viral, the social media playing field will likely not be as favorable to SSM advocates with this newest issue in the battle over marriage.

References

Associated Press. (2013, May 11). Ginsburg: Roe gave opponents target. *Politico*. Retrieved from http://www.politico.com/story/2013/05/ruth-bader-ginsburg-roe-v-wade-abortion-091218

Bakshy, E., Karrer, B., & Adamic, L. A. (2009). Social influence and the diffusion of user-created content. In *Proceedings of the ACM Conference on Electronic Commerce*, pp. 325–334. Stanford: The Association for Computing Machinery.

Baunach, D. M. (2011). Decomposing trends in attitudes toward gay marriage, 1988–2006. *Social Science Quarterly*, 92(2), 346–363. http://doi.org/10.1111/j.1540- 6237.2011.00772.x

Berger, J., & Milkman, K. L. (2012). What makes online content viral? *Journal of Marketing Research*, 49(2), 192–205.

Bond, R. M., Fariss, C. J., Jones, J. J., Kramer, A. D. I., Marlow, C., Settle, J. E., & Fowler, J. H. (2012). A 61-million-person experiment in social influence and political mobilization. *Nature*, 489, 295–298. DOI:10.1038/nature11421

Casillas, C. J., Enns, P. K., & Wohlfarth, P. C. (2011). How public opinion constrains the U.S. Supreme Court. *American Journal of Political Science*, 55(1), 74–88. DOI:10.1111/j.1540-5907.2010.00485.x

Castells, M. (2007). Communication, power, and counter-power in the network society. *International Journal of Communication*, 1, 238–266.

Chadwick, A. (2008). Web 2.0: New challenges for the study of e-democracy in an era of informational exuberance. *Journal of Law and Policy for the Information Society*, 5, 9–41.

Chapman, H. & Coffé, H. (2016). Changing Facebook profile pictures as part of a campaign: Who does it and why? *Journal of Youth Studies*, *19*(4), 483–500. DOI:10.1080/13676261.2015.1083962

Dahlgren, P. (2009). *Media and political engagement*. Cambridge: Cambridge University Press.

Egan, P. (2013, June 27). What if marriage equality is Loving instead of Roe? *The Monkey Cage*. Retrieved from http://themonkeycage.org/2013/06/what-if-marriage-equality-is-loving-instead-of-roe/

Fox, J., & Warber, K. M. (2015). Queer identity management and political self-expression on social networking sites A co-cultural approach to the spiral of silence. *Journal of Communication*, 65(1), 79–100.

Franck, M. J. (2010, August 30). Same-sex marriage and public opinion: Spirals, frames and the Seinfeld effect. *Public Discourse*. Retrieved from http://www.thepublicdiscourse.com/2010/08/1551

Friedman, B. (2009). *The will of the people: How public opinion has influenced the Supreme Court and shaped the meaning of the Constitution*. New York, NY: Farrar, Straus and Giroux.

Gallup. (2017, May 15). U.S. support for gay marriage edges to new high. Retrieved from http://www.gallup.com/poll/210566/support-gay-marriage-edges-new-high.aspx

Gearhart, S., & Zhang, W. (2014). Gay bullying and online opinion expression: Testing spiral of silence in the social media environment. *Social Science Computer Review*, 32(1), 18–36. DOI: 10.1177/0894439313504261

Gearhart, S., & Zhang, W. (2015). Same spiral, different day? Testing the spiral of silence across issue types. *Communication Research*. DOI:10.1177/0093650215616456

Giles, M. W., Blackstone, B., & Vining, R. L. (2008). The Supreme court in American democracy: Unraveling the linkages between public opinion and judicial decision making. *The Journal of Politics*, 70(2), 293–306.

Hampton, K.N., Rainie, L., Lu, W., Dwyer, M., Shin, I., & Purcell, K. (2014). Social media and the 'spiral of silence.' Pew Research Center. Retrieved from http://www.pewinternet.org/2014/08/26/social-media-and-the-spiral-of-silence

Harrison, B. F., & Michelson, M. R. (2017). *Listen, we need to talk: How to change attitudes about LGBT rights*. Oxford University Press. DOI:10.1093/acprof:oso/9780190654740.001.0001

Hart-Brinson, P. (2014). Discourse of generations: The influence of cohort, period and ideology in Americans' talk about same-sex marriage. *American Journal of Cultural Sociology*, 2(2), 221–252. DOI:10.1057/ajcs.2014.3

Hayes, A. F. (2007). Exploring the forms of self-censorship: On the spiral of silence and the use of opinion expression avoidance strategies, *Journal of Communication*, 57, 785–802.

Hayes, A. F. , Glynn, C.J., & Shanahan, J. (2005). Validating the willingness to self-censor scale: Individual differences in the effect of the climate of opinion on opinion expression. *International Journal of Public Opinion*, 17, 298–323.

Ho, S. S. & McLeod, D. M. (2008). Social-psychological influences on opinion expression in face-to-face and computer-mediated communication. *Communication Research*, 35(2), 190–207.

Hoffman, J. (2012, May 14). Sharing our way toward equality: Social media and gay rights. *Nonprofit Quarterly*. Retrieved from https://nonprofitquarterly.org/2012/05/14/sharing-our-way-toward-equality-social-media-and-gay-rights

Katz, E. (1983). Publicity and pluralistic ignorance: Notes on the 'Spiral of Silence.' In C. D. Whitney, E. Wartella, & S. Windahl (Eds.), *Mass communication review yearbook* (pp. 89–100). Beverly Hills, CA: Sage.

Khoo, A. (2013, May 1). Painting the Internet red. *Stanford Social Innovation Review*. Retrieved from http://www.ssireview.org/blog/entry/painting_the_internet_red

Khoo, A. (2013, June 22). How support for marriage equality went viral on Facebook. *The Huffington Post*. Retrieved from http://www.huffingtonpost.com/anastasia-khoo/how-support-for-marriage-_b_3483736.html

Klarman, M. (2015, July 6). The Supreme Court is most powerful when it follows public opinion. *The New York Times*. Retrieved from https://www.nytimes.com/roomfordebate/2015/07/06/is-the-supreme-court-too-powerful/the-supreme-court-is-most-powerful-when-it-follows-public-opinion

Metzger, M. J. (2009). The study of media effects in the era of Internet communication. In R. L. Nabi & M. B. Oliver (Eds.), *The Sage handbook of media processes and effects* (pp. 561–576). Los Angeles, CA: Sage.

Montgomery, P. (2017, July 7). Brian Brown says NOM will target SPLC & HRC. *Right Wing Watch*. Retrieved from http://www.rightwingwatch.org/post/brian-brown-says-nom-will-target-splc-hrc/

Morini, M. (2017). Same-sex marriage and other moral taboos: Cultural acceptances, change in American public opinion, and the evidence from the opinion polls. *European Journal of American Studies*, 11(3). DOI:10.4000/ejas.11824

Noelle-Neumann, E. (1974). The spiral of silence: A theory of public opinion. *Journal of Communication*, 24, 43–51. DOI:10.1111/j.1460–2466.1974.tb00367.x

Noelle-Neumann, E. (1993). *The spiral of silence: Public opinion – Our social skin* (2nd ed.). Chicago: University of Chicago Press.

Penney, J. (2015). Social media and symbolic action: Exploring participation in the Facebook Red Equal Sign profile picture campaign. *Journal of Computer Mediated Communication*, 20(1), 52–66. http://doi.org/10.1111/jcc4.12092

Pew Research Center. (2013, March 20). Growing support for gay marriage: Changed minds and changing demographics. Retrieved from http://www.people-press.org/2013/03/20/growing-support-for-gay-marriage-changed-minds-and-changing-demographics

Pew Research Center. (2013, June 6). *In gay marriage debate, both supporters and opponents see legal recognition as 'inevitable.'* Retrieved from http://www.people-press.org/2013/06/06/in-gay-marriage-debate-both-supporters-and-opponents-see-legal-recognition-as-inevitable

Pew Research Center. (2016, May 12). Changing attitudes on gay marriage. Retrieved from http://www.pewforum.org/2016/05/12/changing-attitudes-on-gay-marriage

Pew Research Center. (2016, September 28). Where the public stands on religious liberty vs. non-discrimination. Retrieved from http://assets.pewresearch.org/wp-content/uploads/sites/11/2016/09/Religious-Liberty-full-for-web.pdf

Pew Research Center. (2017, June 26). Support for same-sex marriage grows, even among groups that had been skeptical. Retrieved from http://assets.pewresearch.org/wp-content/uploads/sites/5/2017/06/23153542/06-26-17-Same-sex-marriage-release.pdf

Rees-Jones, L., & Milkman, K. L. (2015, April 14). The secret to online success: What makes content go viral. *Scientific American*. Retrieved from https://www.scientificamerican.com/article/the-secret-to-online-success-what-makes-content-go-viral

Silver, N. (2013, March 26). How opinion on same-sex marriage is changing, and what it means. *FiveThirtyEight*. Retrieved from https://fivethirtyeight.com/features/how-opinion-on-same-sex-marriage-is-changing-and-what-it-means

Tajfel, H. (1982). Social psychology of intergroup relations. *Annual Review of Psychology*, 33, 1–39.

Tannenbaum, M. (2013, March 28). Will changing your Facebook profile picture do anything for marriage equality? *Scientific American*. Retrieved from https://blogs.scientificamerican.com/psysociety/marriage-equality-and-social-proof

Vie, S. (2014). The Human Rights Campaign Facebook logo. *Civic Media Project*. Retrieved from http://civicmediaproject.org/works/civic-media-project/thehumanrightscampaignfacebooklogo

Voeten, E. (2013, June 28). How the Supreme court responds to public opinion. *Washington Monthly*. Retrieved from http://washingtonmonthly.com/2013/06/28/how-the-supreme-court-responds-to-public-opinion

INDEX

Note: italics indicate figures; ‘n’ indicates chapter notes